FAMILY FRANCE

FRANK BARRETT

FAMILY FRANCE

FRANK BARRETT

BOXTREE

First published in Great Britain in 1993 by Boxtree Limited

10 9 8 7 6 5 4 3 2 1

Typeset by Intype, London
Printed in England by Clays Ltd, St Ives plc

Boxtree Limited
Broadwall House
21 Broadwall
London SE1 9PL

A CIP catalogue entry for this book is available from the
British Library.

ISBN 1 85283 431 5

Cover design by Robert Updegraff

Front cover photograph courtesy of Zefa

CONTENTS

FOREWORD

There are a lot of guides to France. My bookshelves at home are full of them. Cultural guides, food guides, hotel guides, battlefield guides, waterway guides, city guides . . .

It would be foolish for *Family France* to try and cover the ground already thoroughly explored by other more distinguished writers than myself. In this book, for example, you will find no outline of French political history from 1789. There is no glossary of useful phrases ('I wish to have a seat with my back facing the engine'). I can provide no instant appraisal of *nouvelle cuisine* and its leading exponents. Look in vain for an evaluation of the quality of vintage claret.

This is a practical guide for anybody setting out to plan a family holiday to France. Here you will find what I hope is useful advice, hard facts and invaluable information. Who organises riding holidays? Where can you get cheap flights to Paris? Can you save money by taking longer car ferry Channel crossings? Answers to these and other questions are contained within.

In compiling this book I have been helped by more than 200 travel companies specialising in France who took the time and trouble in sending information about their activities.

I must also express my thanks to my wife Sheila who laboured long and hard to input all this information into a database. (Any mistakes in this book, I must say, are all hers . . . !)

I enjoyed putting this book together because I enjoy France. If this book encourages you to experience the pleasures of a French holiday for the first time, please let me know – my life's work will not wholly have been in vain!

To anybody planning to travel to France for a holiday, may I wish you *bonnes vacances*!

Frank Barrett
April 1993

INTRODUCTION

The *Sûreté Nationale* stamp in my passport records the day I first stepped into France. It was 9 August 1962, the port was Calais and I was eight.

Recalling the exact day when a passion commences is normally difficult. But here in my old, dark blue passport, with its faded gold lettering on the cover, it tells me the very date. I have returned to France hundreds of times since, but I have never forgotten that first time.

The passport tells me that my height was four feet two and a quarter inches (the quarter inch must have been of some significance to either me or the Passport Office). The passport photograph shows a rather confused looking child in an over-size, camel-hair coat that I had recently inherited from my older brother (this picture was taken in 1961, remember: in those days nobody worried about children having clothes that fitted!). I had protruding jug-handle ears and a pudding-bowl haircut. Macmillan was prime minister of Britain, de Gaulle was president of France. It was the summer of Telstar, it was the year of the Cuban missile crisis. The Cuban crisis is something I vaguely remember from *Daily Mail* headlines. That first taste of France however is much more sharply recalled.

I particularly remember the elaborate preparations. For my father, a 20-mile trip to Pontypool was a trans-Gobi trek – the journey to France was a moon shot. Weeks ahead of departure we had our continental motoring kit from the Automobile Association (I don't believe they were referred to as the 'AA' in those days). There was a sticker, showing French road signs, that we had to fix to the inside of our windscreen – along with a reminder to drive on the right. We pondered the curious French rules of the road which gave right of way to tractors emerging from tiny lanes on the right. And strangest of all, we were told we had to give priority to cars coming on to roundabouts.

It is hard now to capture the extreme recklessness of this French adventure. In 1962 few people went abroad: the records show that just over four million people took a foreign holiday that year (compared with well over 20 million in 1992). It was still a time of post-war austerity – exchange restrictions existed to discourage people from foreign travel (remember the 'V' form?). With the Government restricting the amount of cash each traveller could take out of Britain, would we have enough money to last us a fortnight? And would we be able to cope with the local money? The French had then recently lopped a zero off their currency, going from Old Francs to New Francs (we assumed that we would be taken for a ride on this at every possible opportunity by sharp-practising French traders).

And what of the French public toilets? Rumour had it that for men these often amounted to indecent, barely concealed urinals; for women there was said to be simply a porcelain trough and a couple of footholds.

But most worrying of all were the French themselves. Would they be sympathetic to British tourists? Would they speak English – our French amounted to nothing more than a few simple sentences gleaned from a phrase book ('We would like to reserve two seats for the opera ... Stop that man he is walking off with my suitcase!').

In these days before the package holiday boom, 'abroad' remained a strange, possibly dangerous place where the food was coated in olive oil and garlic, where the plumbing was suspect and the drinking water was reckoned to be positively poisonous.

After my father had checked five times that the water and electricity in the house were turned off (holidays were spent in the terror of returning home to find it destroyed by fire or water – or perhaps both), neighbours in our Wye Valley village watched us set off with a sort of fascinated horror. Even if we were to reach France – was it possible that we could return? But why would we want to go to France at all?

I remember the endless drive to Kent (car journeys in Britain took an age in the days before motorways): we parked beneath the White Cliffs of Dover and I looked in vain for the bluebirds. I remember the shabby tub of a car ferry: no drive-on, drive-off in those days – a turntable was used to manhandle the car around before it could be driven off.

If things were still tough in Britain in 1962, France by comparison was dirt poor, a sort of poverty shocking even to an eight-year-old. I remember emaciated cattle, farmers cutting their fields with scythes, oxen pulling ploughs, roads practically deserted of traffic. It was a country still heavily marked by the war: pillboxes and other defensive positions remained almost intact. It was as if the German army had only recently been chased away.

I can recall how astonished we were at French life. The smell of

Gauloises, the stink of *pissoires*, the care which people devoted to their food. At our campsite we were astonished to observe neighbouring French families take hours to complete their lunch while we demolished ours in minutes.

In the markets were fruit and vegetables we had never seen before: red peppers, haricots verts, mangetout peas, melons, large peaches, Camembert cheeses, bottles of mineral water (people *buy* water to drink!) and, of course, bottles and bottles of wine. During that first holiday I recall visiting a small town market in Brittany where the France of *Jean de Florette* or even Balzac was still on view, where markets were the most important day of the week.

That holiday provided a clutch of memorable firsts. I can still remember the first smell of fresh coffee, the aroma of Gauloises cigarettes, the whiff of Pernod and Ricard. I will never forget the first taste of hot, crusty French bread or warm croissants. French bread – or what is called French bread – is now freely available at any high street bakers. But our first taste of it in a *boulangerie* remains one of my brightest recollections. We didn't always understand it all. The first carton of yoghurt we tasted we assumed was milk that had been left to go off (little could we have guessed that yoghurt would soon become a daily feature of our diet).

For any eight-year-old going from Britain to France today for the first time, the similarities between the two countries are more obvious than the differences. But nearly 30 years ago in France, we might have been wanderers on another planet. A country without phone boxes, public toilets that consisted simply of a hole and places to park your feet above the flushing deluge, *gendarmes* with guns, Citroens *deux chevaux*, workmen in their *bleus de travail*, *Paris-Match* placards that talked of unknown stars (who *were* Johnny Halliday and Sylvie Vartan?).

We stayed at a pre-erected campsite near Dinard in Brittany, which my mother had booked through a small ad in the *Sunday Times*. The owners of the site were British: the wife asked us to bring them tea and bacon: tea was impossible to buy locally and bacon was prohibitively expensive.

After our week in Dinard, we went on to Paris. This memory is a bit hazy, but I have the certain recollection of my father trying to drive us up the wrong side of the Champs-Elysées in our Commer Cob van: we must have looked rather like the Clampetts turning up in Beverly Hills. Our arrival coincided with what turned out to be the aftermath of yet another *Day of the Jackal*-style assassination attempt on General de Gaulle. My first holiday in France was also almost my last.

This 1962 holiday cost a combined week's wages of my parents' policeman and teacher salaries: for the two week trip, including the stop-over in Paris, it was reckoned to be a bargain.

Until the mid-seventies, British holiday-makers to France divided into two fairly distinct groups. The relatively affluent who could afford to stay in hotels in the established resorts like Monte Carlo, Nice, Cannes, Juan-les-Pins, Biarritz or La Baule. And there was another group for whom France was a place for inexpensive camping and caravanning holidays. These weren't necessarily people of restricted incomes: in the queue for the water or the toilets on many French campsites one would meet all manner of professional types who drove Rovers and Jaguars. They camped because they liked camping: the privations of a public school education are not only a good training for imprisonment, they also seemed to provide an appetite for the dubious pleasures of life under canvas, where all your meals are fry-up's and all your showers are cold.

But in the mid-seventies, France suddenly became the middle-class holiday destination *par excellence*: the reason was the emergence of the *gîte*. The rapid depopulation of the French countryside after the Second World War was leaving huge numbers of empty country properties. Worried at this growing dereliction, the French government agreed to provide grants for farmers wishing to restore these properties. The only condition was that for a limited period, these properties had to be let as self-catering accommodation to holiday-makers through the national gîte organization.

It marked a significant shift in holidaying sophistication for the British. Most gîtes in France are deep in the countryside, far from the traditional attractions of the seaside. However families were happy to leave the beach and immerse themselves in the pleasures of French village life – independent and unpackaged. People who would normally have booked a two week package to Crete or Rimini, got into their cars, took a ferry crossing and drove south through France.

It was probably not surprising that as a result of this switch, French style began to make itself felt on British life. Houses from Muswell Hill to Manchester began to aspire to kitchens that looked like something we imagined we would find in a Provençal farmhouse. Sainsburys began to fill its shelves with dozens of varieties of French cheese, pâté and fromage frais. High street shops started to sell croissants and baguette sandwiches. Empty cinemas reopened as wine warehouses: we learnt to discriminate between the tastes of chablis and sancerre. We stopped drinking gin and tonics and started to ask for kirs.

And as we increasingly enjoyed the pleasures of France in Britain, it was only natural we would seek to enjoy the pleasures of France, in France. By the early eighties, France had established itself as the natural holiday destination of a major section of the British. In those 30 years, France has gone from being a holiday destination to being *the* holiday destination.

In 1971, for example, 5.2m passengers and 890,000 cars passed through the port of Dover; 20 years later the total reached 15.9m passengers and 2.4m cars. The rate of growth may have been less dramatic through the eighties – but over the past five years during which the package holiday market has rapidly declined – the marvel is that the ferry business managed to grow at all.

In 1992, for example, despite the continuing recession – and in contrast to the slump in the sale of package holidays – France experienced another big rise in the number of British visitors. In 1992 over 8m British people visited France compared with 7.1m in 1991. France now receives 25% of all British people who travel abroad. (It's worth recording that in 1992 tourism became France's biggest industry when the country announced a record number of visitors that made it the world's most visited country.)

Over the past 20 years, while other holiday destinations have waxed and waned in popularity, France has continued to exert a steadily growing fascination on the British. Between 1970 and 1990, France's share of the British foreign holiday market has grown from 12.5%–22%. Over the past 10 years more than 50m British people have had a holiday in France.

Among readers of the *Independent* newspaper, for example, France is the chosen destination – one in five have been there in the past twelve months. You need only to see the speed with which *Independents* and *Guardians* sell out on cross-Channel ferries to hazard a guess at the demographics of the francophile traveller. But the growing appeal of France over the past three years – taking it from 5m to 8m British visitors annually – indicates that the country must now be finding growing favour amongst sub-scribers to the *Sun* and *Mirror*.

Over the past three years, France has attracted 2m first-time travellers. With the opening of Euro Disney last year and the completion of the Channel Tunnel, this trend is certain to grow even more rapidly.

Spain still leads in the package holiday market – but not by as much as it did. This year it is estimated that 2.5m British people will buy holiday packages to France out of an expected total of 8.3m visitors. Spain is likely to attract less than 3.5m package holiday-makers this year. While France suddenly smacked of style and elegance, the Spanish standard sun and sand package came to seem dull and unimaginative. On holiday abroad, did we really want lookalike Spanish tower block resorts with cafés selling English beer and beans on toast? If we are abroad, we want abroad – France, for all that we have changed to imitate it in many ways, is still very much a foreign country.

The depressed state of the British economy of the past few years has certainly benefited France. Compared with an air-inclusive package to Spain, a self-drive French holiday can be a cheap holiday. At the moment, for example, a family of two adults and up to three children can have a fortnight's camping holiday in France, including return ferry crossing, for less than £200. In Spain £200 would barely buy one person a seven-night self-catering package.

And with people booking their holiday later and later – leaving the decision until they feel sufficiently confident that they have the necessary funds – France also benefits. Compared with the problems of organizing a last-minute air package, it is a relatively straightforward matter to load up the car and head for the nearest cross-Channel ferry and to return when you have spent enough. And even during the peak time of July and August, it is possible at the last minute to find low-cost, self-catering accommodation.

But though the British are now visiting France in ever greater numbers, the invasion is bottled up in a few heavily-visited regions. British holiday-makers prefer to head for the seaside towns of Brittany and other resorts on the western coast from Nantes down to Biarritz; the Mediterranean coast takes longer to reach and is less popular.

Inland, with self-catering properties spread out throughout rural France – but with a bias towards the Dordogne and surrounding regions – British tourists are more widely dispersed. Unlike the Spanish costas or on Portugal's Algarve where the Brits gather in noticeable numbers, in France the British seem to fit in more harmoniously with the landscape.

France's great strength is the diversity of its countryside and the range of its climate. There are its mountains: the Alps, the Massif Central, the Pyrénées; there are the lakes and rivers from the Loire to Lake Annecy; and the plains of Picardy give way to the gentle valleys of the Auvergne. You can shiver beside the sea at Le Touquet or you can bake on the coast of the Riviera.

For activities you can choose from dozens of organized sports, from parapenting to walking along the thousands of well-signposted footpaths in the excellent Grande Randonnée network. France is a paradise for cyclists, a veritable Eden for canoeists and horse-riders.

So far the British have discovered only a relatively small part of what France has to offer the traveller. We know about gîtes and logis hotels; we have discovered Brittany and Bordeaux. The real invasion has yet to begin.

THE GÎTES PHENOMENON

I came to gîtes relatively late. My first was in 1983: a handsomely-converted house in Brittany, the second home of the man who owned the Peugeot garage in a nearby village. With his wife, he met us at the house on our arrival and plied us with bottles of local cider and sweet Breton cake. Our next gîte in the Dordogne was rather less well appointed. Shortly after we arrived, ants took possession of the kitchen. Not the modest common or garden domestic British ant – these were teenage mutant ninja ants, about four feet long and armed to the teeth. Open the larder door and they would be looking back at you as they trashed the jam: 'Outta my face. Don't mess with this ant, bro'!'.

Insect life was at large in the bedrooms too. What I thought were heat bumps on my legs, were eventually re-diagnosed as flea bites. But the worst horrors weren't the fleas or the ants, but the people next door. When you drive several hundred miles to south-west France, what you don't want to find next door to your away-from-it-all rural retreat is a car with a GB plate.

Jean-Paul Sartre got it almost right when he said that hell was other people – hell is being next door to a gîte with other British people with children called Tamsin and Gawain. Other British people, in fact, who are really just as boring as you and I – and who can't wait to tell you about favourite *boulangeries* and to moan about dreadful restaurants where the cheeseboard is taken straight out of the fridge. And they were listening to the news on Radio Four last night, amazing reception, and it was 89° in Birmingham apparently, and the tarmac has been melting on the runway at Heathrow airport . . .

One wonders what the French must make of we British on holiday. At the gîte we rented in the Dordogne last summer, the couple who owned it admitted that their British tenants were hard to fathom. We were all very polite, said the *patronne* – but why did the British never seen to be enjoying themselves on holiday? They always seem so *distrait*, so intense.

What the French can't understand, and what I didn't try to explain, is that the British holiday-maker has two settings: glum and hysterical. The rampant British traveller, whether he's a lager lout in Spain or a hooray Henry on the slopes of Zermatt, is not a pretty sight. Better the depressed souls in their dirty trainers, dark socks and short shorts that you can encounter in the market places of the Dordogne.

THE LOVE AFFAIR GOES ON

Will our holiday love affair with France continue? The signs are that it will. The strength of France as a holiday destination is its diversity. Those of us who first went to France on camping holidays, have experienced a progression. From tents we went to gîtes. From gîtes to other possibilities: canal holidays, cycle tours, walking or horse-riding.

In the early eighties, we discovered the small, charming French hotel. Led by the discriminating eye of Richard Binns with his influential self-published *Hidden France* and *French Leave* books, the British were encouraged to venture off the beaten track. For those who wanted to be led by the nose, Arthur Éperon pointed the way with his best-selling *Traveller's France* book. We learnt that we could probably spend the rest of our lives holidaying in France and never repeat ourselves or get bored.

France after all is a big country – twice the size of the UK with the same population – with a hugely varied landscape. From the Cornwall-like windblown coasts of Brittany to the palm-fringed beaches of the Riviera, there is an ever-changing scene – each region with its own particular attraction and style. There are many parts of Britain that I loathe, but I have never yet found a piece of France I didn't like. Even charmless Le Havre, a sort of Swindon by the sea, has a special place in my affections.

Certainly France is bound to become less foreign but for the holiday things that count: the weather, the food and the wine, Britain will be Britain and France will always be France. And never the twain will meet, even with a Tunnel. The things that made France attractive as a holiday destination 30 years ago remain as alluring today. The main difference is that France is no longer an experience enjoyed by a few adventurous travellers.

And this year, as I have done almost every year since 1962, I shall return to France for a holiday. My new passport photograph this summer will show a different person to that nine-year-old in 1962 – the pudding-bowl haircut and the protruding ears are less obvious although I still look confused – but my excitement at the prospect of visiting France remains exactly the same.

THE BEST OF FRANCE

In this book I hope to alert you to the best of the holiday possibilities offered by France. To provide a taster of what the country has to offer, here is my selection of French superlatives – I would be pleased to hear your nominations (the best recommendations will earn a free edition of the revised *Family France*).

Best Ferry Company

Cross-Channel ferries used to be basic in the extreme. Since most post-war vessels used for this purpose were probably converted navy-surplus craft, their lack of facilities is not surprising. Even 15 years ago the idea of even trying to select a 'best' cross-Channel company would have been preposterous. All ferries were dreadful. The only major difference worth commenting on was that one might have been less worse than another. But with only a couple of notable exceptions, cross-Channel ferries offered a profoundly depressing travel experience.

Since the ferry companies were compelled by law to compete with each other following the break-up of their cartel at the end of the seventies, the transformation has been wonderful to behold.

The introduction of the new Brittany Ferries ship *Normandie* on the Portsmouth to Caen route last year highlighted just how far things have changed. The *Normandie* is the largest ferry to operate between the UK and France with capacity for 2,200 passengers and 630 cars. It has 10 decks, 220 cabins providing 780 berths, 400 reclining seats – as well as cinemas, restaurants, coffee and tea shops, a duty-free shopping mall, a children's playroom and small hospital. On the Western Channel, Brittany Ferries reigns supreme. On the Eastern Channel out of Dover, P&O European Ferries remains the market leader and principal innovator.
See page 19

Best French Self-catering Specialist

VFB Holidays (0242 526338) has been voted favourite tour operator so often by readers of *Holiday Which?* magazine that by now the Cheltenham-based tour operator ought to have been given the trophy outright.

There is no great secret to VFB's success. The company which began business over 20 years ago as Vacances Franco-Brittaniques, has attracted a devoted following through its honest endeavours to offer genuine value for money and by paying attention to its customers needs and desires. (Want to know what the property you fancy really looks like? VFB will send you a selection of colour photographs to study.) VFB properties are not necessarily cheap – but when was cheap ever good? Each of the places it offers is carefully checked out, the property's French owners have probably been personally visited by VFB's owners Mike Bruce-Mitford and his French wife Françoise.
See page 91

Best French Hotel Chain

As far as I am concerned you can keep your Relais et Château and your Logis de France – give me a modern French chain hotel anytime. They are so civilised: no bossy *patronne* fussing about whether the children are wandering in and out of the hall with wet feet or if you are going to take their over-priced dinner this evening.

What I like is that there are so many different chains covering every sector of the market. At the bottom end you have Formule 1 (the complete do-it-yourself £13-a-night hotel where you even check yourself in with a credit card) up to luxury top-of-the-range places in the Meridien and Pullman/Sofitel chains.

Two-star Ibis and Urbis are perfectly fine but if you fancy pushing the boat out to the world of three star, go for Novotel. A supermarket-style trolley to get your bags from car to room, a mini bar, satellite television, buffet breakfast – and all for around £40 a room. (London bookings for Novotel, Ibis/Urbis, Pullman/Sofitel through Resinter 071 724 1000).
See page 60

Best French Restaurant Chain

A couple of years ago in the *Independent* we had a passionate correspondence on the subject of what vegetarians can do in France to avoid serious malnutrition. Dozens of readers wrote as one to advise: 'Go to Flunch!'

Flunch ('All lovers of good food find their way there' says its slogan) provides the best-value eating places to be found anywhere in France. There are over 100 Flunch's throughout France, self-service cafeterias, mostly attached to hypermarkets (at your first Flunch ask for a map which shows you where the rest are).

A family can dine out handsomely for less than £20: as well as low-cost dishes of the day (usually including a vegetarian meal) there are ridiculously cheap children's meals, good salads and luscious desserts. The only problem is that the French, knowing a good thing when they see it, pack the places to the rafters. Finding a table and enduring the queue (French queues are a torment devised by the devil) can take years off your life. It's worth having your lunch at 11.30am to beat the crowds.
See page 36

Best French Guidebook

If you like your information in no-nonsense chunks, Michelin does the business: the *Red Guide* (£11.95) for hotels, the *Green Guides* (£6.95) for the major tourist regions. No smart lines, no snide comments – just honest to goodness facts and a one to three star rating that one imagines is fixed by a solemn meeting of 100 august worthies in a Parisian salon.

There are more guides to France than any other destination in the world: silly really, as all you really need are the Michelins – plus, of course, the appropriate Michelin road maps (£1.75 or £3) or for sheer luxury, the hardback Michelin French road atlas (£20). For some smart lines – and the occasional snide comment – indulge in the *Rough Guide to France* (£9.99). Walkers should invest in the appropriate Grande Randonnée guide from Robertson McCarta (£8.95).

Best Holiday Region

Normandy is the region of France you usually drive through at breakneck speed in order to get to your proper holiday destination. Le Havre is certainly no St-Tropez, and Cherbourg will never be mistaken for La Rochelle – but don't judge a place by its ports. (After all, what sort of advert for Kent is provided by Dover?)

But why dash through Normandy? It is in many ways the perfect holiday place. It has excellent beaches (good gently-shelving sandy beaches that provided the perfect location for the D-Day Landings), world-class resorts like Deauville, the views along the Seine inspired the impressionist painters – for goodness sake, Normandy even has its own outrageously picturesque hilly region (grandiloquently described as 'La Suisse Normande'). There are fields filled with apple trees, there is the *bocage* country with its distinctive, high hedgerows, there are quaint fishing ports like Honfleur, medieval town centres like Rouen and more damn fine country towns than you ever saw in your life.
See page 141

Best French Inland Waterway

France has Europe's most marvellous system of inland waterways – 5,000 miles of navigable canals and rivers – yet the French seem almost completely indifferent to the idea of canal holidays. As a result, with a few exceptions, the canals are criminally underused.

The Canal du Midi and the Burgundy Canal are two of the busiest, particularly the Midi – negotiating locks here in August can be like circumventing Piccadilly Circus in the rush hour. My favourite waterway is the deserted Saône, an exquisite river in France's delectable Franche-Comté: lush woods, soaring eagles, plunging herons and perfect peace.

French Country Cruises (081 995 3642) features the Saône: a Penichette 1107 which is 36 feet long, has three double beds and

one single bed, toilet, shower and large kitchen area costs from
£547 to £1120 per week for the boat hire: inclusive prices with
ferry travel are available.
See page 112

Best City Break
It is hard to think of any French place in which I would not want
to spend a weekend. Even the most unlikely places – such as Le
Havre or Calais – have a wealth of redeeming features.

Paris is the perfect choice for a couple of nights, so perfect that
it might have been tailor-made for a weekend break package. And
you can return again and again and still find something new to
enjoy.

If I had to choose one place outside Paris for a weekend, I
would head for Le Touquet. If I wanted to be sure of the sun,
I would head south: Perpignan, Montpellier, Nîmes, Avignon,
Toulon, Nice, Menton are all fine. Best of all is Antibes, where
Graham Greene lived his final years – and which F Scott Fitzgerald
visited and described in *Tender is the Night*. Two nights at the Hôtel
du Cap (rooms from £250 per night) would suit me down to the
ground.
See page 115

Best Bargain
On a pence per mile basis, train travel in France is much, much
cheaper than it is in Britain. Many stations also offer cycle hire
from around £5 per day.
See page 31

Best Drive
The Loire Valley, chock-full of fairy-tale castles sounds nauseat-
ingly twee and far too touristy for any serious traveller to under-
take. In fact the country west of Tours is perfect for leisurely drives
through forests, beside rivers (like the Cher, Indre and Vienne),
past fields of golden sunflowers, among neat vineyards. The most
chocolate-boxy of all the castles: the Château d'Ussé – Charles
Perrault's inspiration for *Sleeping Beauty* – is truly a delight.
See page 140

THE WORST OF FRANCE
• Stately homes and castles: most historic French buildings which
open to the public are almost unbelievably shambolic. They seem
for the most part to be in private ownership and run by ancient
retainers who operate at eccentric opening hours. Here's a tip for
Jack Lang – or whichever French minister is responsible – send

someone to have a look at the National Trust or English Heritage. We may not be able to do much else in Britain but we run a ripping stately home.

• The Périphérique, the ring road around Paris: the motorway from hell. Avoid this at every possible cost unless you enjoy driving through your worst nightmare.

• Some say France would be a great country if it wasn't for the French. Are they rude, supercilious, intolerant, self-satisfied, arrogant, cunning, abusive, insensitive, chauvinistic? Or are these just the nice ones . . . ?

• Public toilets: while the French are happy to relieve themselves on the side of the road *en plein air*, they may be surprised to hear that the rest of Europe is less keen. France should build more public toilets and forget about having them patrolled by a ferocious concierge demanding large sums of cash for admission.

• Vegetarians: somebody please tell the French that an increasing number of people do not wish to eat deceased cows and pigs and if customers want just salad and chips the waiters can serve it up without sighing plaintively and rolling their eyes.

• Fresh milk: if the French are so worried about their stomachs, how is it they have such an affection for UHT milk? Can they really have it on their cornflakes? Advice to small French shopkeepers: get your summer orders in now for pasteurised milk.

• French pop music: those French pop stars in full – Johnny Halliday . . . er, that's it.

I hope you enjoy *Family France*: if you have any comments, suggestions or recommendations, please write to Family France at PO Box 67, Bath.

1

PLANNING YOUR HOLIDAY

So you have decided that you want to spend your holiday in France. This is the easy part. The more difficult questions are: what sort of holiday do you want, in which part of France and – if you plan to drive – which is the best way of getting across the Channel.

More British holiday-makers visit France than any other country in the world. Not surprisingly, perhaps, there are more different types of holiday available to France than anywhere else. In this guide, we offer a wide selection of the enormous variety available.

The best holidays tend to be the ones that are most carefully planned. Before choosing, decide exactly what you want. This may seem obvious but it is surprising how many people pick the wrong holiday simply because either they didn't give it much thought or else they failed to consult the other members of the family.

I have to confess that I tend towards the concept of benign dictatorship in selecting a holiday (I'm arrogant enough to believe that I know best!). But you do need at least to go through the motions of consulting one's nearest and dearest before coming to a conclusion. Do the children want to be near the seaside? Will they want access to a swimming pool? Will you want to lie on the beach or will you want plenty of interesting towns, museums and castles to visit?

The more effort you put into picking your actual destination and the type of holiday you want, the more fun you will actually have when you get there. And, of course, planning the holiday can be half the fun too.

TAKING THE CAR
Firstly, you have to make a decision: do you want to take your car? The advantages of driving to France are flexibility and economy. A car is more or less indispensable if you want to take a gîte holiday based in what is likely to be relatively isolated countryside. If you have small children it is a great advantage to be able to load the kids – and their many belongings – into the back of the car and

14

drive straight to your holiday destination. Having a car is the best way of exploring rural France off the beaten track. You could of course fly to your destination and hire a car locally, but you should be warned that car hire in France is expensive (even more expensive than Britain).

But a car is not the only way of travelling. Rail and bus transport in France offer a comprehensive means of seeing the country – and the countryside. France is perfect walking territory and an ideal place for cycling. And don't forget the canal and river network which can be enjoyed without the necessity of a car.

However don't dismiss the idea of taking a car to France because you are anxious about driving abroad. Any reasonably competent driver should have not the slightest difficulty in adapting to the French roads. Driving on the 'wrong' side seems strange at first but you will be surprised by how quickly you adapt (after the first hour driving the wrong way around roundabouts will come to seem the most natural thing in the world!).

If you do not speak French, taking your car might seem to pose other complications. For example, what about when you have to stop for petrol? You might be reassured to know that France, like Britain, has mostly self-service petrol stations. Fill up and pay at the cash desk either with cash or your Access or Visa card. You can say *bonjour* if you wish – and you should say *bonjour* and *au revoir*, the French are scrupulously polite – but you can get away with saying absolutely nothing if you prefer. And it is worth noting that while only 6% of the British speak French, 53% of French people now speak English.

Unless you have compelling reasons for not driving to France (not having a car would be a good reason), my advice would be to take your car. A drive of several hundred miles to the Mediterranean may be a bit ambitious for your first outing, though it is much easier than you might imagine and tremendous fun. If you are worried about whether you are up to the driving, why not dip your toe in with a short hop to Brittany or Normandy?

WHAT TYPE OF HOLIDAY?
The question of whether you might fancy a trip around the battlefields of the Somme or a tour of the vineyards of Bordeaux is a question we will examine later (see chapter six). The first thing to decide is whether you want a hotel or a self-catering holiday. This is not just a matter of price, though on the whole it is cheaper to stay in a rented house or apartment than it is to stay in a hotel.

Self-catering is usually preferred by families with children. The kids are able to eat what they like, when they like. They can race about without disturbing anybody. Parents can enjoy the excellent food and wine sold in the local shops, markets and hypermarkets. This is the best way of immersing yourself in French life.

But before picking a gîte holiday, decide whether you and your family are keen to be in the heart of the countryside. If your children really are fond of the beach, and they yearn for the company of other children, the pleasures of French rural life are likely to pall rather quickly. There are plenty of self-catering places near the sea, though these tend to be conventional self-catering apartments and villas rather than lower-priced gîtes.

But for a holiday, the main drawback of self-catering is that it offers no break from the daily chores of cooking, cleaning and washing up. Hotels offer the advantage of a chore-free break: someone to cook the dinner, someone to make the bed. Hotels, of course, are more expensive – but not necessarily that much more expensive. The new French breed of low-cost hotels and motels offer good quality family rooms from under £30 per night. More agreeable hotels in more attractive locations serving good food are likely to cost from around £60 per night (see chapter five). A hotel of course can also offer entertainment. A swimming pool, tennis courts, bicycles, even satellite TV with EastEnders and Neighbours beamed straight from London. If you want a touring holiday, driving round from place to place, then a hotel is the only practicable option.

In this book we offer a comprehensive guide to both hotel and self-catering accommodation: carefully consider which type of holiday would suit you best.

GETTING ACROSS THE CHANNEL

Choosing your route
It is worth devoting a lot of consideration to choosing the correct route to your destination in France. Taking time to pick the right crossing, not only saves time and money – it can also mean less driving and a more cheerful start to the holiday.

Start first with the total cost: don't just look at the ferry fare when you choose a crossing. A short-sea crossing is usually cheapest (though not much cheaper than the longer crossings), but how much money will you save if it results in additional petrol costs and extra motorway tolls? Cross-Channel car travellers tend to be creatures of habit. Someone who makes his first crossing from Dover to Calais, often goes on using Dover-Calais regardless of whether or not it is the best choice given his final destination.

Consider for example Mr and Mrs Smith, from Manchester, who are planning to travel to their gîte near Bordeaux in their 4.5m long, 30 miles per gallon car.

If they travel Dover-Calais, the peak time one-way fare will be £145. The mileage to Dover from Manchester is 254 miles; Calais to Bordeaux is 551 miles: total mileage 805. Petrol costs for the journey will be around £56. Autoroute costs will amount to around £50. They will need at least one overnight stop en route; the cost for a reasonable hotel for one night would be around £40. Total cost for the journey will be £291.

If they travel Portsmouth-Caen, the peak time one-way fare will be £153. The mileage to Portsmouth from Manchester is 220; Caen to Bordeaux is 367 miles: total mileage 587. Petrol costs for the journey will be around £40. Autoroute costs will amount to around £20. Instead of an overnight hotel, they could travel overnight on the ferry: a cabin for two with washbasin would cost £32. Total cost for the journey will be £245.

Not only does the Portsmouth crossing mean a saving of more than 200 miles driving one way (more than 400 miles for the return trip), the total journey itself is cheaper even though the actual Channel crossing is more expensive (by some curious economic process, fares for Western Channel journeys are roughly the same as short-sea crossings, even though the Western Channel trips are up to five times as long).

The short-sea crossings have undoubted advantages however – not the least of which is the frequency of service. If you miss a sailing at Dover, for example, there's another one along in another hour – if you miss the boat at Portsmouth you are likely to have a delay of several hours. The other attraction of Dover is that the loading and unloading of cars is fast and efficient. Unless you pass through at peak times, you are likely to speed through the port much more quickly than Portsmouth or other ports on the longer crossings. Thanks to improvements to the M20, Dover and the other short-sea crossing ports are also now much more accessible to other parts of the country.

One disadvantage of the short-sea routes used to be the boisterous armies of school parties and day-trippers. With the introduction of motorist-only rooms and 'Club' lounges, it is now possible to escape the madding crowd and spend the journey in peace.

Points to consider
• Look at a large map which shows Britain and France: put a straight line between your starting point in Britain and your destination in France. Find where the most direct ferry crossing lies.

• Study the motorway network both in Britain and France. You have to pay motorway tolls in France but if time is of the essence, the charges are worth paying. Motorways in France offer very fast travel (contra-flows seem non-existent on the autoroutes).

• Compare prices: the main ferry operators charge more or less the same fares but sometimes there may be special offers and good savings available by taking particular crossings. By travelling in the middle of the night out of Dover, your return fare can be cut by up to half.

• On short-sea crossings seek the tranquility of the motorists' lounge. On longer crossings during the day, take a cabin to avoid the madding crowd – day cabins are much less expensive than overnight cabins.

The operators

North Sea Ferries	(0482 77177)
Olau Line	(0795 666666)
Sally Line	(0843 595522)
Hoverspeed	(0304 240241)
Brittany Ferries	(0705 827701)
P&O European Ferries	(0304 203388)
Stena Sealink Line	(0233 647047)
Truckline	(0202 666466)

The Channel Tunnel

Unlike the ferry companies who deposit several hundred cars and passengers in Calais every hour – Eurotunnel will have the capacity to unload similar numbers every fifteen minutes. When demand increases, shuttle services could operate every six minutes.

This 'Le Shuttle' service, as it is to be called, will be operated independent of the inter-city rail services run by the British, French and Belgian railway companies which will link Waterloo station in London with Paris Gare du Nord in three hours and Brussels Midi in three hours ten minutes (the opening of the highspeed rail link from London to the Tunnel will eventually trim thirty minutes off these times). The Shuttle terminal will handle motorcyclists but there is no facility to handle foot passengers and cyclists. Eurotunnel expects local companies to offer bus services which will use the Tunnel: these will also supply transport for cyclists.

If Eurotunnel achieves the level of speed and efficiency it is planning, the ferries will have to work hard to compete. The projected one hour, 'motorway to motorway', Le Shuttle Tunnel journey from Cheriton to Sangatte, near Calais, compares to at least two hours for a motorway to motorway crossing by ferry –

A COMPARISON OF PEAK JULY/AUGUST 1993 CHANNEL FERRY FARES AND SERVICES

Route	Operator	Daily sailings	Journey time	Return fare (4.5m car & 2 adults)
Hull–Rotterdam	North Sea Ferries	1	14hrs	£358
Hull–Zeebrugge	North Sea Ferries	1	14hrs	£358
Felixstowe–Zeebrugge	P&O Ferries	2	5hrs 45mns	£269–294
Harwich–Hook of Holland	Stena	2	6hrs 30mns	£236–292
			8hrs 30mns (night)	
Sheerness–Vlissingen	Olau	2	7hrs	£202–228
			8hrs 30mns (night)	
Ramsgate–Dunkerque	Sally	5	2hrs 30mns	£185–247
Dover–Oostende	P&O Ferries	8	4hrs	£125–290
Dover–Calais	Hoverspeed SeaCat	8	50mns	£216–324
	H'cft	12	35mns	£287–324
Dover–Calais	Stena	22	1hr 30mns	£124–290
Dover–Calais	P&O Ferries	25	1hr 15mns	£125–290
Folkestone–Boulogne	Hoverspeed SeaCat		55mns	£179–261
Newhaven–Dieppe	Stena	5/6	4hrs	£176–294
Portsmouth–Le Havre	P&O Ferries	4	5hrs 45mns	£197–297
Portsmouth–Caen	Brittany Ferries	3	6hrs	£232–306
Portsmouth–Cherbourg	P&O Ferries	2/3	4hrs 45mns	£156–274
Portsmouth–St Malo	Brittany Ferries	3	9hrs	£289–328
Portsmouth–Bilbao	P&O Ferries	1	28hrs	£592–655
Southampton–Cherbourg	Stena	2 pr week	8hrs (night)	£192–270
		1/2	6hrs (day)	
Poole–Cherbourg	Truckline Ferries	1/2	4hrs 15mns	£212–281
Plymouth–Roscoff	Brittany Ferries	1/3	6hrs	£247–324
Plymouth–Santander	Brittany Ferries	2 pr week	24hrs	£521

19

frequently this Dover to Calais journey can take up to three hours.

Where the Dover to Calais run has been something of an obstacle course – show your ticket, get your boarding card, show your passport, show your boarding card: all hurry up and wait – the Tunnel journey is designed to be sweet simplicity. There will be no advance booking – although you can pre-pay if you wish. You leave the M20, pay the fare, clear immigration (British and French passport checks will be carried out before boarding), drive aboard the next Shuttle and head for France – where once off the train you drive straight on to the autoroute. Whether things run as smoothly as Eurotunnel hopes, remains to be seen.

The ferries will survive. Many people like the sea trip: they enjoy having a meal at the cafeteria or restaurant; they love browsing in the shops and duty-free supermarkets; they appreciate having a chance to relax after perhaps a long drive to the port.

But this affection shouldn't be overrated. It will probably not take people long to realise that they can take the Shuttle to Calais and if they want a break for shopping they can head for the nearest Mammouth or Auchan hypermarket – or linger over an excellent meal in some jolly country restaurant just off the autoroute.

But what of the claustrophobes, those people – particularly women, it appears – who say that wild horses, let alone a high speed train, would not drag them through the blackness of the Tunnel? This anxiety is largely based on misapprehension about what Tunnel travel will actually be like for motorists. During the journey through the Tunnel, which will take 35 minutes, car passengers will have to remain in the Shuttle coach with their cars. This conjures up a rather forbidding image of being trapped inside a car in the dark confines of a cattle wagon – albeit a very hi-tech cattle wagon. At the Eurotunnel exhibition centre at Cheriton, a full-size mock up of a car-carrying Shuttle wagon shows that these are well-lit and surprisingly cheerful.

You do not have to remain inside your car – although there will be nowhere else to sit. Despite the protests of the French who considered toilets unnecessary on such a short journey, a compromise was reached with a toilet being available in every other carriage. On the train, car radios can be tuned to a Le Shuttle radio service which will offer en route information. Electronic signs in the wagons show how far you have to travel to your destination.

Faced with the possibility of a prolonged wintery storm-tossed crossing of the Channel by ferry or a rapid transit by train through the Tunnel – it seems likely that even the most ardent claustrophobe will opt for the Tunnel.

Those who live in London and the South will no doubt quickly adjust to the fact that through the Tunnel, Bruges is nearer than Blackpool – that Calais can be reached as quickly as Bristol. The British Tourist Authority says it expects the Tunnel to generate an additional 1.5m tourists to Britain. But clearly given the novelty of the Tunnel it is impossible to have any serious idea of just how many new people will be attracted to travel – in either direction.

Certainly many will be curious to make the trip to see what the Tunnel crossing is like. If it was just a question of trying it out – popping over and back – clearly the Tunnel could be just a nine day wonder. What is more likely is that thousands, probably hundreds of thousands, perhaps millions of British motorists will, for the first time, cross the Channel to France for a day or even two days.

But in the short term, the first wave of Tunnel Travellers will head for the coast and other towns and cities within easy driving distance. To the north of Calais a string of attractive Belgian cities beckons: Bruges, Ghent, Ostend, Liege and, the capital, Brussels; each have enough art galleries, museums, cathedrals and picturesque squares and cobbled streets to last a lifetime of weekend breaks. Belgium's most overlooked delights are its seaside places from Knokke-Heist to De Panne, all full of good value hotels, Michelin-starred restaurants and magnificent cycle paths.

South of the Tunnel lie Boulogne and Le Touquet within easy driving distance, further away is Dieppe – and across the Seine are the delightful towns of Honfleur, Deauville and Cabourg. When the new autoroute from Calais to Rouen opens, shortly after the opening of the Tunnel, Normandy will be less than 60 minutes' drive away.

In just a year from now, the Tunnel should have transformed itself from just a hole in the ground to a thrilling pathway to a Brave New World.

MILEAGES FROM CHANNEL PORTS

Paris	Miles
Calais	180
Dunkerque	190
Dieppe	124
Le Havre	125
Caen	152

Nice	
Calais	762
Dieppe	703
Caen	731

Rennes

Calais	312
Le Havre	176
Caen	116
Cherbourg	125
St Malo	43
Roscoff	136

Bordeaux

Calais	551
Le Havre	403
Caen	367
Cherbourg	384
St Malo	318

WHAT YOU WILL NEED TO TAKE

• British driving licence.

• The vehicle's registration document: it's advisable to have a letter of authorisation with you if the vehicle is not registered in your name.

• Green card: this should be available free of charge from your insurance company: without notifying your insurance company to tell them you are taking your car abroad you may be automatically reduced to the minimum Third Party insurance abroad.

• Passport: a British visitor's passport available from main post offices is sufficient.

• GB sticker: ask for a free one from your ferry company.

• Car breakdown insurance: such as AA Five-Star.

• Personal and medical insurance: don't go on holiday without it.

• Beam deflectors for your headlights to stop them blinding oncoming passengers when dipped: you will be driving on the 'wrong' side of the road and lights dip in the wrong direction. Car accessory shops sell these kits – it's easier and cheaper to use black insulating tape.

• Warning triangles, spare bulbs, fire extinguishers and first aid kits: all may prove to be useful.

• It's worth timing your car's next service to be carried out shortly before you set off on holiday.

• Decide how you will take your spending money. Access and

Visa cards are widely accepted: if you know your PIN number these can also be used to withdraw money (in local currency) from French bank cash machines (check the machines to see whether they have the Visa or Mastercard sign). Since I discovered my PIN number, on trips abroad my credit card has become the principle source of spending money. Travellers' cheques offer a reliable back up; Eurocheques, available from your bank, are also worth thinking about. You will need local currency before you arrive – don't change money on the ferries: they tend to offer the most ungenerous exchange rates.

• Invest in some good maps: a good, large Michelin map for route planning and larger scale maps to cover your destination. The *Red Michelin Guide to France* is invaluable not only for its information about hotels and restaurants, but also for its excellent town plans. The regional *Green Guides* are the best for general tourist information about the area.

FLYING TO FRANCE

About 15 years ago, flying to France used to involve a trip to London where you could expect to find a flight to Paris and perhaps a couple of other French cities served irregularly throughout the week.

These days there are not only hourly flights to Paris from Heathrow, but frequent services to the French capital from Gatwick, Stansted and London City airports – as well as provincial departures from Jersey, Southampton, Cardiff, Bristol, Birmingham, East Midlands, Leeds, Bradford, Manchester, Newcastle, Edinburgh, Glasgow, Aberdeen and Belfast. In the past five years a comprehensive network of services has grown up from London to provincial cities in France. There are now direct flights available to places like Brive, Toulouse, Bordeaux, Lourdes, Montpellier, Narbonne, Nantes, Rouen, Brest, Caen, Clermond-Ferrand, Deauville, Lille, Metz, Strasbourg, Mulhouse, Nice – as well as to major cities like Marseilles and Lyons.

For the cheapest fares it pays to shop around. For example, official British Airways deals for London to Paris cost from £102 for a return booked 14 days in advance, involving a Saturday night stay, travelling Monday to Thursday; a return involving travel on Friday to Sunday costs from £113. A less restricted Euro Budget return costs from £200, while the completely unrestricted Club class return costs £318. French low-fare specialist Nouvelles Frontières (071 629 7772) has charter flight returns available from as little as £69.

Further information: Air France (071 742 6600); British Airways

(0345 222111); British Midland (071 589 5599); Brymon Airways (0345 090000).

FRANCE BY RAIL

Air France rail

For holiday-makers to France, this is one of the best deals on the market. Air France has teamed up with SNCF French Railways to offer a combined fare to any destination on the French rail network. A return ticket from London to Dijon in Burgundy, for example, costs £139 including a flight to Paris and a TGV high-speed train journey from Paris to Dijon (the child fare is £89). For an additional payment, you can fly to Paris from Birmingham, Bristol, Edinburgh/Glasgow, Manchester or Southampton.

The Air France Rail deal also allows travellers to combine a return flight to Paris with the SNCF Euro Domino unlimited rail pass: a flight from Bristol, for example, combined with a three-day pass (three days rail travel in a one month period), costs £215 for over–26s, £198 for 21–26 year olds and £131 for 2–11 year olds.

Further information: Air France Rail reservations (081 571 1413; 071 499 1075 brochures.)

Euro Domino Rail Pass

Three days unlimited rail travel in a period of one month costs £102; five days £141; and ten days £221. For under–26s the pass costs £84, £124 and £194 respectively.

Further information French Railways, French Railways House, 179 Piccadilly, London W1V 0BA (0891 515477). Information and bookings for rail travel to France available at the International Rail Centre, Victoria Station, London SW1 1JY (071 834 2345 enquiries; 071 828 0892 credit card bookings). Bookings and enquiries can also be made at selected British Rail stations and travel agents appointed by British Rail International.

COACHES TO FRANCE

Eurolines (071 730 0202) operates regular services to Paris and over 30 other destinations in France. Services from London include regular coaches to Paris, Euro Disney, Lyon, Bordeaux, Bayonne, Lourdes, Strasbourg, Marseilles, Nice, Chamonix, Perpignan, Montpellier, Toulouse – as well as Channel Hopper services to Le Havre, Calais, Cherbourg, St Malo, Roscoff and Caen. There is also a service from Bristol to Paris via Le Havre and Rouen. Return fares from London to Paris, for example, cost from £52 (£49 for under-25s).

MOTORAIL

In principle, the idea of Motorail is perfect. You present yourself and your car at Calais or Dieppe – your car goes on a transporter while you accommodate yourself in first or second class sleeping compartments. The train crosses France at night while you sleep: in the morning you arrive refreshed at your destination and drive your car off to begin your holiday (the concept is particularly attractive to people with young children and old cars).

Every rose, however, has its thorns. For a service which sells itself on speed, it can often seem to run at an infuriatingly unhurried pace when it comes to loading and unloading cars. The accommodation on the Motorail train is good but fairly basic – even in first class. If you are a light sleeper, you can expect a disturbed night's sleep: the train rattles about considerably, and often comes to a halt for no obvious reason. Washing facilities are basic (one wonders why the water for the wash basins is *non potable*). Take plenty of mineral water and lots of food: food on the train is sometimes available on a self-service restaurant car but it is not brilliant.

But despite the problems, there is much to like about Motorail. Even with all the unexplained delays and the lack of efficient organisation during the unloading process, having your car Motorailed to the south of France gets you to your holiday destination very quickly – and spares you the labour of a long drive. There are particular attractions for people with young children; and for people with elderly cars which they don't want to risk on a long, hot motorway journey.

Also, any excuse to gaze at France from a train is an opportunity worth taking. Rattling into the Dordogne at dawn, for example, it is marvellous to throw up the blind and look at the countryside shrouded in morning mist. On the return trip, it is a pleasure to lie on the couchettes watching the sunset. The country flashes past like a series of Cartier Bresson postcards: a wedding party, a *bal musette*: the sound of a small dance band playing in a crowded square, the smell of food cooking, coloured lights twinkling through the gathering dusk.

Motorail however is not necessarily a cheap way to travel. A return trip from Calais to Brive for a family of four costs from around £700 including the Channel ferry crossing and couchette accommodation. There is no question that it would be far cheaper to drive down – even if you ate at good restaurants and stayed at a very expensive hotel en route you would still end up paying less than the Motorail fare.

But that's not really the point. People don't seem to use Motorail to save money. Many do it for very sensible reasons that have to do with travelling with children or infirm cars. But one suspects that many do it for no better reason than that they like it.

Motorail routes from the channel ports
Calais to: Avignon; Biarritz; Bordeaux; Brive; Fréjus/St Raphaël; Moutiers; Narbonne; Nice; Toulouse.
Dieppe to: Avignon; Fréjus/St Raphaël.
There is also a wide choice of Motorail services from Paris, Lille and Nantes.
Further information: French Railways has special discount cross-Channel fares with Brittany Ferries, Hoverspeed, Stena Sealink and P&O European Ferries which offer substantial savings. Railsavers (0253 300080) offers discounts on Motorail for travel in the UK and on the Continent.

Motorbikes
Motorbikes are transported on all routes within France.

Bicycles
These must be transported inside your vehicle. Bicycles carried on specially designed roof- or boot-racks will be refused on Motorail and will be forwarded as registered luggage on the next available parcels train (subject to a handling fee and delivery within five days).
Further information: Motorail brochures are available from high street travel agencies or direct from French Railways, 179 Piccadilly, London W1V 0BA (071 409 3518; fax 071 409 1652); brochure requests (071 499 1075).

2

GETTING AROUND IN FRANCE

ON THE ROAD

Motorways

In those not so long ago days before motorways, driving in France was frequently a nightmare. The main holiday routes had two settings: dead stop (the jams were appalling) and terrifying (the traffic would occasionally speed up encouraging madmen to over-take on blind bends). In the summer the daily toll of casualties on French roads used to read like a body count from the Battle of Verdun.

The construction of the motorway system has transformed motoring in France. Shifting the bulk of the traffic, particularly holiday traffic, on to the motorways has freed the ordinary roads to allow a more comfortable passage for the driver happy to take his or her time.

The French motorway system is magnificent: over 3,000 miles of fast, efficient modern highway. If you want to reel off the miles, you can clock up big distances on the motorway. One summer Saturday I joined the autoroute at Nîmes in the south of France at about 7am and reached the ferry port at Calais slightly less than 12 hours later at about 6.45pm. Allowing for a number of comfort stops – and a break for about 90 minutes at the Cora hypermarket (worth a detour at the Auxerre Nord turn off) to shop and have lunch at the cafeteria – the journey of 627 miles took around 10 hours. If the port of Calais had not been turned into a madhouse by a strike which affected the French half of Sealink, we would have been home in Bath by midnight. (We caught a later ferry and arrived home at 2.30am).

Yet it is not so long ago when a drive to the south of France was like taking the road to hell. The RN7 from Paris to the Mediter-ranean was possibly the worst road in the world. Overtaking was a dice-game with death – the roadside scrap-heaps of smashed-up cars suggested that it was a game many people lost. Anyone planning a drive from Calais to somewhere like Nîmes would have had to allow at least two full days of driving.

For the whole of the journey from the gîte in France to our home in Bath, all but 40 or 50 miles was on motorway. Some people begrudge the motorway tolls in France – the journey from Nîmes to Calais costs around £35 – but you cannot criticise the excellent state of the French motorways. In 627 miles there were no road-works – not one single contra-flow. And the imposition of tolls seems to cut down the amount of traffic on the French motorways – on weekdays there appear to be very few lorries compared with British motorways – one presumes that lorry drivers on the Continent prefer free-of-charge passage on the ordinary highways with their convenient Routiers restaurants. On weekends most lorries are banned from French motorways.

If there is one criticism of the French motorways, it is that traffic goes too fast. Germans in their Mercedes, no doubt accustomed to their speed-unlimited autobahns, hug the fast-lanes at speeds which must exceed 120mph. If they can keep that up without attracting the attention of the French traffic police – who seem to maintain a low profile on the autoroutes – that would be Nîmes to Calais in five hours, Nîmes to Bath in about eight hours. I expect someone will write to tell me that they have done the journey faster than that.

I wouldn't recommend hammering up and down France via the motorway. Firstly, it's dangerous: all the research suggests that the more you drive, the more tired you get, and the more likely you are to have an accident. Secondly – and more importantly – if you are on the motorway, you see nothing of the wonderful French countryside. While you can do 500 miles in one day on the motorways, it would make better sense to do it in two days – schedule a break off the motorway in some charming, small hotel.

Life in the fast lane
You may have to pay to drive on French autoroutes but you will find them much more user-friendly than British motorways. The fact that people have to pay means that the autoroutes are generally less busy (though you may find this hard to believe on an August holiday weekend when you are stuck in a 12-mile jam outside Lyons).

There are regular service stations (*aires de service*) roughly every 25 miles, selling petrol and diesel – usually with good quality and good value cafés and restaurants. In between the service stations, you will also find *aires de repos*: rest areas with toilets and children's playgrounds where you can take a break. Since they can attract thieves, you would be advised not to sleep overnight in the car in rest areas.

Paying the motorway toll is straightforward. When you join the motorway you will normally encounter a machine with a knob (of course, this will irritatingly be on the wrong side of the car – you will need the assistance of co-operative spouses or children). Press the knob and a ticket will appear – keep the ticket in a safe place until you are asked to produce it at the payment booth (which will also be on the wrong side of the car). If you lose the ticket, you will have to pay the maximum possible toll (so don't let it blow out of the window as I did once). Once you have presented the ticket, an electronic indicator will show the amount you have to pay. If you have no cash, Access and Visa cards are accepted. Many payment areas have automatic machines which accept coins which you toss into a basket sending the barrier up. If you do not have the right change, head for the booth with an attendant.

As on British motorways, there are emergency telephones if you need assistance – usually two kilometres apart (about one and a quarter miles). And, as in Britain, you would be wise not to linger too long on the hard shoulder – if you do have to stay on the hard shoulder because you have broken down, wait behind the barrier well away from the traffic.

MOTORWAY TOLLS

From	To	Toll
Calais	Paris	£11
	Reims	£10.50
	Troyes	£16
	Dijon	£23
Paris	Mâcon Nord	£12
	Lyons	£14.50
	Le Havre	£ 3.50
	Caen	£ 6.50
	Chartres	£ 3
	Tours	£10
	Bordeaux	£25
	Nantes	£16
Lyons	Orange	£ 7.50
	Salon	£10
Salon	Brignoles	£ 3.50
	Cannes	£ 8
	Nice	£ 9.50
Reims	Strasbourg	£14
Rouen	Caen	£ 4

29

Mâçon	Annecy	£ 6
Beaune	Strasbourg	£ 9
Orange	Montpellier	£ 4
	Perpignan	£10.50
	Narbonne	£ 8
Bourdeaux	Narbonne	£16.50
Clermont-Ferrand	Paris	£17
	St Etienne	£ 6

Rules and regulations
• Children under 10 are not allowed in the front seats; children in the back seats must wear seat belts or approved child restraints.
• Minimum age of drivers: 18 years of age.
• Speed limits: on the Paris Périphérique, the city's ring road, the speed limit is 50mph (80km/h) – it has to be said that the Parisians seem to treat this as a lower rather than a higher limit. The speed limit in built-up areas is 31mph (50km/h), 56 mph (90km/h) elsewhere, 69mph (110km/h) on dual carriageways with a central reservation, 81mph (130km/h) on motorways. In wet weather (defined by the need to have your windscreen wipers on) speed limits are reduced: on roads outside built up areas the limit is reduced to 50mph (80km/h), 62mph (100km/h) on dual carriageways and 69mph (110km/h) on motorways. Drivers with less than a year's experience are not allowed to exceed 56mph (90km/h).
• Police are ready, willing and able to exact draconian on-the-spot fines. Common offences include failing to come to a complete halt at 'stop' signs – also be careful not to cross solid single lines in the middle of the road which prohibit overtaking.
• Car crime is as common in France as it is in Britain: British cars seem more at risk because their GB plates invite particular attention (they suggest rich pickings – the French clearly haven't heard about our hard life under Norman Lamont). Never leave your car parked on the street overnight if you can avoid it: find out if there is somewhere offering secure off-road parking – or choose a hotel that has its own safe parking area. Never leave anything of value in the car while it is unattended at any time, day or night. Car alarms may not prevent an attempted break-in but they could deter a casual thief so think about having one installed before your holiday if you do not already have one.
• In France petrol is *essence*: the ordinary grade is referred to simply as *essence*, the higher is *super*. Unless you have the right engine, do not fill up with *gas-oil* (also called *gazole*) which is

diesel. Unleaded petrol is *sans plomb*. *Faites le plein* means 'fill her up'.

• Traffic lights follow the British pattern except they go straight from red to green. If the amber traffic light is flashing (a common phenomenon at many traffic lights outside the rush hour), it means 'proceed with caution'.

• The two most commonly signposted places in France are *centre ville* and *toutes directions*: if you want to go to the town centre or city centre follow *centre ville* – if you are heading on somewhere else, follow the *toutes directions* signs until you see your destination signposted. French signposting can be infuriatingly erratic – signs for Tours or Clermont-Ferrand will suddenly vanish just when you need them most. For this reason have a good map handy.

On the rails

SNCF French Railways operates a reliable, efficient and generally good value service – particularly the excellent TGV high speed trains which operate at over 150mph from Paris to more than 40 towns and cities including Le Mans, Nantes, Rennes, Brest, Tours, Bordeaux, Hendaye, Dijon, Lyon, Marseille and Chambery – and from 1993 north from Paris to the English Channel.

Car hire

Expect to pay from around £200 per week for the smallest size car (Ford Fiesta, for example). Companies to contact include Avis (081 848 8733); Budget (0800 181181); EuroDollar (0895 233300); Europcar InterRent (081 950 5050); Hertz (081 679 1799); Holiday Autos (071 491 1111); Trans Hire (071 978 1922).

Buses

Unlike Britain, the French rail network is so comprehensive and fares are such good value that long-distance coach services are unnecessary. Information about local bus services is available locally from tourist offices.

Bicycles

Bikes can be hired at over 200 railway stations in France at modest rates. Mountain bikes can also be hired from an increasing number of shops.

3

LIFE IN FRANCE: SHOPPING AND EATING

In France, shopping is a business which is still taken very seriously. Unlike Britain where it is seen as a chore which must be completed with all possible haste (the Sainsbury's 200m sprint on a Saturday morning), the French seem to take a special pleasure in their food purchases.

On the British high street, the specialist food shop has become practically extinct. But in France, even the smallest town can boast an array of butchers, bakers and cake shops – each with a window display designed to set the mouth watering. And while France still clings to its small specialist shops, it has also turned its face to the future – leading Europe with the size and quality of its modern out-of-town hypermarkets and shopping centres.

The holiday-maker in France therefore can add the delight of shopping to all of France's other attractions.

THE HIGH STREET SHOPS OF FRANCE

Britain's high street shops these days are full of TV dealers, fashion retailers, jewellers, shoe shops and building societies. It is a place of chain stores: Dixons, Currys, W H Smith, Our Price, Boots, Next, Argos, Marks & Spencer. If you were placed blindfolded in a British city centre you would be unable to tell where you were by simply looking at the shops.

France is quite different. The big retailers stick to the outskirts, sharing space in large out-of-town shopping centres with the major hypermarket chains like Mammouth, Carrefour, Continent, Auchan and Leclerc. The town centres remain dominated by the independent retailer: the ironmonger, the newsagent, the tobacconist – but above all the food shops. This is why walking down a French high street in any town is more interesting – the mouth-watering displays in the food shops are a true delight. And on market days, town centres are transformed into new worlds of delight: stalls piled high with large, red strawberries, yellow peaches, fat peppers, ropes of garlic, home-grown lettuces, bottles of walnut oil, tubs of fresh herbs and boxes of free-range eggs.

Shopping is not a chore to be dispensed with as quickly as

possible, it is an integral part of social life. Buying a piece of cheese demands careful consideration and discussion with the shopkeeper. In between discussing the cheese, there will be time to chew over the local news and to digest nuggets of gossip and scandal.

If you don't speak fluent French, don't be put off. Everyone will be keen to help (admittedly in Paris, people are less keen in this respect). The first rule to remember is: be polite. Etiquette demands that you formally greet everybody in the shop when you enter: *Bonjour messieurs-dames* (they will all say 'hello' to you). Requests for everything must be heavily larded with please (*s'il vous plaît*) and thank you (*merci*). Say goodbye (*au revoir*) to everybody as you leave. The failure to utter these courtesies will be construed as either gross rudeness or incipient lunacy. And while by simply pointing at what you want in the shops you can get by, knowing a few simple phrases will oil the wheels of communication immensely. *Une tranche de celui-là s'il vous plaît* (a slice of that one please), *un comme ça* (one of those) and *c'est tout* (that's all), will all come in very handy.

Hypermarkets keep very long hours: most stay open from 9am to 9pm Monday to Saturday: large supermarkets in the main holiday areas open on Sundays during the season. Town centre shops also open early and stay open late – most food shops will also open on a Sunday morning (bread shops have a rota like emergency chemists!).

Boulangeries

The bâton of crusty bread is the symbol of French life. Real French bread, fresh from the oven, is a true delight. It does not remain fresh very long: after six hours you could use it to hammer nails. If you want fresh bread with a meal (and the French do), you have to buy bread twice a day. Every village therefore has either its own bakery or a *dépôt de pain* where fresh bread is delivered (supermarkets usually fulfil the role of *dépôt de pain* in many small towns).

French loaves come in various shapes and sizes, but the traditional bread is the long thin crusty white *baguette*. But a trip to a *boulangerie* will reveal that French sticks have different names according to their dimensions: there is also *le bâtard, la flute* and *la ficelle*. Getting a sliced loaf used to be impossible. However, incredible as it may seem, there appears to be a growing taste for what is called 'the English loaf' which you can see on sale in hypermarkets. One presumes that the French buy it for making toast. There is no accounting for taste.

At the baker's, you will also be able to buy your breakfast

33

croissants (opt for *croissants au beurre* for the genuine article). You can also get *pains au chocolat* and *pains aux raisins*.

Remember that the *boulangerie* in France opens at the crack of dawn. If you rise early (as I do), in France it is always a treat to head down to the baker's at seven o'clock to pick up still hot bread and croissants.

Boucheries

With the exception of pork, obtainable from the *charcuterie*, French butchers' shops sell all the meats you would expect to find in a British butcher's including *volaille* (poultry) *agneau* (lamb) *bifteck* (cheap steak) and *filet* (fillet steak). Don't be surprised to see rabbits and hares on sale as well as *poussin* (baby chicken), *pintade* (guinea fowl) and *caille* (quail). Tripe should also be available, but you may be pleased to know that you have to go to a special butcher's (*boucherie chevaline*) for horse meat.

Charcuteries

These delicatessens sell pâtés, terrines, sausages, ready-made *hors d'oeuvre*, quiches and pizzas, pastries, puddings and pies.

Pâtisseries

The chief delight of the French high street is the cake and pastry shops. Don't look for the stodgy old cream horns with fake cream or stale doughnuts that get served up in British cake shops. The French *pâtisserie* is a place where the cake- and pastry-maker's art is practised with tremendous skill. Feast your eyes (and digestive system) on exquisite small tarts with real fruit, *brioches* and croissants, eclairs, choux buns, *petits fours* and beautiful light home-made cakes. At Easter there are chocolate rabbits and hens, at Christmas luxurious chocolate logs and every weekend there is a special display for Sunday lunch (the French rarely make their own desserts).

Milk and tea

These are the two things that British holiday-makers in France most complain about. Given that the French show such exquisite good taste in other gastronomical matters; it seems curious that they should wish to dilute their excellent coffee with the witches' brew that is UHT milk.

While UHT milk might just about be bearable in coffee, I would rather have engine oil on my breakfast muesli. Happily hypermarkets and supermarkets stock real milk (*lait frais*) in the refrigerated cabinets. In smaller shops, particularly in the warmer southern regions, they might not have it at all: if you can't find it, ask.

The other French blind spot is tea. What they call *thé* (tea) is some wretched herbal infusion which is apparently served to elderly women on their death beds. If you can't do without a proper cup of tea for two weeks (and let's face it, who can?), bring your own tea or tea-bags with you.

Other hard-to-get British comestibles worth bringing with you to France include baked beans, instant coffee, bottles of tomato sauce and jars of Marmite.

EATING OUT IN FRANCE

People will tell you that French restaurants are not what they were. Twenty years ago you could turn up at any French restaurant, a family of four could eat their way through a superbly-ordered and magnificently-prepared meal, drink a couple of bottles of fine wine – and still have change from a 100 Franc note.

Things *are* different today. There are more higher-priced eating places than there were 20 years ago (as is the case in Britain). The rise of the food snob has been as irresistible in France as elsewhere: the concept of *nouvelle cuisine*, which means you eat less but for more money, has much to answer for in this respect.

But it isn't worth regretting changes (we can all sigh for the days when the English were World Cup soccer champions or when beer was a penny a pint and Woodbines a half-penny). It is true that eating out in France is one of life's great pleasures – and it will be a high point of your holiday in France. Whether your meal is an extravagant bash in a haute cuisine dinery or a more modest but no less satisfying picnic of fresh bread, ripe cheese and *vin ordinaire* – food in France will be a pleasure.

Food is important to the French. A family meal is an important occasion to be savoured at length. And whereas we confine meals out to birthdays, high days and holidays, the French routinely dine out, especially on Sundays when a whole family will descend on a restaurant en masse. As a result there are more restaurants, and better-run restaurants. But it should be said that there are also plenty of bad restaurants, and bad, expensive restaurants.

However there is plenty of choice, and the choice goes on growing. As well as many formal restaurants, there are an increasing number of informal eating places: most towns now have a pizzeria – and the main cities have hamburger places and other fast food joints. Most places have food stalls serving up *frites*, pancakes, hot dogs and French bread sandwiches all day.

In finding a restaurant, the *Michelin Red Guide* is a sound source of advice. It's worth spending some time understanding the guide's entries which explain the price of a set meal, degree of comfort, specialities, location on map (if in a town), days closed and so on. (The knife and fork symbols indicate how smart the restaurant is, the stars are for outstanding food.) The other worthwhile guide for those who speak French is *Gault Millau*, named after its original authors, two leading food writers. Without a guide or recommendation the best way to go about choosing a place is by looking at the menu and the clientele. Don't take the decor as a guide to culinary standards; good food is often found in basic or uninspired settings.

In most restaurants the fixed price menus offer the best value: several courses with a narrow choice of dishes, at a fixed all-in price. (A list of individually-priced dishes from which you can choose at random is a *carte*.) Restaurants tend to keep rigid hours. Lunch is generally served earlier in France than it is in Britain. Popular restaurants start filling up soon after 12 noon and think about shutting up shop shortly after 2pm. Dinner is usually served from around 7pm or 7.30pm until 8.30pm or 9pm; in some areas it's difficult to get dinner after 8pm, and in any restaurant the set menus may be unavailable if you arrive late.

Cafés are usually open all day, starting by serving coffee and croissants for breakfast. During the day they will have a limited food menu of French bread sandwiches and *croque-monsieur* (toasted cheese and ham sandwich). A *brasserie* (a larger, smarter and less intimate version of a café) is usually open all day for snacks or more substantial meals.

Hypermarket eating

If you want to spend a £100 per person on a meal, you will have no trouble in finding plenty of swanky restaurants in France which can serve you up haute-cuisine and bottles of the very finest wine at suitably inflated prices. But you will equally have no problem in eating cheaply. The very best value family restaurants can be found attached to the hypermarkets in the large out-of-town *centres commerciales* (shopping centres) located on the outskirts of most French towns and cities.

These self-service restaurants offer tremendous value for money: there are children's meals for a couple of pounds – but even adult meals are barely more expensive. It is possible for a family of four to have a good lunch or dinner (most French hypermarkets remain open until 9pm or 10pm) for around £15. And the food is of very high quality – you only need to see the local French queuing in droves to be sure of this.

The best-known of these hypermarket restaurant chains is Flunch, owned by the Auchan chain – but you can also find Flunch's next to Continent, Carrefour, Mammouth and Leclerc hypermarkets. There are also a number of Flunch's in city centre locations. If you are driving through France, it is worth keeping an eye out for a Flunch: children particularly enjoy eating there – not only is there a special low-price children's meal, but they get giveaways like balloons, toys and sweets. At your first Flunch ask for a map which shows how to find the other Flunch's (this is also a good indicator to the whereabouts of the nearest hypermarket). Here is a directory of Flunch locations in France:

FLUNCH RESTAURANTS IN FRANCE

Aix-en-Provence, 2 Avenue des Belges
Angoulême, Auchan La Couronne shopping centre, RN10
Annecy, 23 Rue Sommeiller, city centre
Annecy, Auchan shopping centre, Epagny
Antibes, Carrefour shopping centre
Aubagne, Auchan Barneoud shopping centre
Aulnay-sous-Bois, Parinor shopping centre
Avignon, 11 Boulevard Raspail, city centre
Avignon, Auchan shopping centre, Le Pontet, RN542
Avignon, Mistral 7 shopping centre, RN7
Bayonne, BAB 2 shopping centre, Anglet
Belfort, 18 Faubourg de France
Béthune, Auchan La Rotonde shopping centre
Bordeaux, 4–6 Cours de L'Intendance, city centre
Bordeaux, Auchan shopping centre, Quartier du Lac, Le Lac
Bordeaux, Meriadeck shopping centre
Bordeaux, Carrefour shopping centre, Chemin de Mirepin, Merignac
Boulogne, Auchan shopping centre, RN42
Bourges, Record shopping centre, St-Doulchard
Brest, 20 Rue Jean Jaures, city centre
Brest, Euromarche Arche shopping centre, de l'Iroise
Bretigny-sur-Orge, Auchan shopping centre
Caen, Carrefour shopping centre, Hérouville
Calais, Avenue Guynemer
Cambrai, Auchan shopping centre, Escaudoeuvres
Cergy, Les 3 Fontaines shopping centre, Pontoise
Châlons-sur-Marne, Carrefour shopping centre, Croix Dampierre
Chambery, Avenue des Ducs de Savoie
Cholet, Continent shopping centre, route d'Angers
Clermont-Ferrand, 8 Avenue des États-Unis
Colmar, 8 Avenue de la République
Compiègne, Carrefour shopping centre, RN31
Dijon, 24 Boulevard des Brosses, town centre
Dijon, Carrefour shopping centre, 16 Rue deshopping centrehalands
Dunkerque, Auchan shopping centre, G Synthe, RN40
Évry, Évry 2 shopping centre, 107
Fontenay-sous-Bois, Auchan shopping centre
Givors, Givors 2 Vallées shopping centre

Grenoble, Continent shopping centre, St-Egreve
Henin-Beaumont, Auchan shopping centre, RN43
Le Havre, Auchan shopping centre, Avenue du Bois-au-Coq
Le Mans, Auchan de la Chapelle St-Aubin shopping centre, La Milesse
Lens, Lens 2 shopping centre, Vendin-le-Vieil
Les Ulis, Carrefour Ulis 2 shopping centre
Lievin, Carrefour shopping centre
Lille, Galerie du 57, Rue de Béthune, city centre
Lille, Auchan shopping centre, Englos, RN352
Lille, Avenue Charles St-Venant, Gare
Lille, Auchan shopping centre, Villeneuve Auchan shopping centre
Limoges, Boisseuil shopping centre, RN20
Lorient, K2 shopping centre
Lyon, Le Perollier Carrefour shopping centre, Écully
Lyon, Mammouth shopping centre, Limonest
Lyon, Auchan shopping centre, St Priest, A43
Mantes-La-Jolie, Auchan Buchelay shopping centre
Marseille, 8–10 Rue St-Ferreol, city centre
Marseille, le Merlan Carrefour shopping centre, Nord
Marseille, Carrefour shopping centre, Vitrolles, RN113
Martigues, Canto Perfrix Auchan shopping centre, Route d'Istrès
Maubeuge, Europe 14 shopping centre, Louvroll, CD121
Maurepas, Auchan shopping centre
Melun, Boissenart Auchan shopping centre, Cesson
Metz, 17 Rue deshopping centrelercs
Metz, Auchan shopping centre, Voie Romaine, Semecourt
Montluçon, Centres St Jacques
Montpellier, Le Polygone shopping centre
Montpellier, Avenue de Montmorency, city centre
Mulhouse, Europe 14 shopping centre, Boulevard de l'Europe
Nancy, 9 bis, Rue Maurice Barres, city centre
Nancy, Rue du Grand Rabbin Haguenauer, St-Sebastien
Nantes, 4–6 Rue de Feltre
Nantes, Leclerc shopping centre, Reze
Nantes, La Petite Jaunaie Auchan shopping centre, St-Sebastien
Nice, SNCF railway station
Nice, 7 Rue Halevy
Nice, Carrefour shopping centre, Lingostière, RN202
Nice, La Trinité-Victor Auchan shopping centre, Trinité
Nîmes, 10 Boulevard de l'Admiral Courbet
Ollioules, Continent shopping centre, Toulon
Orléans, Auchan shopping centre, Avenue de Verdun, Olivet
Orléans, St Jean-de-la-Ruelle Auchan shopping centre, St-Jean
Paris, 5–7 Rue Pierre Lescot, Forum des Halles, 1er
Paris, 11 Boulevard Poissonière, 2e
Paris, 5 Rue de Berri, 8e
Paris, 1–3 Rue de Caulaincourt, 18e
Paris, St-Denis Basilique shopping centre, St-Denis
Pau, 2 Rue du Marechal Joffre, city centre

Pau, Carrefour shopping centre, Lescar, route de Bayonne
Périgueux, Auchan shopping centre, RN9
Plaisir, Auchan shopping centre, CD161
Poitiers, Rue du Petit Bonneveau
Rembouillet, Carrefour Le Bel-Air shopping centre, RN10
Reims, Continent shopping centre
Roanne, Record Mably shopping centre
Roubaix, Auchan shopping centre, Rue Pierre Catteau, Leers
Rouen, 66 Rue deshopping centrearmes, city centre
Rouen, Carrefour shopping centre, Mesnil-Roux, Barentin
St-Brice-sous-Foret, Continent shopping centre, RN1
St-Nazaire, Auchan shopping centre, Z.A.C. de la Fontaine au Brun, Trignac
Strasbourg, 31 Place Kleber, city centre
Strasbourg, Auchan Hautepierre shopping centre, Hautepierre
Toulouse, 28 Allées Jean Jaures, city centre
Toulouse, Labège shopping centre, Z.A.C. de la Grande Bordge, Labège
Toulouse, Carrefour shopping centre, Portet-s-G
Tourcoing, Auchan shopping centre, Boulevard d'Halluin, Roncq
Tours, 14 Place Jean Jaures
Tours, St-Pierre-des-Corps shopping centre
Troyes, Carrefour shopping centre, Saint-Andre-les-Vergers
Valence, 19–21 Boulevard Maurice Clerc
Valenciennes, Val d'Escaut shopping centre, Place Charles de Gaulle
Valenciennes-P-Foret, Auchan shopping centre, RN45
Villiers-en-Biere, Carrefour shopping centre, RN7

4

Ports of call

For most cross-Channel travellers, the French ports are an inconvenience – an irritating interruption in the mad dash to the final destination further south. In fact unlike the English ports such as Dover and Portsmouth which really are as bad as they look, the French ports are worth lingering in if you have the time. Places like Dieppe and St Malo are a positive pleasure.

In fact, if I was asked to name my favourite trips of the past 10 years, at least half of the top ten would probably be short-breaks across the Channel. Where did we have one of our best family holidays: Florida? the Caribbean? Well, Le Touquet actually: day after day in the Aqualud water fun place going down the slides on a rubber tyre. I also have very fond memories of weekend outings to Bruges, Dieppe, Rouen, Caen and Le Havre. Yes, you read right: Le Havre – I accept that I am probably the only fully paid up member of the Le Havre Appreciation Society. And if I had to pick one favourite part of France, it would be Normandy. The high-hedged meadows with slumbering cows, the apple orchards, the small villages with their churches and châteaux – and the countryside is at its best in the autumn with the smell of wood fires on the evening air.

It seems incredible, yet the idea of taking a cheap short-break across the Channel is little more than 10 years old. It wasn't until the Government forced the cross-Channel car ferry companies to start competing for business at the end of the seventies that it occurred to them to offer cut-price deals during the off-peak periods. This now seems curious because until the invention of the bargain break, cross-Channel ferry companies languished in the doldrums of the off-season for most of the year. Their complaint was that they had to invest in expensive ferry capacity to cope with a six-week rush during July and August – for the rest of the year their ferries were rarely more than one-third full.

Even when the ferry companies began offering cut-price deals, there was some doubt as to whether anyone would really want to buy them. Remember the joke? First prize: a weekend in Belgium; second prize: two weekends in Belgium ... And for that matter, who really wanted to go to Dunkerque, Calais or Le Havre – no matter how cheap the fare.

Much to the surprise of the ferry companies, people did want to pop across the Channel for the weekend. Food writers went to Belgium, for example, and were publicly astonished to discover more Michelin-rosetted restaurants than you could shake a garlic crusher at – was this the boring Belgium of legend? We also began to revise our opinions about the Pas de Calais and Normandy. We discovered that the most interesting parts of France were not necessarily the sun-kissed bits south of the Loire Valley. Until the thirties, the fashionable resorts of France had been on the Channel: elegant places with smart casinos like Deauville and Le Touquet. Inspired by the renewed interest of the British, these and other places along the coast are undergoing a revival. And, of course, there is Brittany – Cornwall with the smell of Gauloises and French bread – sometimes remote, occasionally extraordinary and often magical.

In many ways a weekend across the Channel is the perfect short-break. It is certainly good value: ferry fares are remarkably cheap, hotels and restaurants are good and reasonably priced. And there is the added bonus of being able to hit the local hypermarket for beer, wine, 24-packs of croissants for the freezer and other delights.

For the cross-Channel traveller the variety of short-breaks is infinite. If money is no object, there are many château hotels offering gastronomic big bangs for over £100 per person per night. For those minding the pennies, there are plenty of places with rooms from £10 per night. (Try the Formule 1 chain – where you check yourself in with a credit card – with rooms sleeping three for £13 a night.)

If you prefer to have arrangements made for you, buy an inclusive package from a ferry company or one of the specialist operators – but there is good fun to be had in simply turning up at a Channel port and taking off on the next available ferry and seeing where the fancy takes you.

DUNKERQUE

It may not be on anybody's list as a future European City of Culture; Dunkerque nevertheless has its attractions. It has a pleasant laid-back atmosphere but few sights beyond the modern art museum, the view from the lighthouse and a stroll around the port.

Your first glimpse of the place from the long drive into town from the ferry port is not encouraging – a bleak industrial landscape. But Dunkerque has its moments: a short way from the

41

centre, it even has its own resort Malo-les-Bains – a surprisingly characterful spot.

But Dunkerque's main attraction is that it is within a very short drive of greater delights. No other French Channel port is within a half hour's drive of as many Michelin-starred restaurants (mostly just over the border in Belgium). If you want charming towns take a five mile drive to look at Bergues, completely surrounded by 17th-century walls and a moat. Also worth a detour is the nearby 800-year-old windmill at Hondschoote. Cassel, 15 miles from Dunkerque, is an attractive hilltop town with good views over the flatlands of Flanders.

Hypermarkets: The best is Auchan, on the RN1 close to the Sally ferry terminal. The others are Cora, at Coudekerque-Branche on the road out to Bergues; and Carrefour in the *centre commercial* Saint Pol, Petite-Synthe.

Market: Wednesdays and Saturdays in the Place du General de Gaulle in the town centre.

Hotels: The best of Ostende's hotels is the Europ Hotel, 13 Rue du Leughenaer (28 66 51 80) with double rooms from £32.50 a night. More expensive and four miles from the centre of Dunkerque is La Meunerie at Teteghem, 174 Rue des Pierres (28 26 14 30), a Michelin-starred restaurant with rooms in the luxury class complete with black-marble bathrooms, from £53 per night.

Restaurants: Michelin recommends Dunkerque's railway station restaurant: the Richelieu, Place de la Gare (28 66 52 13) which offers something more than all-day Inter-City sizzlers: set menus from around £15. Top-rated out of town eatery is La Meunerie (see above).

Tourist office: Beffrio de Dunkerque (28 66 79 21).

CALAIS

How far east from Dover do you have to go these days to discover a society languishing under the iron heel of communism? If you guessed China, you guessed wrong. The answer is much nearer home: Calais. From the heights of the White Cliffs of Dover on a clear day, communist-controlled Calais stares you right in the face. But there is no sign that it is languishing under anybody's iron heel. 'Perhaps you shouldn't mention that Calais has a communist council,' suggested the nervous spokesman for the Calais chamber of commerce, 'people get the wrong idea. It's not quite like it sounds.'

It would be fair to say that Calais' problem is not that people have the wrong idea about it but that they have no idea about it at all. For 11 million British travellers Calais is a sort of continental Crewe Junction. The place where they leave the ferry and join the autoroute (reversing this process when they return home). As far as these millions are concerned, Calais' greatest contribution to human happiness was constructing the highly effective bypass to the motorway which has reduced any view of the town to nothing more than a brief glimpse through the car window. For another substantial army of British travellers – around three million this year – Calais is simply a place to go for cheap booze. They know nothing more than that it is an extended bargain basement off-licence where beer comes in cardboard boxes and costs as little as 10p per bottle.

This general ignorance is a shame. Not even the Calais chamber of commerce can pretend that this largely inelegant port is worthy of the soubriquet 'the Venice of the English Channel', but the place deserves more serious consideration.

Calais looks dull but that's because Allied bombers flattened it during the last war. In the park near the railway station, an old German blockhouse has been turned into a fascinating museum which vividly details Calais' grim wartime experiences.

The English have always had an intimate relationship with Calais – for 200 years it was ruled by England until the French won it back in 1558 (in the process engraving the name of Calais on Tudor Queen Mary's heart). But while it is effectively at the frontier with Britain, it is only over the past five years that Calais has taken on the character of a frontier town. It used to be content to please itself, there was no obvious effort to accommodate *les anglais* – now it seems to do as much as it can to please the British trippers. Given that we annually inject around £60m into Calais' economy – amounting to 20% of local business turnover – it should not be so surprising that the British are now being warmly welcomed.

At the Holiday Inn – one of a crop of smart new hotels that has recently opened in Calais – a young Englishman who worked locally asked me what I thought of the town. I said I liked it. 'I hate the place. There's nothing to do,' he complained. 'There's a couple of clubs; but they charge you ten quid to get in and fifty quid for a bottle of drink. The locals don't go near – they're for English trippers.'

If your interests lie beyond nightclubs, there is much to amuse you. In front of the handsome town hall, there is Rodin's famous statue of the six burghers who in 1347 were prepared to give up their own lives to save Calais from being massacred by Edward III's English army. (Rodin's models and studies for the statue can be seen in the town's excellent museum in Rue Richelieu.)

Calais also supports a large number of restaurants – including an astounding variety of very good pizzerias – whose menus in English indicate the national provenance of their customers.

The town's chief charm is in its unexpected sights. The attractive fishermen's houses on the harbour front, for example, with their steep pantiled roofs. There is the beach (yes, a beach at Calais!) with a monument commemorating Captain Webb's first Channel swim in 1875. Take a look at the Gare Maritime which tells of another glorious era of cross-Channel packet steamers met by trans-European night trains heading for Nice and Ventimiglia.

There are only a couple of main shopping streets: the Rue Royale which runs on beyond the town hall to become Boulevard Jacquard: this intersects with Boulevard Gambetta running west and Boulevard La Fayette heading west. If time is limited stick to the shops on Rue Royale which seems to have the better bars and restaurants.

Finding the centre: After driving through passport control, the road to the centre (*centre ville*) lies immediately to the right (if you follow the traffic to the motorway to Paris, you could be out of town and thoroughly lost in minutes). Remember that all signposting for 'ferry port' appears to be designed to cause maximum confusion to visitors and minimum inconvenience to residents: consult a map before you arrive.

Hypermarkets: The Continent hypermarket is a mile and a half from the ferry port, just off the road to Dunkerque. From the outside it looks old and shabby, but inside it is well-kept with the usual wide range of hypermarket goodies. Perhaps its most compelling attraction is the Flunch restaurant which offers good food at ridiculously low prices.

The Mammouth is two miles out of town on the N1 to Boulogne: open Monday to Saturday 9am to 9pm. It is newer and more salubriously located than the Continent but the range of goods – and the prices – are more or less the same (in fact, the Continent has a better choice of wine). Remember a 2p piece will release a trolley (you will get your 2p back when you return your trolley – not somebody else's 10 Franc coin!).

Market: Thursday and Saturday mornings in the Place Creve-coeur.

Hotels: Calais has two check-yourself-in hotels: the Hotel Liberte on Quai Danube (21 96 10 10) near the station, simple but clean rooms from £16 a night; the better-known Formule 1 (21 96 89 89) chain has a place out of town handily-placed next to the Mammouth: rooms from £16 a night. The best place in town is the Holiday Inn (21 34 69 69) with rooms from around £40 per night: lousy breakfasts but good off-the-street parking.

Restaurants: Top eating places include Côte d'Argent on Digue

G-Berthe (21 34 68 07): set menus from £10; and Le Channel on Boulevard Resistance (21 34 42 30): set menus from around £9. Good cheap eating places abound everywhere.

Tourist office: Hard to find but worth searching out at 12 Boulevard Clemenceau (21 96 62 40; fax 21 96 01 92), diagonally opposite the railway station. Opening hours: Monday to Saturday 9am–12.30pm and 2.30–6.30pm (Sunday 4.30–7.30pm).

BOULOGNE

Boulogne is just half an hour's drive from Calais but in terms of style and character they are world's apart. Boulogne was heavily bombed in the war but afterwards they tried to put it back the good way it looked before the war. Boulogne is middle class and handsome, while Calais is working class and plain. But while Calais has a good-natured cheerfulness about it, Boulogne can sometimes seem a bit too pleased with itself.

In Philippe Olivier's famous cheese shop on Rue Thiers, the staff are dressed for the operating theatre and have that particular French hauteur which suggests they might still be bearing grudges over Agincourt. When I tasted a few cheeses but didn't buy, the lady on the cash desk looked ready to phone the police.

While Calais is best for a day trip, Boulogne is the place to go for a weekend. It's a great town to amble about in: the haute ville, with its 13th-century ramparts, is a great place to idle away an afternoon. The principal attraction for tourists up here is Notre-Dame cathedral with its distinctive Italianate dome which looks like the result of a marriage between St Peter's in Rome and St Paul's in London.

Not content to rest on its Italianate laurels, Boulogne has invested £16m in a stunning new tourist attraction. Nausicaa sounds like a particularly vicious form of seasickness, in fact it is a magnificent aquarium. To call it an aquarium doesn't do the place justice as this suggests a place with gloomy fish-tanks containing a few moth-eaten tropical fish. Nausicaa is much more than this: it has more than 5,000 fish ranging from terrifying 2.5m sharks to amazing technicolor inhabitants of coral reefs – all presented in as natural a setting as possible. Nausicaa also has a very well regarded restaurant (yes, fish is a speciality).

And once you've exhausted the extensive charms of Boulogne, the surrounding countryside – Le Boulonnais – beckons: Le Touquet, Hardelot, Montreuil, Agincourt . . . With a car, as they would tell you at Nausicaa, the world is your oyster.

My advice would be to head for Le Touquet, 20 miles down the coast. You might imagine that Le Touquet is one of those once fashionable seaside places that have now gone to seed: in Britain, after all, it's difficult to think of any once fashionable seaside place that hasn't gone towards rack and ruin.

So the drive towards the centre of Le Touquet is a grand surprise. Neat, tree-lined avenues of smart villas built in what one supposes was meant to be English stockbroker style: some half-timbered, others thatched. Much of the architecture has a tongue-in-cheek wit: the curious neo-Jacobean *Hôtel de ville*, an extraordinary art deco market place and several helpings of pastiche Black Forest. There are golf courses, good shops, fine hotels and an excellent range of restaurants. And best of all a long sea-front with a wide promenade. It's hard to believe that Folkestone lies just over the horizon.

Another possible base is Montreuil, once a port but now just a pleasant, old town with well-preserved ramparts, picturesque cottages and cobbled streets.

Hypermarkets: Auchan, situated on the road to St Omer about five miles from the centre of Boulogne, is the best shopping place: well worth the drive from Calais. It is vast: 14,000 square metres, compared with just 7,000 square metres at Calais' Mammouth: open 9am to 10pm Monday to Friday; Saturday 8am to 10pm. It also has a superb Flunch cafeteria and plenty of parking space.

Market: In Boulogne, every Wednesday and Saturday morning in the Place Dalton, a short walk from the ferry terminal.

Hotels: Boulogne's biggest drawback is a lack of decent hotels: the two best are the Ibis on Boulevard Diderot (21 30 12 40), rooms from around £30 per night; and the Metropole on Rue Thiers (21 31 54 30) with rooms from £35 per night. In Le Touquet the smartest place is the Westminster, Avenue Verger (21 05 48 48) with double rooms from around £100 per night. The Novotel has rooms from £48 per night. In Montreuil the Château de Montreuil (21 81 53 04), owned and managed by Christian Germain, who trained with the Roux brothers, is the top choice. Double rooms from around £85.

Restaurants: The smartest and most expensive places are La Liegoise in Rue Monsigny (21 31 61 15): set menus from around £20; and La Matelôte in Boulevard Ste-Beuve (21 30 17 97): set menus from £18. For cheaper good quality food try the restaurant at the Nausicaa (21 33 24 24) on the sea-front: set menus from around £10 (children's meals from £5).

Good shops: Maison Tellier, 7 Rue Porte Neuve (21 31 65 47): upmarket food and wine shop immediately behind the old town. Philippe Olivier's Fromagerie, 45 Rue Thiers (21 31 94 74).

Tourist office: Quai de la Poste (21 31 68 38). Opening hours 9am to 7pm: closed Sundays, Mondays and Bank Holidays.

DIEPPE
Of all the Channel ports, Dieppe is probably the only one that could be described in any way as charming. At the harbour front where the Newhaven ferry ties up – it looks, feels and smells like a proper fishing port should. The other side of town, on the sea front, has something of a genteel English seaside resort about it. Dieppe, in many ways, is the perfect place for a weekend escape. Small, self-contained, with good shopping and plenty of atmosphere.

Dieppe was once the haunt of the fashionable and the bohemian: Oscar Wilde is said to have written *The Ballad of Reading Gaol* during his exile here – it was also a favourite place of Walter Sickert and other artists who met at the Café des Tribunaux.

It also provides a good base for exploring further afield. Rouen is about an hour's drive from Dieppe with more than enough to keep you occupied for a full day. For a blast of fresh air, the 'Alabaster Coast' is a 59-mile stretch of coastline between Dieppe and Étretat where the cliffs and the cliff-top views are often spectacular.

Hypermarket: Mammouth at the Val Druel *centre commercial* on the RN27 road towards Rouen, a few minutes' drive from the centre of town.

Market: The main market is on Saturday in the Grande Rue.

Hotels: *Hôtel de l'Univers*, 10 Boulevard de Verdun, 76200 Dieppe (35 84 12 55): room with sea-view costs from £42 per night half-board for two people. Stay here for the *fin-de-siècle* atmosphere: what it lacks in modern refurbishment, it makes up for in amiability. We also liked *Hôtel Aguado*, 30 Boulevard Verdun (35 84 27 00), a classic early-sixties French hotel but still pleasantly characterful: bed and breakfast for two people costs from £38 per night. At the bottom end of the range, the Ibis at le Val Druel (35 82 65 30) offers exceptionally good value, with rooms from just £32 a night.

Restaurants: Not surprisinly sea food plays a leading role on most menus: a regular speciality is *marmite dieppoise*, a fish stew of local sole, turbot and angler fish cooked in, amongst other things, white wine, cream, celery, leeks, onions and fennel. The top-rated eating place, according to Michelin, is the one-star La Melie, 2 Grande Rue Pollet (35 84 21 19): fixed-price meals start at around £19 per person.

Sightseeing: The town has few 'sights' to see. St-Jacques church is worth a peek. The 15th-century castle is also interesting with its museum which includes the Dieppe Ivories as well as a collection of prints by Georges Braque, one of the originators of cubism.

Tourist office: Syndicat d'Initiative de Dieppe, Boulevard General-de-Gaulle BP 152, 76204 Dieppe (35 84 11 77).

LA HAVRE

It wasn't Le Havre's fault that the Allies bombed the place flat in order to flush out the Germans at the end of war. You can however blame Le Havre for putting the plans for its post-war reconstruction into the hands of someone keen to build what looks like France's answer to Gotham City.

I first discovered Le Havre when I went there with the school dramatic society, staying in a beaten-up youth hostel in the shadow of St Joseph's church (Le Havre's principal landmark – from far away at sea it looks a bit like an ecclesiastical Empire State Building. We were there to perform *Henry IV Part II*. Goodness knows what the locals made of it all – I was Doll Tearsheet: it was a boys' school – but the Havrais were exquisitely polite. A photograph of one of my scenes was run across five columns of page seven in *Havre Libre*. After the show, the communist mayor entertained us with a champagne reception in his grand *Hôtel de ville* – a stark piece of Stalinist architecture (the city is twinned with Leningrad and Southampton). Tipsy on half a glass of fizz, we returned to our doss house and gathered around a tinny transistor to enjoy the Eurovision success of 'Puppet on a String'. Bliss was it in that dawn to be alive.

Ever since, Le Havre has held a special place in my affections. Not everybody loves it: in fact the only other person I've ever heard say nice things about Le Havre is Auberon Waugh – and it's often hard to know whether he's teasing or not. While I may not be quite ready to rebuild my life in Le Havre, I'd happily spend a day or two there, and not just to recapture the smell of the greasepaint and the roar of the crowd (the indifferent applause of the crowd, at least).

Much of its attraction for me lies not so much in what Le Havre is now (even its most devoted admirer would have to admit that it's one of the ugliest towns in Europe – in some ways worse than Portsmouth even) – the pleasure lies in glimpses of Le Havre's past. Maupassant's *Pierre et Jean* was one of my French set texts: its evocative portrait of *fin de siècle* Havrais life provides an intriguing glimpse of the past – as powerful as the works of the many notable impressionist painters who came to paint this and other parts of Normandy.

Looking at Le Havre now, a town built almost wholly in reinforced concrete to a plan drawn up by Auguste Perret, it's hard to imagine that it was once a bright, frothy place. At the André Malraux Fine Arts Museum, across the road from the P&

O terminal, there are glimpses of what life was like here before Le Havre was reduced to rubble by Allied bombing. Dufy's paintings of Le Havre, his birth place, with their exuberant washes of blue provide an extraordinarily vivid picture of the town in the early years of the century. Also on display at the museum are vibrant pre-Impressionist and Impressionist works of Boudin, Pisarro, Sisley and Renoir.

Looking at the paintings, it's easy to imagine the excited comings and goings at the harbour front at the turn of the century: the fishing smacks tying up beside the huge three-masted schooners; and the paddle boats steaming in and out, on their way to the seaside towns of Trouville and Deauville across the Seine estuary: the ladies elegant in their large hats, full skirts and colourful parasols.

At the Museum of Old Havre – a restored 17th-century house – there are intriguing glimpses of a more recent past. Le Havre was the main transatlantic port for the great liners of the twenties and thirties: the *Île de France* ('with all the gulls around it . . .') and the *Normandie*. The *gare maritime* built to service these magnificent ships was a masterpiece of *art deco* – so was the main railway station with its swaggering clock tower. Before and after photographs at the museum show the dreadful extent of the destruction of Le Havre: after the final bombardment of September 1944 hardly one stone was left standing.

From Le Havre you can go eastwards up the coast towards Dieppe, or westwards across the Tancarville bridge towards Caen: both equally agreeable journeys. My advice however is to follow the Seine upstream for 30 miles to Caudebec-en-Caux. For reasons I find hard to explain, this part of Normandy is perhaps my favourite piece of France. The town itself isn't much to look at, pleasantly rebuilt after heavy wartime damage: it's more the atmosphere. The Seine provides much of that atmosphere: the river is busy with large ocean-going ships that pass alarmingly close to shore. At the Marine hotel they used to give clients ear plugs to block out the sound of the ships' early morning fog horns.

But best of all is the small village of Villequier, five minutes' drive along the river towards Le Havre. High on the wooded hillside above the village used to be a magnificent country house hotel, the Domaine de Villequier – sadly this closed a few years ago. The village of Villequier was where Victor Hugo's daughter and her husband were drowned in a boating accident six months after their marriage. Hugo expressed his grief in one of his best known poems 'Les Contemplations'. A statue of Hugo marks the place of the accident: the village also has a Hugo museum.

The last time I was there, two boys straight out of a Truffaut film, were sitting on the river bank absorbed in the business of poking the body of a drowned cat with a long stick, *'Oh, c'est gonflé,'* they gasped to each other: isn't it swollen? Behind them, in the gardens of the restaurant, a wedding reception was proceeding with dignified hilarity. Across the road, an old woman in black was chasing a hen up the hill back to her garden. Ah, souvenirs of France.

Hypermarket: The Auchan hypermarket at the Mont Gaillard *centre commercial* in the *haute ville*, is about 15 minutes drive from the ferry terminal and town centre.

Market: The main market in Le Havre takes place on Tuesdays, Thursdays and Saturdays in the Cours de la République. The market in Caudebec is on a Saturday: this is a fine old country market in the best Norman tradition.

Hotels: Staying in Le Havre tends to be what marketing experts describe as a 'distressed purchase': people do it because they have to (staying overnight to catch an early morning ferry, for example) rather than because they want to. Accommodation is mostly geared to bed and breakfast needs. Apart from a reasonable Mercure, Chausée d'Angoulême (35 21 23 45) with double rooms from £40, Le Havre is short of good accommodation. Best of the places in town is the Bordeaux, 147 Rue Louis Brindeau (35 22 69 44) where a room for two costs around £44 a night.

Caudebec has two good hotels: the Normotel (35 96 20 11), formerly the Marine, with rooms from £30 per night – and the Manoir de Retival (35 96 11 22) is more of an upmarket bed and breakfast place with rooms from around £70 per night. In Villequier, the Grand Sapin (35 56 78 73) is a 'restaurant avec chambres' with double rooms for £28 a night.

Tourist office: Office de Tourisme, Forum de l'Hôtel de Ville, Le Havre (35 21 22 88).

CAEN

Strictly speaking, Caen isn't a Channel port at all. The Brittany Ferries terminal is at Ouistreham, 15 minutes drive north of Caen on the Côte de Nacre. While Ouistreham has its pleasures – it's just the sort of place where Monsieur Hulôt might have spent his holidays – it is a resort for the summer; Caen is a city for all seasons.

Brittany Ferries' economy with the truth can be excused on two grounds. Ouistreham is a jolly little place to pitch up in when you drive off the ferry (but let's face it, after Portsmouth even Chernobyl would seem like Bourton-on-the-Water). And Caen is such a fine base for a short break that being dropped off just 10 miles short is near enough to make no difference. Of course you may decide not to go near Caen. Turn left at the first available opportunity and you will be on your way to Cabourg (a favourite haunt of Marcel Proust who described it in *A la Récherche du Temps Perdu*), Deauville and neighbouring Trouville. You could happily spend a weekend in any of these three jolly seaside places and return fully satisfied.

Turn right when you get off the ferry and you will be heading along the D-Day coast past memorials and cemeteries that mark the biggest amphibious landing in history. Steer inland a little and you will reach Bayeux, well worth visiting even if you don't bother to see the magnificent Bayeux tapestry: these days handsomely-accommodated in an excellent new museum.

However if you choose to make Caen your base, you will not be disappointed. It has a handful of interesting historic sights – including the tomb of William the Conqueror in the Abbaye aux Hommes – as well as plenty of good shops and restaurants. Since its opening a few years ago, the main attraction is the 'Memorial' – 'a museum for peace' – housed in an extraordinary new building in the north of the city. Rather than offering a simple account of the D-Day landings and their dreadful aftermath, the museum dramatically sets out the events that led to the Second World War, outlines the war as it affected the French themselves – and in one of the most powerful and moving audio-visual presentations I've ever seen, shows the preparation and execution of the D-Day landings.

It's easy to forget the agonies suffered by the French during the German occupation ('les années noires' or 'black years' as they are called). The museum clearly stirred up uncontrollable emotions. An old man seized my arm at one point, desperate to share his memories. 'I'm 79 years old,' he said: 'During the war I was six years in Poland. *Six ans.* You understand? The museum explains the causes of war, but doesn't show how it affected people like me. *Vous comprenez?*' He became slowly incoherent with grief. At another part of the stunningly laid-out exhibition, where an actual recording was played of the French surrender to the Germans, I saw an old French woman weeping silently, tears creeping across wrinkled cheeks. The museum had accounts of the French Resistance – but didn't ignore the extensive collaboration that went on with the Nazis.

A half-hour's drive from Caen is another equally dramatic account of a previous invasion: the Bayeux tapestry which records the Norman conquest of England in 1066. Once housed in an uncomfortable hall, the size of somebody's front room, the Bayeux tapestry now has the thoughtful setting it deserves – complete with an intelligent audio-visual presentation which explains the historical context of the invasion. Interestingly, in the tapestry, the Brits all have drooping, hippy moustaches while the Normans sport hooligan-style skinhead haircuts (one wonders if they charged the beach at Hastings chanting: 'Ici nous allons, ici nous allons . . .').

I first got to know Caen 20 years ago. I can't go there now without thinking of long afternoons spent learning the noble art of table football ('baby foot') in a bar near the castle, where the air was full of the unforgettable smell of *anis* and Gauloises cigarettes. There was a young Frenchman on the pinball machine who, according to my recollection, always seemed to be singing along with Jimi Hendrix: 'Hey Joe, where you goin' with that gun in your 'and . . .'

In some ways Caen hasn't changed at all since the sixties. On the face of things, it's still the same rather unexciting-looking place that it was then. After the D-Day landing of June 1944, the city was over three-quarters destroyed and 10,000 of its population killed – in the circumstances perhaps it's a wonder that it was rebuilt at all. But whereas 20 years ago Caen was a rather guileless Norman town, today it has discovered a more confident, more prosperous style. Now so near to Paris – less than two hours' drive on the autoroute – it was perhaps inevitable that Caen would prosper from this rapprochement.

Travelling to Caen from Portsmouth, it's difficult not to make comparisons between the two cities. Much of the city centre rebuilding carried out in Portsmouth since the war has been vile: grotesque tower blocks and hideous shopping centres, the worst of which are now facing demolition. Caen, on the other hand, has continued to evolve.

If you have the time, and the inclination, there is plenty of sightseeing to be done in and around Caen. But if the weather's good, leave the city and enjoy the pleasures of the Norman countryside – in autumn it's particularly agreeable. South of Caen is *bocage* country, fields divided by thick hedgerows; everywhere the distinctive *chaumière* black and white half-timbered cottages. By the end of September, it all has a dreamy over-ripe feel: the trees full of fat cider apples, plump, lazy cows sat comfortably on the lush grass, the sweet smell of apple-tree logs burning on the chill evening air. It's difficult to imagine why the Normans ever bothered to conquer England.

Hypermarket: The best hypermarket in town is the Carrefour at the *centre commercial* in Herouville. The Continent, near the Novotel on the road to the Côte du Nacre, is dreadful.

Market: Friday morning at the Place St-Sauveur; Sunday morning at the Place Courtonne.

Hotels: The best of the city-centre hotels is the bright and cheerful Relais des Gourmets, 15 Rue de Geole (31 86 06 01) where a double room costs from £30 per night – but it has no car park. The Mercure, 1 Rue de Courtonne (31 47 24 24) has its own private garage: a double room costs £42 per night. On the outskirts of the city, my choice is the Novotel, Avenue de la Côte de Nacre (31 93 05 88): a double room costs £50 per night. If money is no object, the star hotel in the area is the Manoir d'Hastings (31 44 62 43) at Benouville, five miles north of Caen; a one-rosette Michelin 'restaurant with rooms' housed in a 17th-century priory. Double rooms cost from £70 per night.

Restaurants: The top-rated restaurant in the city is La Bourride, 15 Rue Vaugueux (31 93 50 76) with two Michelin rosettes and fixed-price menus starting at around £47.

Tourist office: Office du Tourisme, Place Saint-Pierre, Caen 14300 (31 86 27 65).

CHERBOURG

The road to and from the ferry port skirts the town so effectively, you could live the whole of your life without knowing that the centre of Cherbourg really exists. Let's not kid ourselves, across the little *port de plaisance* you are not going to find Barcelona but there is a pleasant little burg full of cheerful hustle and bustle.

Much of Cherbourg town centre has been pedestrianised, which is fine as long as you can find somewhere to park your car. If you are only visiting for a short time, best to leave your car in the Continent hypermarket car park and walk into town across the bridge. The heart of the town is the Place General de Gaulle, the market place, which is dominated by the handsomely restored municipal theatre. There are several good shops and a good selection of restaurants and bars.

Napoleon liked Cherbourg. Near the sea-front on the Quai de Caligny is a statue of the great man, astride a horse, pointing out to sea. On the plinth is the inscription: *J'avais resolu de renouveler à Cherbourg les merveilles de l'Egypte* (I had resolved to renew in Cherbourg the wonders of Egypt). Napoleon had plans to use Cherbourg as a naval base linking France with his planned empire in Egypt. Well, not tonight, Josephine.

Cherbourg may not provide a base for exploring Egypt, it can serve however as a serviceable base for visiting the Cotentin peninsula. You will probably not to want to venture too far west to Cap de la Hague where you will eventually encounter the Cap Hague nuclear re-processing plant: the French version of Sellafield, which is said to discharge 'low level' radiation into the sea.

Further south, away from the low-level radiation is the pleasant

53

resort of Barneville-Carteret which looks across to Jersey. An hour or so further south is Mont St Michel, which during the main holiday season is a tourist beer garden: out of season visitors may see it in a better light.

Heading eastwards from Cherbourg probably offers better possibilities. A short drive east along the coast from Cherbourg is the small port of Barfleur, famous as the place from which Duke William sailed to conquer England. A few miles south of Barfleur is St-Vaast-la-Hougue which has the sort of fishing harbour guidebooks describe as 'picturesque' and being full of 'gnarled old fishermen'. What with EEC fishing quotas and the rest, you don't often see gnarled old fishermen these days, so it's worth a visit on this score alone. Another reason is the admirable hotel France et Fuchsias where the food is excellent.

Further south is Utah Beach, one of the five landing beaches of the Allied invasion. There are memorials and viewing platforms at La Madeleine. Those who saw the film of the invasion *The Longest Day*, will also want to visit Saint-Mère-Eglise, where the first parachutists landed on 6 June. One of the most memorable moments of the film is the soldier whose parachute caught, as he landed, on the church steeple. In a tribute of dubious taste, a dummy 'parachutist' still hangs from his parachute stuck to the church steeple. 'It's been done for the tourists,' explained a man in the bar opposite, with a shrug of his shoulders. When it comes to amusing tourists, he seemed to be saying, no taste can be too bad.

Hypermarket: The Continent hypermarket (the second road to the right after leaving the ferry terminal) deserves some award as the least prepossessing structure in France.

Market: Tuesdays, Thursdays and Saturdays in the Place General de Gaulle.

Hotels: The Hôtel Mercure, Gare Maritime (33 44 01 11) – across the water from the ferry terminal – is the typical Lego kit French chain hotel but in a glorious spot: the interior and exterior look is meant to echo that of a transatlantic liner. Double rooms cost from around £50 per night. Probably the best hotel on the Cotentin peninsula is the Hôtel de France (33 54 42 26) in St-Vaast-la-Hougue: a pretty port, a fine family-run hotel with an excellent restaurant – a winning combination. Rooms with baths from £24 per double per night. The other chain hotel in town is the Climat de France at Equeurdreville (33 93 42 94), which also offers very good value with double rooms from £29 per night.

Restaurants: Two of the more highly-rated places are Grandgousier, 21 Rue de l'Abbaye (33 53 19 43) with set menus from £14,

and L'Ancre Dorée, 3 Rue Abbaye (33 93 98 38) with menus from
£11.
Tourist office: Office de Tourisme de Cherbourg et du Nord Cotentin, 2 Quai Alexandre III, Cherbourg (33 43 52 02).

St Malo

To borrow that favourite travel writing cliché, St Malo is a place
of contrasts and enigmas: old but new, beautiful and yet rather
plain.

In his efforts to wrest the city from the Germans in 1944, General
Patton practically razed the place to the ground. Showing the sort
of dogged determination that other war-damaged places would
have done well to imitate – particularly in Britain – the Malouins
rebuilt the old walled city as faithfully as they could to the original
design and shape.

They did a good job. But outside the elegantly revamped ramparts of the citadelle, the new parts of St Malo are common or
garden French suburbs. Pleasant enough but not worth a detour.
If you are planning to stay in St Malo therefore, station yourself
in the 'intra muros' citadelle.

The best alternative base lies across the river Rance in Dinard.
(Cross over the tidal power dam which was built in 1966 but for
technical reasons has never been able to work at full capacity.
Dinard was a popular place with the English at the turn of the
century. It has managed to hang on to its good looks: there is a
casino, pleasant beaches and some attractive Hansel and Gretel
cottage-style villas.
Hypermarket: There is a Continent hypermarket in the La Madel-
eine area in the south-west of the city.
Market: In the 'intra muros', market days are Tuesday and
Friday.
Hotels: In the old city top hotels include the Central, 6 Grande
Rue (99 40 87 70): double rooms from £32 per night; and La Cité,
26 Rue Ste-Barbe (99 40 55 40), doubles from £40 per night.
Restaurants: The Duchesse Anne, 5 Place Guy La Chambre (99 40
85 33) is a one-star Michelin restaurant, set meals from £22.
Tourist office: Office de Tourisme, Esplanade St-Vincent (99 56 64
48).

Roscoff

If you are looking for an away-from-it-all Channel port where you
are unlikely to be disturbed by British hoolies on the rampage for
cases of bargain price beer, then Roscoff is your destination. In
winter it practically languishes into hibernation. It is certainly the
least well-known and least visited of all the ferry ports, although

it was once a main port of entry for France. Mary Stuart came through Roscoff in 1548 on her way to be presented to the King of France. Bonnie Prince Charlie also sought refuge here after his defeat at the Battle of Culloden.

However Roscoff diminished in importance and might have continued in relative obscurity if local farmers had not become frustrated at the lack of French government support in finding new markets overseas for their produce. In a bold move, the farmers cooperative decided to set up their own ferry company to take their cauliflowers, artichokes and other produce to Britain. A deep-water harbour was constructed in Roscoff in 1973 and Brittany Ferries was born.

Any new development however has been away from the well-preserved town and its picturesque old houses. Roscoff has an attractive Vieille Porte surrounded by cafés and bars, a popular gathering place in the evening.

Nearby places worth visiting include Morlaix 15 miles southeast of Roscoff – popular with British trippers for its hypermarket. A ferry ride from Roscoff is the Île de Batz.

Hypermarket: The nearest is the Euromarche in Morlaix.

Market: There is a market in nearby St Pol de Leon on Thursday mornings.

Hotels: Top-rated hotels include the Brittany, Boulevard Ste Barbe (98 69 70 78) with an indoor swimming pool: double rooms from £50 per night; the Urbis-Le Corsaire, Place Eglise (98 61 22 61) is open all year with doubles from £33.

Restaurants: The best of the town's restaurants is probably Le Temps de Vivre, Place Eglise (98 61 27 28) with set meals starting at around £12.

Tourist office: Office de tourisme, 46 Rue Gambetta (98 61 12 13).

5

WHERE TO STAY?

The choice of accommodation in France is enormous: hundreds of thousands of hotel rooms, tens of thousands of self-catering properties, thousands of campsites. Choosing a place to stay is not just a matter of price (the most expensive self-catering places can set you back £10,000 a week – much more expensive than the most expensive hotel).

HOTELS

France is where we expect to find the perfect country house hotel, the stuff that day-dreams are made of. An avenue of plane trees, a drive of crunchy, clean gravel and at the end of it a small, cosy château with a mansard-roof pierced by windows and guarded by pepper-pot towers.

You will be met by the owner-manager who will personally assist you with your luggage. Before you go to your room he will welcome you with a glass of kir. Your bedroom will be comfortably furnished with a large double bed with crisp, neatly turned-down white linen sheets. Throw open the windows and there is a view of a formal garden – and beyond a large park bordered by a lake or a river. There will be a pool and swinging hammocks in which you can relax in the afternoon heat while waiters bring you freshly-squeezed lemonade. The food will be magnificent. Breakfast will be home-baked croissants or still warm pains aux raisins. Dinner will be unforgettable. And, best of all, the price at the end of your stay will be laughably cheap.

I discovered this perfection not once, but twice in the same trip 10 years ago – both by chance. The first was an exquisite mansion perched high above the Seine between Rouen and Le Havre. We could sit on the terrace of our room at dusk and watch the lights of barges as they drifted up and down the river far below. During the day we rode bikes, loaned by the hotel, through the Norman countryside. The days spent at the Domaine were dreamlike in their *dolce far niente*.

The second hotel, like most of the best things that happen when you travel in France, we came upon by accident. We were near

Chinon in the Loire Valley in search of a modest *logis et auberge*, when we spotted a sign for the *Château de Marçay*: Relais et Châteaux, and imagined that it would be much too expensive. It couldn't do any harm to see how much it cost. The car park was full of Mercedes and BMWs, our dusty VW Polo looked conspicuously inelegant. The château is a magnificently restored 15th-century fortress.

I was given a Basil Fawlty once-over by the man at the desk, who clearly didn't much like the look of me. He grudgingly admitted they did have a room; and it was surprisingly cheap. You were expected to dine at the hotel however. And the price of dinner would have cleared the national debt of several Third World Countries. 'Will you be dining?' *Mais naturellement,*' I said sweetly.

The next three days remain firmly written in my memory: I have total recall. Blistering August days, too hot to do much beyond sitting in the luxurious gardens. I can remember everything, even the books I read lounging in the swinging hammock drinking long cold glasses of *citron pressé*. And when it was too hot, an afternoon in the cool of our stone-walled bedroom. We ate in our room too: like inmates of Greyfriars school, a secret supply of tuck – French bread, cheeses, peaches – home-made kir from paper cups.

But there was time to see the Cinderella castles and fascinating places like Richelieu: a Renaissance 'new town', and the eponymous home of the famous Cardinal. I remember an evening in the hot, cobbled streets of Chinon, the sound of a Phil Collins record playing through an open window. Seven years later I can even tell you what was on Radio 4's *Pick of the Week* that Friday night as we drove home through the golden fields as the sun went down.

Most of all, perhaps, I remember the bad looks from the manager each morning when he asked what time we would be dining. '*Ah, pas ce soir,*' I would tell him. My wife feels a little '*malade*': she is pregnant. And she was: you can't get more romantic than that.

This was 10 years ago when French hotels – even Relais et Château ones – were a bargain. We paid around £20 a night for a superb room and memorable breakfasts on the terrace. This summer, you would have to pay at least four times as much.

These days travelling with children, for reasons of economy and practicality, we stay at chain hotels. If France is streets ahead of us in the business of running small, independent hotels – they are also much, much better at running cheap and cheerful chain hotels.

The Accor group covers the spectrum from basic one-star to executive class luxury. The Accor group's Formule 1 chain really is basic one-star – a do-it-yourself hotel where you check yourself in, with a credit card, and help yourself to breakfast. It may not be the George V, but it is cheap: a room for one, two or three people costs just £15.50, breakfast is £2.50 per person.

When choosing a hotel, particularly of the traditional variety, it pays to do some research. There are bad hotels in France, just as there are bad hotels in Britain – they are not all uniformly perfect. There are members of the Logis consortium that are shabby and sad rather than cheap and cheerful. And at the other end of the spectrum there are countless members of the Relais et Château group that are distinguished more by richly vulgar decoration and snobby attitudes than by real excellence.

Hotel Tips
• If you have children ask for a family room (this usually means a porter bringing along a couple of Z-beds). Unless you ask you will be given two rooms (depending on what sort of fight you put up they may well insist you have two rooms anyway!).
• Breakfast normally costs extra (and is disproportionately expensive).
• If you are arriving late rooms can be held by giving your credit card number as a guarantee.
• Pillows are usually to be found in the wardrobe.

Traditional French Hotels

Logis de France: Over 4,000 privately owned one- and two-star hotels in 3,000 French towns and villages who are members of the National Fédération of Logis de France. The guide used to be free from the French tourist office: now they make a charge of £6.50 (£7.50 by post: make cheque payable to 'Maison de la France'). Prices at Logis de France hotels cost from £20 per person for half-board accommodation.

Relais et Châteaux: Famous consortium of 150 leading French country house hotels: prices range from around £50 to over £200 per room per night. A guide available from the French Government Tourist Office (address below) price £4 (£5 by post: cheque payable to 'Maison de la France').

Château Welcome (0491 578803): Bed and breakfast in French châteaux: prices start at around £30 per night.

Château Hôtels Independants et Hostelleries d'Atmosphere (010 33 1 43 54 74 99): A consortium of over 200 châteaux and country house hotels. Rooms from around £60 per night.

Les Etapes François Coeur (010 33 1 47 95 05 47): Up market bed and breakfast in châteaux and other large houses.

Relais du Silence: A group of nearly 150 two- three- and four-star hotels selected for 'friendly atmosphere, superb service and quiet location'. Reservations office in Paris (45 66 77 77). Rooms from around £35 per night.

Booking agency: Hotels Abroad (0689 857838) provides a booking service for overnight stops and longer stays for a range of hotels.

Useful books: The *Michelin Red Guide to France* is the one book you must have, if only for the invaluable town plans and a wealth of other useful information. However, it does not always list the modern chain hotels for each town. Other useful guides include *Charming Small Hotel Guide to France* (Duncan Petersen, £7.99) and the *French Entrée* series (Quiller Press) by Pat Fenn: the latest guide to Normandy, for example, costs £5.95.

Main French Modern Hotel Chains

Many of the new breed of chain hotels seem to be found out-of-town near main motorway junctions and business parks. Room rates are kept low by offering the minimum of facilities: you take your own luggage to your room, you are unlikely to find room service on offer. Before taking a room, check whether there are any special rates on offer. Hotels mainly used by businessmen normally have good deals on offer during August. At other times children under 16 usually stay free and at some places are allowed a free breakfast: they may offer you an adjoining room at no extra cost. If you don't ask, you won't get.

Accor group: Bookings and information on all chains from London Resinter office (071 724 1000). The group's chains are artfully banded to cover the various market sectors, from the basic one-star of Formule 1 to the more luxurious Sofitel hotels. With the exception of Sofitel, the hotels generally have a pre-fabricated look. One assumes that there is a factory somewhere in France turning out hotel kits which are then bolted together on site. But who's complaining; if you are looking for a cheap, convenient overnight stop – particularly if you have children. Many have secure parking areas. The chain includes:

Formule 1: Over 200 one-star hotels. Basic rooms with wash-basins and TVs – but without en suite facilities – with one double bed and one single bed. Rooms cost £15.50 per night.

Hôtel Ibis and Urbis: Over 240 two star hotels. Every room has an en suite bathroom and satellite TV. Hotels also have restaurants. Rooms accommodating up to three people from around £35 per night.

Hôtel Mercure (now merged with the Altea group): Over 100 three-star hotels. Children sharing their parents room stay free.

Rates vary according to season, but average rates are around £50 per room per night.

Novotel: Over 100 three-star hotels. Children under 16 stay free and have free breakfast. Meals available from 6am to midnight. Average price of rooms around £55 per night.

Sofitel (now merged with the Pullman chain): Over 30 four-star hotels in the main French cities. Room rates from around £60 per night.

Other Chains

Campanile: Over 200 two-star hotels: rooms from around £30 per night. (UK reservations 081 569 6969; Paris 64 62 46 46.)

Climat de France: Over 130 two-star hotels: rooms from around £28 per night. Reservations in the UK through Voyages Vacances (071 287 3181).

Arcade: Over 70 two-star hotels: rooms from around £35 per night. (Reservations 071 724 1000.)

Fimotel: Over 50 two-star hotels: rooms from around £28 per night. (UK reservations 081 785 2977; Paris 47 72 67 79.)

Les Relais Bleus: Over 60 two-star hotels: rooms from around £25 per night. (Reservations office in Paris 46 86 51 30.)

Resthôtel Primevère: Over 100 two-star hotels: from around £30 per night.

A Guide to the Chains

The main hotel guides like Michelin and Gault Millau frequently omit the cheaper hotel and motel properties. Unless you have each chain's guide, finding them can sometimes be a hit or miss affair.

This is a list of where to find the main chain hotels:

Abbeville
Formule 1
Ibis

Acheres
Formule 1

Agen
Formule 1
Campanile
Ibis

Aix-en-Provence
Campanile

Campanile (Aix-la-Beauvalle)
Campanile (Meyreuil)
Ibis
Novotel (Beaumanoir)
Novotel (Fenouillères)
Mercure-Altea

Aix-les-Bains
Campanile

Albertville
Formule 1
Ibis

Albi
Formule 1
Campanile
Mercure-Altea

Alençon
Formule 1
Campanile
Ibis

Alès
Ibis
Mercure-Altea

Amboise
Novotel

Amiens
Formule 1 (Est)
Campanile (Boves)
Ibis

Angers
Formule 1 (Angers Ouest)
Formule 1 (Angers Sud)
Campanile (Sud)
Ibis (Le Château)
Mercure-Altea (Centre)
Mercure-Altea (Lac de Maine)

Angoulême
Formule 1
Campanile (Saint-Yrieix)
Ibis
Mercure-Altea

Annecy
Formule 1
Campanile (Sud)
Ibis
Mercure-Altea

Annemasse
Formule 1
Campanile (Genève-Est)
Mercure-Altea

Archamps
Ibis (Porte de Genève)

Arcueil
Campanile (Paris-Sud)

Argenteuil
Campanile (Paris-Nord)

Arles
Ibis
Campanile
Mercure-Altea

Armbouts-Cappel
Campanile (Dunkerque)

Armentières
Formule 1

Arnage
Campanile (Le Mans-Sud)

Arques
Formule 1

Arras
Formule 1
Campanile (Saint-Nicolas)
Ibis
Mercure-Altea

Artigues
Campanile (Bordeaux-Est)

Atalante
Campanile (Rennes-Nord-Est)

Aubagne
Formule 1

Auch
Campanile

Aulnay
Formule 1 (Garonor A1)
Formule 1 (Garonor A3)

Aurillac
Campanile

Auxerre
Formule 1 (Nord)
Campanile (Moneteau)
Ibis
Mercure-Altea (Nord)

Avallon
Campanile (Sauvigny-Le-Bois)

Avene-Les-Bains
Mercure-Altea

Avermes
Campanile (Moulins-Nord)

Avignon
Formule 1 (Avignon Nord)
Formule 1 (Avignon Rochefort)
Campanile (Sud)
Campanile (Nord)
Ibis (Avignon Ville)
Ibis (Avignon Sud)
Novotel (Nord)
Novotel (Sud)
Mercure-Altea (Centre)
Mercure-Altea (Sud)

Avranches
Ibis

Bagnolet
Campanile

Bailleul
Formule 1

Balaruc-Le-Vieux
Campanile (Sete)

Bastia
Ibis

Bayeux
Campanile
Novotel
Mercure-Altea

Bayonne
Formule 1

Campanile
Mercure-Altea

Beaucaire
Ibis

Beaucouze
Campanile

Beaune
Formule 1
Campanile
Ibis
Novotel
Mercure-Altea (A6)
Mercure-Altea (Centre)

Beauvais
Formule 1
Campanile (Sud)
Mercure-Altea

Belfort
Formule 1 (Sud Bavilliers)
Campanile (Nord)
Mercure-Altea

Bellefort Centre
Formule 1

Bellegarde
Campanile

Bellerive
Campanile

Belleville-sur-Saône
Campanile

Belley
Ibis (Centre)

Bergerac
Campanile

Besançon
Formule 1 (Planoise)
Formule 1 (Centre)
Campanile

Ibis (Marchaux)
Ibis (Valentin)
Novotel
Mercure-Altea (Centre)
Mercure-Altea (Parc Micaud)

Bessoncourt
Campanile

Béthune
Formule 1 (Beuvry)
Formule 1 (Fouquières)
Campanile

Beziers
Formule 1 (Est)
Campanile
Ibis (Est)

Biarritz
Ibis (Anglet)
Campanile
Novotel (Anglet Aéroport)

Blois
Formule 1 (Nord)
Formule 1 (Vineuil)
Campanile
Ibis
Ibis (Centre)
Novotel

Bobigny
Ibis
Campanile

Bonneuil-sur-Marne
Campanile

Bordeaux
Formule 1 (Aéroport)
Formule 1 (Est Artigues)
Formule 1 (Nord Lormont)
Formule 1 (Ouest Eysines)
Formule 1 (Quai de la Souys)
Formule 1 (Sud Villenave
    D'Ornon)
Campanile (Le Bouscat)
Campanile (Le Lac)

Campanile (Cestas)
Campanile (Gradignan)
Campanile (Pessac)
Campanile (Merignac)
Campanile (Artigues)
Ibis (Aéroport)
Ibis (Le Lac)
Ibis (Meriadeck Centre)
Ibis (Pessac)
Ibis (Saint-Jean)
Novotel (Aéroport)
Novotel (Centre Meriadeck)
Novotel (Le Lac)
Mercure-Altea (Aéroport)
Mercure-Altea (Le Lac)
Mercure-Altea (Pont d'Aquitaine)

Boulogne sur Mer
Formule 1
Campanile
Ibis (Centre)
Ibis (Plage)

Bourg en Bresse
Formule 1
Campanile
Ibis
Mercure-Altea

Bourges
Formule 1
Campanile
Ibis
Novotel

Bourgoin-Isle-d'Abeau
Campanile

Bouscat
Campanile

Brest
Formule 1
Campanile
Ibis (Plougastel)
Novotel
Mercure-Altea

Brétigny sur Orge
Formule 1

Briançon
Mercure-Altea

Brie-Comte-Robert
Campanile

Brignoles
Formule 1
Ibis

Brive
Formule 1 (Ussac)
Ibis
Mercure-Altea (Ussac)

Buchères
Campanile

Cabourg
Mercure-Altea

Caen
Formule 1 (Mondeville)
Formule 1 (Nord Memorial)
Campanile
Ibis (Centre)
Ibis (Centre Paul-Doumer)
Ibis (Herouville Saint-Clair)
Novotel
Mercure-Altea (Port de Plaisance)

Cahors
Formule 1
Campanile

Calais
Formule 1 (Coquelles)
Campanile
Ibis

Cambrai
Formule 1
Campanile
Ibis

Cannes
Formule 1

Campanile
Ibis (La Bocca)
Ibis (Le Cannet)
Novotel (Montfleury)
Mercure-Altea (Mandelieu)

Carcassonne
Formule 1
Campanile
Ibis

Carnac
Ibis (Plage)
Novotel (Plage)

Cavaillon
Ibis

Cergy
Formule 1 (Saint Christophe)
Campanile
Ibis
Novotel

Cestas
Campanile

Chaintre
Campanile

Châlons-sur-Marne
Formule 1
Campanile
Ibis

Châlon-sur-Saône
Formule 1 (Nord)
Campanile
Ibis
Mercure-Altea (Nord)

Chambery
Formule 1 (Nord)
Formule 1 (Sud)
Campanile
Ibis
Novotel
Mercure-Altea (Centre)

Chambly
Formule 1

Chambray-Les-Tours
Campanile

Chamonix
Novotel

Chanas
Formule 1 (A7)
Campanile
Chanteloup Les Vignes
Formule 1

Chantepie
Campanile

Chantilly
Campanile

Chapelle-St-Mesmin
Campanile

Charleville-Mézières
Formule 1
Campanile
Mercure-Altea

Chartres
Formule 1
Ibis (Centre)
Ibis (Luce)
Novotel
Mercure-Altea (Centre)

Chasse-sur-Rhône
Campanile

Chasseneuil-du-Poitou
Campanile

Château-Thierry
Campanile
Ibis

Châteauneuf-de-Grasse
Campanile

Châteauroux
Campanile
Mercure-Altea

Châtelaillon
Ibis (Plage)

Châtellerault
Formule 1 (Nord)
Campanile
Ibis

Châtillon-en-Michaille
Campanile

Chaumont
Formule 1

Chaville
Campanile

Cherbourg
Formule 1
Campanile (La Glacière)
Mercure-Altea

Cholet
Formule 1
Campanile

Cleon
Campanile

Clermont
Formule 1

Clermont-Ferrand
Formule 1 (Est)
Campanile
Ibis
Novotel
Mercure-Altea (Arverne)
Mercure-Altea (Gergovie)

Cleunay
Campanile

Cognac
Ibis

Colmar
Formule 1 (Aéroport)
Campanile
Ibis
Novotel
Mercure-Altea (Centre)
Mercure-Altea (Champ de Mars)

Compiègne
Formule 1
Campanile
Ibis

Conflans-Ste-Honorine
Formule 1
Campanile

Contrexeville
Campanile

Corbeil
Formule 1 (Sud)
Formule 1 (Tarterets)
Campanile

Correze
Mercure-Altea (Tulle)

Coulommiers
Formule 1

Courchevel
Mercure-Altea

Cran-Gevrier
Campanile

Crêche
Campanile

Creil
Formule 1

Creteil
Ibis
Novotel (Le Lac)

Cuincy
Campanile

Deauville
Campanile
Ibis
Mercure-Altea

Denain
Formule 1

Dieppe
Formule 1
Ibis

Digne-Les-Bains
Campanile

Dijon
Formule 1 (Nord)
Formule 1 (Sud)
Campanile (Nord)
Campanile (Sud)
Campanile (Est)
Ibis (Centre)
Ibis (Sud)
Novotel (Sud)
Mercure-Altea

Dinard
Formule 1

Dizy
Campanile

Dôle
Formule 1
Campanile

Douai
Formule 1 (Flers)
Campanile
Ibis (Espace Le Romagnant)

Dreux
Formule 1
Campanile

Dunkerque
Formule 1 (Grande Synthe)
Campanile
Mercure-Altea (Le Lac)
Mercure-Altea (Reuze)

Ecouen
Campanile

Ecully
Campanile

Egletons
Ibis

Elbeuf-Cleon
Campanile

Englos
Formule 1

Épernay
Campanile
Ibis

Épinal
Campanile
Ibis (Centre)
Mercure-Altea

Épinay sur Orge
Formule 1
Campanile

Épinay sur Seine
Ibis

Épone
Formule 1

Ermont-Sannois
Campanile

Essay
Campanile

Évreux
Formule 1
Campanile
Ibis
Mercure-Altea

Évry
Formule 1 (A6)
Formule 1 (N7)

Ibis
Novotel

Ferney-Voltaire
Campanile

Ferte-Bernard
Campanile

Feyzin
Campanile

Fleurines-Senlis
Formule 1

Flins Les Mureaux
Formule 1

Foix
Campanile

Fontainebleu
Formule 1 (Chailly en Bière)
Ibis
Novotel (Ury)

Fontenay-Tresigny
Formule 1

Fos-sur-Mer
Mercure-Altea

Fougères
Campanile

Fouquières-Les-Bethune
Campanile

Fourmies
Ibis

Franqueville
Campanile

Fresnes
Campanile

Futuropolis
Campanile

Gap
Formule 1
Ibis

Genève
Formule 1 (Aéroport Ferney
  Voltaire)
Formule 1 (St Julien en Genevois)
Campanile (Est)
Campanile (Ouest)

Gennevilliers
Campanile (Barbanniers)
Campanile (Port)
Ibis

Glisy
Campanile

Gonesse
Campanile

Gonfreville
Campanile

Gouesnou
Campanile

Goussainville
Formule 1
Campanile

Gradignan
Campanile

Grasse
Formule 1 (Mouans Sartoux)
Campanile (Est)
Ibis

Grenoble
Formule 1 (Fontanil)
Formule 1 (Seyssins)
Formule 1 (Université)
Campanile (Nord)
Campanile (Nord-Ouest)
Campanile (Seyssins)
Campanile (Est)
Ibis (Université)

Ibis (Centre)
Mercure-Altea (Centre)

Gueret
Campanile

Hautpierre
Campanile

Hem
Campanile

Hendaye
Campanile

Henin-Beaumont
Campanile

Honfleur
Campanile
Mercure-Altea

Hyères
Formule 1 (Le Lavandou)
Ibis (Plage)
Ibis
Mercure-Altea

Illkirch-Graffenstaden
Campanile

Illzach
Campanile

Issoire-Coudes
Formule 1

Issy-les-Moulineaux
Campanile

Ivry-sur-Seine
Campanile

Joinville-le-Pont
Campanile

Joue-les-Tours
Campanile

Kremlin-Bicetre
Campanile

La Baule
Ibis (Pornichet)

Labege
Campanile

La Grande-Motte
Mercure-Altea

Lançon
Mercure-Altea

Landerneau
Ibis

Lanester
Campanile

Langueux
Campanile

Laon
Campanile
Mercure-Altea

La Rochelle
Formule 1 (Angoulins)
Campanile (Est)
Campanile (Puilboreau)
Ibis (Centre)
Ibis (Vieux Port)
Novotel (Centre)
Mercure-Altea (Sud)
Mercure-Altea (Centre)

La Roche-Sur-Yonne
Formule 1
Campanile
Ibis (Nord)
Ibis (Sud)
Mercure-Altea

Laval
Formule 1
Campanile
Ibis (Le Realis d'Armor)

La Cannet des Maures
Formule 1

Le Blance Mesnil
Campanile

Le Bourget
Novotel

Le Creusot
Novotel (Montchanin)

Le Havre
Formule 1
Ibis (Centre)
Ibis (Sud Harfleur)
Mercure-Altea

Le Mans
Formule 1 (Nord)
Formule 1 (Sud Arnage)
Campanile (Sud)
Campanile (Est)
Ibis (Centre)
Ibis (Est Pontlieue)
Novotel (Est)

Lens
Campanile

Le Puy-en-Velay
Ibis (Centre)
Ibis (Saint-Laurent)

Lesquin
Formule 1

Les Sables d'Olonne
Mercure-Altea

Les Ulis Courtaboeuf
Formule 1

Le Touquet
Ibis
Novotel

Levallois
Campanile

Lievin
Formule 1

Lille
Campanile (Sud)
Campanile (Est)
Campanile (Villeneuve d'Ascq)
Campanile (Nord)
Campanile (Nord-Est)
Campanile (Roubaix)
Ibis (Centre)
Ibis (Opera)
Ibis (Villeneuve d'Ascq)
Novotel (Aéroport)
Novotel (Centre Palais des
    Congres)
Novotel (Lomme)
Novotel (Tourcoing)
Mercure-Altea (Aéroport)
Mercure-Altea (Centre)
Mercure-Altea (Lomme)

Limoges
Formule 1
Campanile (Nord)
Ibis (Centre)
Ibis (Nord)
Novotel (Zone Industrielle)

Linas Montlhery
Formule 1

Lingolsheim
Campanile

Lisieux
Campanile

L'Isle d'Abeau
Ibis

Lorient
Formule 1
Campanile
Ibis
Novotel
Mercure-Altea

Loudun
Mercure-Altea

Lourdes
Campanile
Ibis

Louviers Val de Reuil
Formule 1

Luneville
Campanile

Lyon
Formule 1 (Isle d'Abeau Ouest)
Formule 1 (La Tour de Salvagny)
Formule 1 (Est Beynost)
Formule 1 (Meyzieu)
Formule 1 (Nord Dardilly)
Formule 1 (Saint Priest)
Formule 1 (Solaize)
Formule 1 (Sud Ollins)
Formule 1 (Vaulx-en-Velin)
Campanile (Centre)
Campanile (Centre Perrache)
Campanile (Nord)
Campanile (Feyzin)
Campanile (Chasse-sur-Rhône)
Campanile (Saint-Foy)
Campanile (Ouest)
Campanile (Isle d'Abeau)
Campanile (Bron)
Campanile (St Laurent)
Ibis (Bron Eurexpo)
Ibis (Bron Monchat)
Ibis (Est Beynost)
Ibis (Gerland)
Ibis (Nord)
Ibis (Part-Dieu Sud)
Ibis (Université)
Novotel (Bron)
Novotel (Nord: Porte de Lyon)
Novotel (Tassin Vaise)
Mercure-Altea (Charbonnières)
Mercure-Altea (Gerland)
Mercure-Altea (L'Isle d'Abeau)
Mercure-Altea (Le Part Dieu)
Mercure-Altea (Lumière)
Mercure-Altea (Park Hotel)

71

Mercure-Altea (Nord)
Mercure-Altea (Sud)

Mâcon
Formule 1 (La Salle A6)
Formule 1 (Nord)
Campanile (Nord)
Campanile (Sud)
Ibis (Sud)
Novotel (Nord)
Mercure-Altea (Bord de Saône)
Mercure-Altea (Saint-Albain)

Maffliers
Novotel (Château de Maffliers)

Manosque
Campanile

Mantes
Formule 1 (Magnaville)
Ibis (Sud)

Marne la Vallée
Formule 1 (Collegien)
Formule 1 (Noisy Le Grand)
Ibis
Novotel (Collegien)
Novotel (Noisy Mont d'Est)

Marseille
Formule 1 (Est)
Formule 1 (Valentine)
Formule 1 (Plan de Campagne
   Cabries)
Formule 1 (Plan de Campagne Les
   Pennes Mirabeaux)
Formule 1 (Septèmes)
Formule 1 (Aéroport)
Campanile (Saint-Antoine)
Campanile (Vitrolles-Anjoly)
Campanile (Nord)
Campanile (Ouest)
Campanile (Est)
Ibis (Bonneveine)
Ibis (Centre)
Ibis (La Timone)
Ibis (Prado)
Ibis (Provence Aéroport)

Ibis (St-Menet-La-Valentine)
Novotel (Aéroport)
Novotel (Centre)
Novotel (Est)
Mercure-Altea (Bonneveine)
Mercure-Altea (Centre)

Martigues
Formule 1
Ibis

Massy Palaiseau
Novotel

Maubeuge
Formule 1 (Louvroil)
Campanile
Mercure-Altea

Maurepas
Formule 1

Mayenne
Campanile

Meaux
Formule 1 (Nord Penchard)
Formule 1 (Meaux Sud Esbly)
Campanile
Campanile (Nanteuil-les-Meaux)

Melun
Formule 1 (Moissy Cramayel)
Formule 1 (Nord)
Formule 1 (Senart)
Campanile
Ibis

Merlebach Saarbrucken
Formule 1

Metz
Formule 1 (Actipole)
Formule 1 (Ennery)
Formule 1 (Nord Devant les
   Ponts)
Formule 1 (Sud)
Campanile (Dammarie-les-Lys)
Campanile (Technopole)

Campanile (Nord)
Campanile (Sud)
Ibis
Ibis (Centre Gare)
Novotel (Centre)
Novotel (Hauçoncourt)
Mercure-Altea (Nord)
Mercure-Altea (Saint-Thiebault)

Meurdon-La-Foret
Ibis

Mons en Baroeul
Formule 1

Montargis
Ibis

Montbeliard
Ibis

Mont-de-Marsan
Campanile

Montauban
Campanile

Montelimar
Formule 1 (Nord)
Ibis (Nord)

Montluçon
Formule 1
Campanile
Ibis (Centre)

Montpellier
Formule 1 (Ouest St Jean de
  Vedas)
Formule 1 (Montpellier Sud)
Formule 1 (Vendargues)
Campanile (Nord)
Campanile (Sud)
Campanile (Ouest)
Campanile (Est)
Ibis (Fabregues)
Ibis (Sud)
Novotel
Mercure-Altea (Antigone)
Mercure-Altea (Aéroport)

Mont St Michel
Mercure-Altea

Morangis
Campanile

Moulins
Formule 1 (Sud)
Campanile (Nord)
Ibis (Centre)
Ibis (Nord)
Ibis (Sud)

Moutiers
Ibis (Sud)
Ibis (Tarentaise)

Mulhouse
Formule 1 (Bale Aéroport)
Formule 1 (Île Napoleon)
Formule 1 (Ouest)
Campanile (Nord)
Campanile (Morschwiller)
Ibis (Sausheim)
Novotel
Mercure-Altea (Centre)
Mercure-Altea (Sausheim)
Mercure-Altea (Sausheim)

Mutzig
Formule 1

Nancy
Formule 1 (Nord Bouxière aux
  Dames)
Formule 1 (Sud)
Campanile (Vandoeuvre)
Campanile (Ouest)
Campanile (Est)
Ibis (Brabois)
Ibis (Centre Gare)
Novotel (Ouest)
Novotel (Sud Houdemont)
Mercure-Altea (Centre)
Mercure-Altea (Thiers)

Nantes
Formule 1 (Carquefou)
Formule 1 (Est)

Formule 1 (Ouest St Herblain)
Formule 1 (Sud Bouguenais)
Campanile (Sud Ouest)
Campanile (Ouest)
Campanile (Est)
Campanile (Sud Est)
Ibis (Beaujoire)
Ibis (Centre)
Novotel (Carquefou)
Novotel (Centre)
Mercure-Altea (Carquefou)
Mercure-Altea (Ouest)

Narbonne
Formule 1 (Sud)
Ibis
Novotel (Sud)

Nemours
Formule 1
Ibis
Mercure-Altea

Nevers
Formule 1 (Nord)
Campanile
Ibis

Nice
Campanile
Ibis (Aéroport)
Novotel (Cap 3000)
Novetel (Centre)
Mercure-Altea (Baie des Anges)
Mercure-Altea (Massena)
Mercure-Altea (Opera)

Nîmes
Formule 1 (Est Marguerittes)
Formule 1 (Ouest)
Campanile
Novotel (Centre)
Novotel (Ouest)
Mercure-Altea (Centre)
Mercure-Altea (Ouest)

Niort
Formule 1 (St Maixent)
Campanile

Ibis
Mercure-Altea

Nuits Saint-Georges
Ibis

Oléron
Novotel (Saint-Trojan)

Orange
Campanile
Ibis
Mercure-Altea

Orgeval
Novotel

Orléans
Formule 1 (Charbonnière)
Formule 1 (La Chapelles St
    Mesmin)
Formule 1 (Olivet)
Campanile (Nord)
Campanile (Sud)
Campanile (Ouest)
Ibis (Centre)
Ibis (Nord Saran)
Novotel (Charbonnière)
Novotel (La Source)

Oyonnax
Ibis

PARIS
Campanile (Bastille)
Campanile (Bobigny)
Campanile (Boulevard Berthier)
Campanile (Boulogne)
Campanile (Issy-les-Moulineaux)
Campanile (Italie Gobelins)
Campanile (Levallois)
Campanile (Nation)
Campanile (Orly)
Campanile (Pantin)
Campanile (Porte de Bagnolet)
Campanile (Porte d'Italie)
Campanile (Porte d'Ivry)
Campanile (St Denis Basilique)
Campanile (St Denis Quai)

Campanile (Tour Eiffel)
Ibis (Alesia)
Ibis (Bagnolet)
Ibis (Bercy)
Ibis (Gentilly)
Ibis (Jemmapes Louis-Blanc)
Ibis (La Défense)
Ibis (La Fayette)
Ibis (Maine-Montparnasse)
Ibis (Montmartre)
Ibis (Nanterre)
Ibis (Nation Avron)
Ibis (Orly)
Ibis (Pont de Suresnes)
Ibis (Porte d'Orléans)
Ibis (Roissy Charles de Gaulle)
Ibis (République)
Ibis (Sacre Coeur)
Ibis (Italie Tolbiac)
Ibis (Vanves)
Ibis (Parly 2)
Novotel (Bagnolet)
Novotel (Bercy)
Novotel (Charenton)
Novotel (La Défense)
Novotel (Les Halles)
Novotel (Orly Rungis)
Novotel (Roissy Charles de
  Gaulle)
Novotel (Suresnes Longchamp)
Mercure-Altea (Bercy)
Mercure-Altea (Blanqui)
Mercure-Altea (Étoile)
Mercure-Altea (La Defense)
Mercure-Altea (Montmartre)
Mercure-Altea (Montparnasse)
Mercure-Altea (Monty)
Mercure-Altea (Place d'Italie)
Mercure-Altea (Ronceray)
Mercure-Altea (Tolbiac)
Mercure-Altea (Vaugirard)
Mercure-Altea (Porte d'Orleans)
Mercure-Altea (Porte de Pantin)
Mercure-Altea (Porte de la
  Plaine)
Mercure-Altea (Saint-Maurice)
Mercure-Altea (Val de Fontenay)
Mercure-Altea (Roissy Charles de
  Gaulle)

Mercure-Altea (Maurepas)
Mercure-Altea (Meulan)
Mercure-Altea (Orly)

Pau
Formule 1
Campanile (Est)
Ibis (Lons)
Novotel (Lescar)
Mercure-Altea

Périgueux
Formule 1
Campanile
Ibis
Mercure-Altea

Péronne
Formule 1 (Assevillers A1)
Mercure-Altea

Perpignan
Formule 1 (Sud)
Campanile
Ibis (Centre)
Ibis (Littoral)
Novotel
Mercure-Altea

Plaisir
Formule 1

Poitiers
Formule 1 (Nord)
Formule 1 (Sud)
Campanile (Nord)
Ibis (Beaulieu)
Ibis (Futuroscope)
Ibis (Sud)
Novotel (Nord)
Mercure-Altea

Pont-a-Mousson
Campanile

Pontarlier
Formule 1
Campanile

Pontoise Saint Martin
Formule 1

Provins
Ibis

Quiberon
Ibis

Quimper
Formule 1
Campanile
Ibis
Novotel

Rambouillet
Ibis

Reims
Formule 1 (Tinqueux)
Campanile (Sud)
Campanile (Taissy)
Campanile (Ouest)
Ibis (Tinqueux)
Novotel (Tinqueux)
Mercure-Altea
Mercure-Altea (Est)

Remiremont St Nabord
Formule 1

Rennes
Formule 1 (Est Vern Sur Seiche)
Formule 1 (Nord Est Chantère)
Formule 1 (Ouest Le Rheu)
Campanile (Sud)
Campanile (Ouest)
Campanile (Nord-Est)
Ibis (Beaulieu)
Ibis (Centre Gare)
Ibis (Cesson)
Novotel (Alma)
Mercure-Altea (Centre)
Mercure-Altea (Parc du
   Colombier)

Roanne
Formule 1
Campanile
Ibis

Rochefort-sur-Mer
Campanile

Rodez
Campanile

Romans Bourg de Peage
Formule 1

Roncq
Formule 1

Roscoff
Ibis

Roubaix
Formule 1 (Centre)
Ibis
Mercure-Altea

Rouen
Formule 1 (Est)
Formule 1 (Sud)
Formule 1 (Val de Reuil)
Campanile (Barentin)
Campanile (Nord)
Campanile (Sud)
Campanile (St Etienne)
Campanile (Sud-Est)
Campanile (Ouest)
Ibis (Barentin)
Ibis (Centre)
Ibis (Parc Expo)
Ibis (Saint-Sever)
Novotel (Sud)
Mercure-Altea

Royan
Novotel

Rueil Malmaison
Novotel

Rungis Orly
Formule 1

Saclay
Novotel

Saint-Avold
Campanile
Novotel

Saint-Brieuc
Formule 1
Campanile

Saint Chamond
Formule 1

Saint Cyprien
Ibis (Residence)

Saint Denis
Formule 1

Saint Die
Formule 1
Campanile
Ibis

Saint-Dizier
Formule 1
Campanile
Ibis

St Etienne
Formule 1 (Aéroport)
Formule 1 (Nord)
Campanile (Nord)
Ibis (gare Châteaucreux)
Ibis (Nord La Terrasse)
Novotel (Aéroport)
Mercure-Altea

Saint-Jean-de-Monts
Mercure-Altea

Saint-Lary
Mercure-Altea

Saint Lô
Formule 1
Ibis (Centre)
Ibis (La Chevalerie)

Saint Malo
Formule 1

Campanile
Ibis (Plage)
Ibis (Quartier de la Madeleine)
Mercure-Altea

Saint-Nazaire
Campanile (Est)
Ibis (Trignac)

Saint Omer
Formule 1
Ibis (Centre)

St Pol sur Mer
Formule 1

Saint-Quentin-en-Yvelines
Campanile (Ouest)
Novotel

Saint-Rambert-d'Albon
Ibis

Saint-Valery-en-Caux
Mercure-Altea

Saint Witz
Formule 1 (A1)
Mercure-Altea

Saintes
Formule 1
Campanile
Ibis

Sallanches
Ibis

Salôn de Provence
Formule 1
Campanile
Ibis

Sarcelles
Formule 1

Saumur
Campanile

77

Saverne
Formule 1

Savigny
Formule 1 (Villemoisson)

Sedan
Campanile

Senlis
Formule 1
Campanile
Ibis

Sète
Formule 1 (Frontignan)
Campanile

Sevran
Campanile

Sisteron
Ibis

Sochaux
Formule 1
Campanile

Soissons
Formule 1 (Crouy)
Campanile

Sophia Antipolis (Antibes)
Formule 1
Ibis
Mercure-Altea

Strasbourg
Formule 1 (Mutzig)
Formule 1 (Nord)
Formule 1 (Pont du Rhin)
Formule 1 (Sud)
Campanile (Ouest)
Campanile (Hautpierre)
Campanile (Sud)
Ibis (Centre)
Ibis (Lingolsheim)
Ibis (Palais des Congres)
Ibis (Petite-France)

Novotel (Centre Halles)
Novotel (Sud)

Survilliers
Novotel
Mercure-Altea (Centre)
Mercure-Altea (Pont de l'Europe)
Mercure-Altea (Sud)

Tain-l'Hermitage
Mercure-Altea

Tarbes
Formule 1
Campanile (Ouest)
Campanile (Sud)

Taverny
Campanile

Thiers
Campanile

Thionville
Formule 1 (Yutz)
Campanile (Yutz)
Thonon-les-Bains
Formule 1 (Est)
Ibis

Toulon
Formule 1 (La Seyne)
Formule 1 (La Valette)
Formule 1 (Sollies-Pont)
Campanile (Centre)
Campanile (Ouest)
Campanile (Est)
Ibis (La Seyne)
Ibis (La Valette)
Novotel (La Seyne)
Mercure-Altea

Toulouse
Formule 1 (Aéroport)
Formule 1 (Le Mirail)
Formule 1 (L'Union)
Formule 1 (Muret)
Formule 1 (Ramonville)
Campanile (L'Union)
Campanile (Nord)

Campanile (Sud)
Campanile (Sud-Ouest)
Campanile (Ouest)
Campanile (Sud-Est)
Campanile (Labege)
Ibis (Aéroport)
Ibis (Le Mirail)
Ibis (Matabiau)
Novotel (Centre Compans
   Caffarelli)
Novotel (Centre)
Novotel (Purpan)
Mercure-Altea (les Capitouls)
Mercure-Altea (Matabiau)
Mercure-Altea (Saint-Georges)
Mercure-Altea (Wilson)
Mercure-Altea (Centre)

Tourcoing
Formule 1 (Gare)
Ibis (Centre)

Tours
Formule 1 (Nord)
Formule 1 (Sud)
Campanile (Sud)
Campanile (Sud-Ouest)
Ibis (Nord)
Ibis (Sud)
Novotel (Sud)
Mercure-Altea (Nord)

Trappes
Formule 1

Trouville-sur-Mer
Mercure-Altea

Troyes
Formule 1
Campanile (Sud)
Novotel (Aéroport)
Mercure-Altea

Val de Reuil
Mercure-Altea

Val d'Isère
Mercure-Altea

Valence
Formule 1 (Nord)
Campanile (Sud)
Ibis
Novotel (Sud)

Valenciennes
Campanile
Campanile (Petite Foret)
Novotel (Aérodrome)

Val Thorens
Novotel

Vannes
Formule 1
Campanile
Ibis

Vernon
Formule 1

Versailles
Novotel (Le Chesnay)
Mercure-Altea

Vesoul
Formule 1
Ibis

Vichy
Campanile (Bellerive)
Ibis
Novotel (Thermaux)

Vienne Chasse sur Rônes
Formule 1

Vierzon
Campanile

Vigneus N6
Formule 1

Villefranche sur Saône
Formule 1
Campanile
Ibis

Villeneuve d'Ascq	**Villepinte**
Formule 1	Formule 1
	Campanile
Villeneuve St Georges Crosnes	Ibis
Formula 1	
Villeneuve-sur-Lot	**Villers-Cotterets**
Campanile	Ibis

HOTEL HOLIDAYS

Operators That Offer Hotel-inclusive Packages to All Parts of France

AA Motoring Holidays (0256 493878)
Rooms in hotels from the France Accueil, Logis de France and Best Western chains, on a pre-booked or go-as-you-please basis. Accommodation vouchers are purchased in the UK, and exchanged in hotels as travellers tour around. Two nights' accommodation with breakfast and dinner for two people at Logis de France or country inns in August costs £322, ferry inclusive.

Air France Holidays (081 742 3377)
Throughout France, Corsica and Monaco: hotels range from two star to four star, with selections in city centres, beach resorts and villages inland. Fourteen nights in the Riviera, staying at the two-star Hôtel Regence in Nice costs from £421 to £645 per person, air inclusive.

Allez France Holidays (0903 742345)
Auberges, château hotels and vineyard hotels in all regions. 'Two nights at a two-star auberge in the Champagne village of Ambonnay with its award-winning chef-patron costs from £123 to £151 per person for a party of four, including ferry crossing and half-board accommodation.'

Bonnes Vacances (081 948 3467)
Accommodation in main tourist areas, particularly Provence, Dordogne, Charente and the Alps. Prices from £32 per couple, per night for bed and breakfast in a converted water-mill hotel in the Dordogne, to £38 per person, per night, half-board in the Alps. Both prices are exclusive of travel.

Brittany Ferries (0752 221321)
Car touring holidays throughout France. Accommodation is in one- two- or three-star hotels as well as country inns. Holiday-makers can choose pre-booked tours or book as they go. A 10-night tour including bed and breakfast accommodation in one-star

hotels and country inns costs from £181 to £247 per person, ferry inclusive.

Cresta Holidays (061 926 9999)

Over 140 hotels throughout France from two star to luxury class. A bed and breakfast package, by air, costs from £273 to £444 per person staying in a three-star hotel in Nice for seven nights.

France Life Holidays (0532 390077)

All types of hotels in most areas. A 14-night holiday in a two-star hotel in Paris costs around £383 per person, ferry inclusive. Fourteen nights in a luxury hotel on the Riviera in high season costs £1137 per person, flight inclusive.

Gîtes de France (071 408 1343)

Chambres d'hôtes: Gîtes de France publishes a brochure listing more than 150 bed and breakfast places throughout the whole of France. Prices range from around £37 per person to £84 per person for two nights bed and breakfast including return ferry crossing.

Hampton House Travel (081 977 6404)

Accommodation is offered in three- four- and five-star hotels, châteaux and country house hotels in all regions. Prices start from £128 per person for two nights in Normandy, including ferry travel, breakfast and gastronomic dinners on each night.

Inntravel (0439 7111)

Family-run hotels, from two star to four star, chosen for location, good food and standard of hospitality, throughout most regions. Combine any to make your own itinerary. A seven-night half-board stay at Hostellerie du Grand Duc, Gincla, costs from £290 to £340 per person, including short-sea ferry crossings.

Maison Vacances (081 540 9680)

Every type of hotel accommodation is offered from luxury hotels to family hotels. Seven nights half-board at a three-star hotel in the Hautes Pyrénées costs from £376 to £506 per person, ferry inclusive.

Meon Villa Holidays (0730 268411)

Holidays to a selection of restored châteaux and manor houses. Prices range from £428 to £476 per person for two weeks on a bed and breakfast basis. The prices include ferry crossings.

North Sea Ferries (0482 77177)

Go-as-you-please motoring holidays with sailings from Hull to Zeebrugge. Vouchers are supplied for accommodation at Logis de France hotels. Prices from £208 per person for a six-night holiday.

Quatre Saisons (0303 221135)

Normandy, Brittany, Dordogne, Provence, Burgundy, Loire, Champagne, Auvergne, Lot and Limousin: Two nights in the Hôtel

L'Hermitage in Pernes-les-Fontaines in Provence costs £159 per person on a bed and breakfast basis, ferry inclusive.
Sunvista Holidays (0985 217373)
Two- and three-star hotels offered throughout France, specifically chosen for touring holidays. Packages range from five to ten nights although this can be extended. Prices include half-board, return ferry crossing and insurance for two adults: five nights in low season costs £600 – ten nights in high season costs £1180.
VFB Holidays (0242 526338)
For touring or residential holidays. Small family-run hotels with the emphasis on good cooking and peaceful locations. A two-night break costs from £104 per person, including half-board accommodation, return ferry and insurance.

Operators Who Offer a Selection of Hotel-inclusive Packages in Particular French Regions

Alps

Sally Holidays (0732 780440)
Seven nights accommodation in a two- or three-star hotel costs from £150 per person for bed and breakfast to £313 per person on half-board, including ferry.
Sandpiper Camping Holidays (0932 868658)
Two weeks half-board in a double room with bathroom and balcony in chalet-style hotels costs £820. Prices are for two adults and include a short sea ferry crossing.

Brittany

Brittany Direct Holidays (081 641 6060)
A seven-night half-board package at the Hôtel Roche Corneille in Dinard costs from £283 to £409 per person, ferry inclusive.
Brittany Ferries (0752 221321)
A 14-night bed and breakfast package at Le Manoir du Menec in Bannalec, a 15th-century manor house, costs from £403 to £525 per person, including return ferry crossing with car. The hotel offers a gym, sunbeds and a heated indoor swimming pool.
Crystal Holidays (081 390 3335)
A 14-night half board package at the Abbaye de Villeneuve costs from £1042 per person, including return air travel from London.
Westbury Travel (0225 444516)
A choice of three hotels, one on the north coast and two on the south coast, all within easy reach of the sea. Prices for two adults

range from £458 to £488 for seven nights in a three-star hotel on a bed and breakfast basis, ferry inclusive.

Burgundy

Crystal Holidays (081 390 3335)
A 14-night bed and breakfast package at the Hostellerie de la Petite Verrerie near Beaune, costs from £467 to £495 per person, including scheduled return air travel from London.

La France des Villages (0449 737664)
Small family-run hotels and chambres d'hôte in manoirs and châteaux. One night's bed and breakfast, based on two sharing costs from £19 per person.

Sally Holidays (0732 780440)
Seven nights bed and breakfast accommodation costs from £240 to £267 per person, including ferry.

Champagne

Hoverspeed Holidays (081 424 2929)
Short-break holidays throughout in towns and rural areas. Prices range from £50 to £139 per person, per night. All prices include a hovercraft or SeaCat crossing, based on two in a car.

Corsica

Allegro Holidays (0737 221323)
Beach hotels, inland inns or luxury hotels in Porticcio or Porto Vecchio. There is a wide range of styles, locations and prices, for example from £299 per person for one week's bed and breakfast in a three-star hotel, to £2000 per person for two weeks half-board in a luxury hotel.

Corsican Places (0424 774366)
Accommodation ranges from auberges to four-star luxury hotels. Seven nights in a three-star hotel on half-board costs from £468 to £600 per person, flight inclusive.

French Affair (071 381 8519)
'Small and friendly auberges': a week's stay at the Hôtel La Rivière in Porto Vecchio on a bed and breakfast basis costs from £320 per person, flight inclusive. This price includes car hire with unlimited mileage.

Simply Corsica (081 747 3580)
Aullene: a mountain auberge, ideal for walkers costs from £667 to £737 per person, based on two sharing. Price includes half-board, return flights from Gatwick and a Group A car hire.

VFB Holidays (0242 526338)
Two- and three-star hotels close to the mountains and the sea: 14 nights from £800 to £1390 per person, including flights, insurance, half-board accommodation and car hire.

Voyages Ilena (071 924 4440)
Twenty hotels in all areas. They range from small auberges to three-star hotels with swimming pools. They also have a small selection of 'hôtels pavillionaire' accommodation offering the flexibility of self-catering with the full range of services offered by a hotel. Prices per week range from £160 per person for bed and breakfast to £550 per person for a stay at one of the 'hôtels pavillionaire'.

Dordogne

La France des Villages (0449 737664)
Small family-run hotels and chambres d'hôte in manoirs and châteaux. One night's bed anad breakfast, based on two sharing, costs from £19 per person.

Sally Holidays (0732 780440)
Seven nights bed and breakfast accommodation in a two- or three-star hotel costs from £312 to £365 per person, including ferry.

Westbury Travel (0225 444516)
Six hotels, all with pools, dotted around the region, including a converted château, an ivy-clad manor house and a former coaching inn. Prices for two adults range from £322 to £406 for a seven-night holiday on half-board, ferry inclusive.

Haute Savoie

Freedom Holidays (081 741 4686)
Summer holidays to a chalet hotel. Prices from £99 per week, per person, on a bed and breakfast basis, excluding travel.

Lakes and Mountains Holidays (0329 844405)
A week's half-board at the Hôtel Les Belles Pistes in Les Carroz costs from £239 to £299 per person, ferry inclusive.

Languedoc

Crystal Holidays (081 390 3335)
A 14-night bed and breakfast package at the Hôtel du Golf in Cap d'Agde costs from £574 to £708 per person, including scheduled return air travel from London.

French Affair (071 381 8519)
Small friendly auberges and hotels located by rivers, lakes and

the sea. A three-night stay at the Hôtel Le Bon Port in Collioure, on half-board, costs from £247 per person. This price includes air travel and car hire with unlimited mileage.

Tailhos (010 33 67 97 27 62)
Chambre d'hôte accommodation in renovated farm buildings. One night's accommodation costs 185F including breakfast.

Loire Valley

Westbury Travel (0225 444516)
A selection of three châteaux hotels and one restored country house with formal gardens, close to the Loire. Prices range from £482 to £652 for two adults, for seven nights' half-board in a three-star hotel, ferry inclusive.

Normandy

Brittany Ferries (0752 221321)
A 14-night bed and breakfast package at the Château du Baffy in Colombiers costs from £403 to £487 per person, including return ferry crossing with car. The hotel was originally a water-mill and has its own tennis courts, archery and boules.

Crystal Holidays (081 390 3335)
A 14-night half-board package at the Hôtel Lutetia in Bagnoles de L'Orne costs from £857 per person, including scheduled return air travel from London.

Hoverspeed Holidays (081 424 2929)
Short-break holidays in towns and rural areas. Prices range from £50 to £139 per person per night. All prices include hovercraft or SeaCat crossing from Dover to Calais/Boulogne, based on two in a car.

La France des Villages (0449 737664)
Small family-run hotels and chambres d'hôte in manoirs and châteaux. One night's bed and breakfast, based on two sharing costs from £19 per person.

Westbury Travel (0225 444516)
A selection of six hotels including a country auberge, a converted corn-mill, an old Normandy farmhouse with its own pool and a château in peaceful surroundings. Prices range from £331 to £550 for seven nights in a two-star hotel for two adults on half-board, ferry inclusive.

Picardy

Crystal Holidays (081 390 3335)
A 14-night bed and breakfast package at the Château de Bellinglise costs from £703 to £778 per person, including scheduled return air travel from London.

Hoverspeed Holidays (081 424 2929)
Short-break holidays throughout the area in towns and rural areas. Prices range from £50 to £139 per person, per night. All prices include hovercraft or SeaCat crossing, based on two in a car.

Provence

Crystal Holidays (081 390 3335)
A 14-night bed and breakfast package at the Noga Hilton in Cannes costs from £888 to £1432 per person, including scheduled return air travel from London.

French Affair (071 381 8519)
Small and friendly auberges and hotels located by rivers, lakes and the sea. A three-night stay at the Hôtel Le Vieux Moulin in Villeneuve-les-Avignon costs from £255 per person on half-board. This price includes air travel and car hire with unlimited mileage.

La France des Villages (0449 737664)
Small family-run hotels and chambres d'hôte in manoirs and châteaux. One night's bed and breakfast, based on two sharing, costs from £19 per person.

Westbury Travel (0225 444516)
Five hotels in quiet surroundings, four with pools and one an 18th-century manor house in a Provençal village. Prices for two adults range from £430 to £746 for a seven-night holiday on a half-board basis, ferry inclusive.

Pyrénées

Borderline (0963 250117 brochures)
Haute Pyrénées: in the spa village of Barèges. A week's stay during the summer at Les Sorbiers, a converted Napoleonic building, costs from £205 to £220 per person on half-board. In winter a week's stay costs from £295 to £393 per person on half-board, flight inclusive. The hotel offers regional south west cuisine and vegetarian menus are always available.

Even Breaks (010 33 68 83 09 91)
Breaks with all sorts of activities for people between the ages of 20 and 40 years. Accommodation is in a restored 12th-century Romanesque chapel on the French/Spanish border. Activities

include sailing, water-skiing, horse-riding or golf. Prices range from £265 to £335 per person for one week's full board, excluding travel from the UK.

Itinerary Ltd (0439 71303)
Fifty hotels using a voucher scheme bookable in the UK. Prices range from £29 to £43 per day, per person. This includes dinner and bed and breakfast, a welcome drink and a bottle of wine with dinner.

Vendée

Brittany Ferries (0752 221321)
A 14-night bed and breakfast package at the Hôtel Lion d'Or in St Gilles Croix de Vie just 2km from the coast costs from £318 to £422 per person, including a return ferry crossing with car. The hotel has a heated indoor swimming pool and is close to the seaside resort of Sables d'Olonne.

SELF-CATERING HOLIDAYS

Most people who take a holiday in France will be staying in some sort of self-catering property. The best known is the gîte. There are over 30,000 gîtes in France: privately-owned, self-contained rural property, modernised with government help and supervised by the non-profit making Gîtes de France organization. Don't expect great luxury from a gîte: they are generally basic, often strong on character and charm – sometimes short on the basic comforts.

The official gîte organization has a wide variety of places from half-timbered houses in Normandy and rustic stone cottages in the Auvergne, to a village house or even an apartment in a Loire château. It could also be a very modern-looking cottage. Although they are regularly inspected, there seems to be quite a wide variation in standards of maintenance and cleanliness.

The attraction of renting a French country cottage from one of the specialist operators (see list below) is that there tends to be a higher degree of quality control. The places are often better furnished with conveniences like dishwashers and washing machines. But of course, the price is higher.

Remember that gîtes are in the countryside. You will have the benefits of peace, tranquility and a chance to immerse yourself into the real life of France. On the other hand, you may find that the peace and quiet amounts to isolation: your children complain that they are bored. The wildlife, which is charming in your gîte garden, becomes less of a delight when it ventures into the house: after you have killed your thousandth fly and your ten thousandth ant, you may begin to pine for urban pleasures.

There is an increasing number of conventional self-catering properties – villas and apartments – both at the seaside and in the cities. Many of the operators listed below can offer places with all mod cons (at a price to match). France also has a growing number of chains specialising in what amounts to suite hotels.

Orion, for example, offers attractive apartments accommodating from one to five people in 28 locations throughout France, including Paris. Seven nights for an apartment in its Deauville property, for example, costs from £176 to £450 depending on season: good value for four people. Information and reservations are available from Orion in Paris (010 33 1 40 78 54 54).

Other companies offering *residences* include: Residentiale (010 33 1 42 25 01 49) and Citadines (010 33 1 47 25 54 54).

Operators With a Wide Selection of Self-catering Accommodation Throughout France

AA Motoring Holidays (0256 493878)
Most holidays are at multi-activity centres; the company also offers self-catering accommodation at Euro Disney. Three weeks in Cannes in a studio and cabin for a family of five from 4 September costs £790 – the third week is free.

Air France Holidays (081 742 3377)
Apartments and studios in both city centre and resort locations. A 14-night self-drive package to Normandy, staying in a modern apartment for four people in Deauville costs from £221 to £419 per person, ferry inclusive.

Allez France Holidays (0903 742345)
Over 500 villas with pools, cottages, gîtes, farmhouses, châteaux, apartments and holiday villages in all holiday regions. Two weeks at a house with its own pool near Dinan in Brittany, costs from £890 to £1310 for a family of five, including ferry crossing with car.

Beach Villas (0223 311113)
Over 80 individually-chosen villas and apartments throughout France. 'We offer all types of accommodation from compact apartments to privately-owned villas for 10 people with a pool. Our prices range from £210 for two weeks rental in Brittany in May, for four people, to £3000 for two weeks in the south of France, for 10 people with a pool.'

Bonnes Vacances (081 948 3467)
Over 200 properties in all areas, particularly in the main tourist

regions. Prices range from £90 per week for a Normandy cottage, sleeping eight, to £1800 per week for a converted farmhouse in the Alps, sleeping six. Prices are for property rental and do not include travel to France.

Bowhill Holidays (0489 878567)

Over 300 farmhouses and villas all over France. Two weeks in a cottage in the Loire costs from £97 per person, including ferry. Two weeks in a Mediterranean villa within walking distance to the beach and with a private pool costs up to £430 per person, ferry inclusive.

Bridgewater Travel (061 707 8547)

More than 250 properties in most regions: two weeks in a traditional house at Erdeven, sleeping six people costs from £660 to £834 for a party of five, including a short-sea return ferry crossing.

Brittany Ferries (0752 221321)

Over 1,300 gîtes, some with swimming pools: two weeks at a gîte with a courtyard and lawn in the Loire Valley sleeping four costs from £156 to £270 per person in a party of four adults including return ferry crossing with car. A number of apartments in Brittany, Normandy and the west coast of France are also offered. Two weeks in a renovated Breton house, sleeping six people costs from £131 to £296 per person in a party of four adults including return ferry crossing with car. Over 400 British-owned holiday homes are featured. Two weeks in a 13th-century windmill in rural Brittany sleeping six or seven people costs from £173 to £414 per person, excluding ferry crossings.

Cresta Holidays (061 926 9999)

Apartments in all popular locations, many on the Riviera and in Brittany. Two weeks at Pierre et Vacances Apartments, Gulf of St-Tropez, sleeping five people, costs from £54 to £372 per person, ferry inclusive.

Destination France (081 689 9935)

Villas, gîtes and apartments in most regions of France. Prices range from £22 per person per week for a restored pigeonnier in Saint Laurent Iolmie in Lot to £207 per person, per week for a villa with a private pool in the region of Var.

Drive France (081 395 8888)

Over 400 properties throughout France: a week's holiday for a family of four in Languedoc-Roussillon costs from £203, ferry inclusive.

Four Seasons (0532 564373)

Apartment accommodation offered in most French resorts. A ferry inclusive price for a family of four ranges from £370 to £1250.

French Life Holidays (0532 390077)
A wide range of villas, gîtes and apartments. A gîte in the Loire Valley, sleeping four to five adults, costs from £339 for a fortnight in low season. The price includes a ferry crossing for two adults and all children under 14 plus one car.

French Villas (081 651 1231)
The company offers villas, gîtes, traditional country-style properties, and seaside and city centre apartments. Prices range from £85 to £2000 per property per week.

Gîtes de France (071 408 1343)
Gîtes are privately-owned properties, modernised with the help of French government grants and supervised by the non-profit making Fédération Nationale des Gîtes de France. 'A gîte may be a small cottage, a village house, a flat in a farmhouse, a chalet, a mill, a manor, or a restored farm building. A countryside setting, often on a farm, is an essential part of a gîte character and low prices reflect their being 'off the beaten track'. A small number are within driving distance of the coast or other popular tourist destinations.' There are more than 2,500 gîtes on offer throughout the whole of France. Prices range from £275 to £1365 for two weeks. The price includes accommodation, return ferry crossing for two adults and a car and Europe Assistance vehicle service. To book a gîte holiday, you need to be a member: this costs £3 per year.

Hoseasons Holidays (0502 500555)
Properties available in Normandy, Brittany, Burgundy, Picardy, Loire, Vendée, Dordogne, Moselle, Haute Saône, Île de France and the Côte d'Azur. Prices range from £96 to £1350 per week, excluding travel costs from the UK.

Interhome (081 891 1294)
Villas, gîtes, castles and apartments. An apartment in Chamonix, for example, for two people costs from £40 per week. A castle in Burgundy sleeping 10 people which has a private tennis court, swimming pool and golf course costs from £3669 per week, excluding the cost of travel to France.

La France des Villages (0449 737664)
Traditional country properties, mostly with pools: two weeks at a farmhouse in Bas Quercy, sleeping six people, costs from £275 to £775, including a short sea ferry crossing for two adults and a car.

Maison Vacances (081 540 9680)
Houses situated in Normandy, Brittany, Auvergne, Dauphiny Alpes, Midi-Pyrénées, Rhone Valley, Franche Comté, Poitou-Charente, Western Loire, Limousin, Quercy and Provence. Two weeks at a converted presbytery, sleeping six persons in the Lot

costs from £262 to £346. The cost is for the accommodation only and is not per person.

Martin Sturge (0225 310822)
The attractive brochure lists over 250 villas, cottages and farmhouses. A week's holiday in western Provence in a secluded farmhouse with a pool sleeping nine people costs £1947 in high season. Prices in May, June, September and October range from 40% to 75% of high season prices.

Meon Villa Holidays (0730 268411)
Over 200 gîtes, apartments, farmhouses and luxury villas with private pools. Most of the properties are in rural areas. Prices range from £478 to £1148 for a family of four for two weeks in a four-star cottage, including return ferry crossing.

Sally Holidays (0732 780440)
Destinations include Picardy, Loire Valley, Brittany, the west coast, Burgundy, Dordogne, the Alps and the south of France. Two weeks in a gîte near Le Touquet, sleeping five people costs from £55 to £358 per person, including a return ferry crossing. Children are free.

VFB Holidays (0242 526338)
Traditional country properties and a small number of villa-type properties (many with pools). Two weeks at a converted chapel, attached to an 18th-century château, with a shared pool, in the Loire, sleeping six people costs from £92 to £275 per person. Two weeks at a thatched farmhouse in Brittany sleeping six costs from £107 to £245 per person. All prices include cottage rental, short sea ferry crossing and personal travel insurance, based on maximum occupancy.

Vacances en Campagne (07987 433)
Country houses, some with pools, in most regions of France including Corsica. Prices range from £299 to £2234 per week, including ferry crossing for two adults and a car. Short breaks are also offered during the low season and cost from £142 for three nights. The price includes a short sea crossing for a car and two adults.

Operators Which Have a Selection of Self-catering Accommodation in Particular French Regions

Alps

Hoverspeed Holidays (081 424 2929)
Savoy Alps. Apartments in Meribel-Mottaret, Val d'Isère, Chamonix and Valmorel. Prices start from around £81 per person for a fortnight, inclusive of Channel crossing.

International Chapters (071 722 9560)
Six chalets and villas, all fully staffed, some with swimming pools. For example, a 200-year-old Savoyard farmhouse with a private swimming pool costs from £2200 to £5500 for two weeks, including staff and breakfast.
SVP France (0243 377862)
Alpes Maritimes: studios for two to four people, with swimming pool in Sospel in the mountains behind the Riviera. Two weeks for up to four people including ferry, costs from £561 to £871.
Sandpiper Camping Holidays (0932 868658)
Apartment holidays in Chatel – a traditional old Savoyard village where activities such as swimming, rafting, tennis, riding and mountain biking are available. Two weeks in a three-room apartment for two adults and three children with their car, including a short sea ferry crossing costs from £599 to £649 for the complete party.
Something Special Travel (0992 505500)
Alpes Maritimes: Thirteen coastal properties and properties around the perfume capital of Grasse. A three-bedroomed villa with a private pool costs from £160 to £600 per person for a party of eight people, for two weeks. This price includes a ferry crossing for two cars.
Stena Sealink Travel (0233 647033)
Ten self-catering apartment residences available in the summer only. A four-person studio at Valmorel costs from £435 to £730, ferry inclusive.
Westbury Travel (0225 444516)
Thirteen chalets in Alpine surroundings. Prices for two weeks range from £580 to £2197 for two adults and all children of 13 years and under, ferry inclusive.

Aquitaine

Aquitaine Holidays (0892 516101)
Over 100 properties. Country cottages, large farmhouses and coastal villas. Two weeks at a converted farmhouse near Bergerac, sleeping six people costs from £150 to £207 per person, including a short sea crossing.
Hoverspeed Holidays (081 424 2929)
Apartments in holiday villages at Hourtin-Port, Carcans-Maubuisson and Moliets. Prices start at £81 per person for a fortnight, inclusive of Channel crossing.
Inntravel (0439 7111)
A converted manor house and outbuildings near Agen. Two weeks in a restored cottage there, with swimming pool, sleeping six

people, costs from £370 to £750 per person, including short sea ferry crossing.

Ardèche

Gîtes Plus (0392 70873)
Over 100 properties in the region of the Ardèche Gorge, some with pools. Many large properties are suitable for two or more families. Prices for two weeks range from £400 for two people to £1500 for a family. 'A daily programme of events and activities is also arranged on an as-you-please basis.'
Westbury Travel (0225 444516)
Sixteen houses and gîtes, some with pools: prices for two weeks range from £561 to £2948 for two adults and all children of 13 years and under, ferry inclusive.

Auvergne

Blakes International Travel (0603 784141)
A two-bedroomed gîte for four people with a shared swimming pool costs from £148 to £229 per person, including a short sea ferry crossing.
SVP France (0243 377862)
Small, very French holiday villages with swimming pools and activities for all ages. A holiday for a family of six costs from £487 to £1057 for two weeks, including ferry crossings.

Brittany

Blakes International Travel (0603 784141)
74 properties all round the coastline of Brittany. Two weeks in a modern house near Vannes, just 200 metres from the beach, for a family of four, costs from £160 to £270 per person, including a short sea crossing.
Brittany Direct Holidays (081 641 6060)
Over 70 properties, in all parts of the region, although most are in south Finistère and Morbihan. A two-week holiday in a detached villa within walking distance of the sea in June costs £750, ferry inclusive.
Clearwater Holidays (0926 450002)
Two weeks at a Breton cottage in the Gulf of Morbihan, south Brittany, will cost from £720 in the low season to £1280 in high season, per cottage, including ferry crossing. 'The Breton-style waterside cottages have three bedrooms, large garden areas

including barbecues and will sleep up to eight people. Dayboats are available for hire, prices according to size and season.'

Crystal Holidays (081 390 3335)
Over 55 properties available: a Breton fisherman's cottage in north Brittany, sleeping four, in a harbour location costs from £434 to £1004 for two weeks with a return short sea ferry crossing for up to four people.

Hoverspeed Holidays (081 424 2929)
Apartments in Perros-Guirec and in the holiday village of Port du Crouesty. Prices start at £81 per person for a fortnight. All prices include hovercraft or SeaCat crossing, based on four persons in a car.

Kingsland Holidays (0752 251688)
Cottages and gîtes throughout the region. Prices from £87 per person for a 'comfortable' cottage sleeping six people for two weeks in the lowest season, ferry inclusive.

Lagrange UK (071 371 6111)
Thirteen resorts along the coastline: an apartment sleeping four people in the resort of Quiberon costs from £155 to £410 per apartment per week.

Les Propriétaires de l'Ouest (0705 755715)
Gîtes and villas, many with swimming pools: two weeks in a gîte sleeping four to six adults costs from £125 to £433 per person.

Pieds-à-Terre (0622 688165)
Twenty-five properties: a traditional four-bedroomed house, six miles from Dinan, costs from £485 to £710 per week, ferry inclusive.

Rural France Direct (0452 812294)
Many restored agricultural buildings, including barns and water-mills, also half-timbered thatched cottages and stone farmhouses. One week in a stone cottage sleeping five people costs from £310 including a short sea ferry crossing.

Stena Sealink Travel (0233 647033)
Over 250 gîtes and seven self-catering apartment residences/holiday villages: two weeks at a gîte sleeping five people costs from £443 to £772, ferry inclusive.

Sunselect Villas (061 655 3055)
Seventy villas and cottages, all near the sea. In north Brittany most properties are on the Emerald Coast and the Pink Granite Coast, in south Brittany properties are between Benodet, Concarneau, and Le Pouldu. Property prices vary from £195 to £800 per week according to size and season. Ferry crossings can be arranged.

Sunvista Holidays (0985 217373)
Cottages and villas, some with pools: two weeks at a house for four people costs £500 in low season; a house for eight in high

season, including the hire of two cars costs £2250. Prices include insurance and a short ferry crossing.
Westbury Travel (0225 444516)
Over 100 houses, with most on or near the coast. A cottage for five has a low season price of £558 for two weeks. This price is for two adults and all children under 13 years and includes a return ferry crossing.

Cévennes

Kingsland Holidays (0752 251688)
Manor houses, farmhouses and gîtes from £87 per person, for a cottage sleeping six people, in the lowest season, ferry inclusive.

Charente

Crystal Holidays (081 390 3335)
Twelve properties situated in La Palmyre and Royan. A villa sleeping six costs from £944 to £1380 for two weeks, including a short sea ferry crossing for up to six people.
Holiday Charente (081 813 5638)
A selection of 14 riverside and coastal cottages all within the départments of Charente and Charente Maritime. Some are actually on the river Charente with moorings, and ideal for fishing, some are situated near local golf courses and some are near the coast. Some have pools. Bicycles and canoes are available for hire with all of the properties and most are available all year round. A two-bedroomed cottage costs from £190 to £315 per week. A four-bedroomed cottage with a pool costs from £325 to £550 per week.
Kingsland Holidays (0752 251688)
Cottages, farmhouses and converted barns from £87 per person for a cottage sleeping six people for a two-week holiday in the lowest season, ferry inclusive.
Rural France Direct (0452 812294)
Restored barns and stables, also stone farmhouses and cottages from £310 per week for a family of five, ferry inclusive.
SFV Holidays (0865 57738)
SFV Holidays specialise in self-catering villas, many with pools, in Charente Maritime. Two weeks in a renovated farmhouse with a swimming pool near Royan, sleeping five people costs from £210 to £386 per person, including a long sea return ferry crossing.
Stena Sealink Travel (0233 647033)
Over 20 gîtes and six self-catering apartment residences/holiday

villages. Two weeks at the Residence Domaine de Bois Soleil in Saint Palais-sur-Mer costs from £444 to £1010, ferry inclusive.

Corsica

Allegro Holidays (0737 221323)
Beachside apartments on the bay of Ajaccio and villas near Île Rousse and Porto Vecchio. One week in a three-star beach apartment near Ajaccio, sleeping up to four people costs from £199 per person, including flights. Two weeks in a villa near Porto Vecchio costs £699 per person, including flights.

Corsican Places (0424 774366)
Villas with pools, medieval village houses, gîtes, studios and apartments: two weeks in a two-bedroomed villa for four with a shared pool in Calvi costs from £368 to £544 per person, including flights.

Simply Corsica (081 747 3580)
Southern Corsica: cottages by the sea with a private beach, sleeping six people cost from £333 to £502 per person, flight inclusive.

Voyages Ilena (071 924 4440)
Cottages, mountain gîtes and villas by the sea. Prices range from £424 per person in a mountain gîte to £1273 per person in a serviced apartment. These prices include two weeks accommodation, flights, car hire and personal insurance.

Côte d'Azur

Continental Villas (071 497 0444)
Over 30 villas and apartments in Cavalaire, Cogolin, Grimaud, Ste Maxime, Plan de la Tour, Les Issambres, Valbonne, Biot, Cannes, Cap d'Antibes, St Paul de Vence and Cap Ferrat. Villa and apartment rents range from £270 per week for two people to £4000 per week for up to 12 people. Some villa owners also offer yachts for charter on a daily or weekly basis – details on request.

Dominique's Villas (071 738 8772)
Villas for two weeks for eight to ten people, including short sea ferry crossings range from £1200 to £4500.

International Chapters (071 722 9560)
Nine properties: for example, a Saracen château in 15,000 acres with its own swimming pool and tennis court costs from £6720 to £11900 for two weeks.

Kingsland Holidays (0752 251688)
A luxurious villa with a swimming pool with views over the Gulf of St-Tropez costs up to £550 per person in peak season, ferry inclusive.

Palmer & Parker (0494 815411)
Fifty properties from Menton to St-Tropez. Prices vary from £620 per week for a three-bedroom villa with private pool to £10400 per week for a villa sleeping up to 13 people in high season. Prices do not include the cost of travel to France.

Riviera Retreats (010 33 93 64 00 80)
Villas and apartments covering an area which stretches along the coastline from Monte Carlo down to St-Tropez and as far inland as Provence. Rentals start at £2000 per month and go up to £95000 per month.

Sunvista Holidays (0985 217373)
Two weeks at a house for four in low season costs £800; a house for eight to nine people with a pool and the hire of two cars in high season costs £4875. Prices include insurance and a short ferry crossing.

Westbury Travel (0225 444516)
Fourteen apartments on the coastal strip from Nice to St-Tropez, all with swimming pools. Prices for two weeks range from £532 to £3539 for two adults and all children of 13 years and under, ferry inclusive.

Dordogne

Blakes International Travel (0603 784141)
Two weeks in a three-bedroomed cottage with a private swimming pool for a family of five costs from £196 to £373 per person, including a short sea ferry crossing.

Crystal Holidays (081 390 3335)
Five properties in rural surroundings. A cottage sleeping seven costs from £464 to £1180 for two weeks. This price is for the property and a ferry crossing for up to seven people.

Dominique's Villas (071 738 8772)
Restored farmhouses: a two-week holiday for eight to ten people including short sea ferry crossings range from £1200 to £4500.

French Affair (071 381 8519)
Twenty-nine properties, many with swimming pools. A manoir with a pool, sleeping 10 people in Haute Brousse, near Mauriac costs from £1022 to £2856 for two weeks. This price includes a short sea ferry crossing for one car and up to five passengers.

International Chapters (071 722 9560)
Ten châteaux and farmhouses. For example, a 17th-century manor house, sleeping 10, on a private 85-acre estate near Bergerac costs from £1950 to £5900 for two weeks.

Kingsland Holidays (0752 251688)
Cottages, converted farmhouses and barns from £87 per person

for a cottage sleeping six people in the lowest season, ferry inclusive.

Les Propriétaires de l'Ouest (0705 755715)
Gîtes and villas, many with swimming pools. Two weeks in a gîte sleeping four to six adults costs from £125 to £433 per adult.

Miss France Holidays (081 452 5901)
Cottages and villas: for example a house with a swimming pool near Beaumont du Périgord, sleeping 11 people, costs from £1100 to £2100 for a fortnight.

Pieds-à-Terre (0622 688165)
Five properties. A traditional stone three-bedroomed house in the grounds of a château with a swimming pool costs from £725 to £1260 per week, ferry inclusive.

Rural France Direct (0452 812294)
Restored barns, stables and water-mills from £310 per week for a cottage sleeping five people, ferry inclusive.

SVP France (0243 377862)
Bungalows for up to six people at Vayrac on the banks of the Dordogne which can be linked to a canoeing holiday. Two weeks for six people, ferry inclusive, costs from £784 to £982.

Something Special Travel (0992 505500)
Five properties, all with pools. For example a four-bedroomed villa with a pool and extensive grounds costs from £200 to £350 per person, for a party of eight people, for two weeks. This price includes a ferry crossing for two cars.

Stena Sealink Travel (0233 647033)
Over 60 gîtes and eight self-catering apartment residences/holiday villages. Two weeks at a gîte sleeping four people costs from £489 to £687, ferry inclusive.

Sunvista Holidays (0985 217373)
Cottages and villas, some with pools. Two weeks at a house for four to five people costs £500 in low season; a house for eight with a pool and two cars costs £1950 in high season. Prices include insurance and a short ferry crossing.

Westbury Travel (0225 444516)
Over 80 villas and country houses, all but 10 with private or shared pools and spread throughout the region. Prices for two weeks range from £436 for a converted house in Beynac to £4185 for a Périgordine house in St Cyprien. These prices are for two adults and all children of 13 years and under, ferry inclusive.

Gascony

French Affair (071 381 8519)
Six properties. A windmill sleeping two people near Auch costs

from £614 to £1073 for two weeks. This price includes a short sea ferry crossing for two adults and a car.

Kingsland Holidays (0752 251688)
Farmhouses and gîtes from £87 per person, for a cottage sleeping six people in the lowest season, ferry inclusive.

Westbury Travel (0225 444516)
Three houses with pools: prices for two weeks range from £630 to £1600 for two adults and all children of 13 and under, ferry inclusive.

Haute Savoie

Freedom Holidays (081 741 4686)
Self-catering studios and apartments from £119 to £199 per person for one week, based on four sharing, ferry inclusive.

Lakes and Mountains Holidays (0329 844405)
Studios and one- and two-bedroomed apartments in St Jorioz (Lake Annecy), Le Grand Bornand and Les Carroz. Two weeks for a family of four in a two-bedroomed apartment in Le Grand Bornand costs from £178 to £298, ferry inclusive.

Languedoc

Crystal Holidays (081 390 3335)
Seventeen villas and one apartment complex. Every property has a private or shared pool. Most are on the Canal du Midi. A villa sleeping six people near Narbonne costs from £524 to £1525 for two weeks. This price includes the villa and a ferry crossing for up to five people.

French Affair (071 381 8519)
Eighteen properties. For example, a 19th-century maison de maître near Carcassonne, sleeping eight people costs from £689 to £1521 for two weeks. This price includes a short sea ferry crossing for up to five people and a car.

Hoverspeed Holidays (081 424 2929)
Apartments at the holiday village of Cap-Coudalère (Port Barcarès) and at Cap d'Agde. Prices start from around £81 per person for a fortnight, inclusive of Channel crossing.

Miss France Holidays (081 452 5901)
Cottages and villas: prices range from £350 for a cottage in the low season.

Stena Sealink Travel (0233 647033)
Nine self-catering apartment residences/holiday villages. Two weeks at the Pierre et Vacances Club Resort at Port Barcarès costs from £488 to £1240, ferry inclusive.

Tailhos (010 33 67 97 27 62)
Three renovated farm buildings: property rental prices from £120 to £350 per week.

Westbury Travel (0225 444516)
Three modern villas on the banks of the Canal du Midi. Prices range from £880 to £1989 for two weeks, for two adults and all children of 13 years and under, ferry inclusive.

Les Landes

Westbury Travel (0225 444516)
Twelve seaside and rural cottages, apartments and houses, some within walking distance of the beach. Prices for two weeks range from £533 to £2183 for two adults and all children of 13 years and under, ferry inclusive.

Loire Valley

Dominique's Villas (071 738 8772)
Entire châteaux or château apartments: prices for two weeks for eight to ten people, including short sea ferry crossings range from £1200 to £4500.

International Chapters (071 722 9560)
Three properties: for example, Château du Planty near Angers, sleeping 16 people, with a swimming pool costs from £3800 to £5900 for two weeks.

Palmer & Parker (0494 815411)
Château with a private pool, tennis court and in 25 acres of grounds costs from £1730 to £5000 per week. Prices do not include travel to France.

Rural France Direct (0452 812294)
Restored barns and stone farmhouses from £310 per week for a cottage sleeping five people, ferry inclusive.

Stena Sealink Travel (0233 647033)
Seven gîtes and nine self-catering apartment residences/holiday vilages. Two weeks at a large residence with swimming pool costs from £463 to £1061 for an apartment for two adults and two children. Ferry prices are included.

Westbury Travel (0225 444516)
Sixteen houses spread throughout the Loire and Burgundy area, some with shared swimming pools. A manor house near Angers, sharing a large garden and pool, sleeping up to 14 people costs up to £2239 in high season. This price is for two adults and all children of 13 years and under, ferry inclusive, for two weeks.

Lot

European Villas (0223 314220)
Nine properties: a deluxe villa for 12 to 13 people in Albas costs from £895 to £1395, weekly rental only.

French Affair (071 381 8519)
Over 40 properties: a stone farmhouse with a swimming pool sleeping eight near Figeac costs from £1203 to £2240 for two weeks. This price includes a short sea ferry crossing for up to five people and a car.

Kingsland Holidays (0752 251688)
Converted barns, manor houses and gîtes from £87 per person, for a cottage sleeping six people in the lowest season, ferry inclusive.

Normandy

Blakes International Travel (0603 784141)
Fourteen properties in both coastal and inland areas of Normandy. Two weeks at a converted water-mill with a shared swimming pool costs from £177 to £331 per person, including a short sea crossing.

Hoverspeed Holidays (081 424 2929)
Apartments in Houlgate and bungalows at Grandcamp-Maisy. Prices start at £81 per person for a fortnight. All prices include hovercraft or SeaCat crossing, based on four in a car.

Normandie Vacances (0922 20278)
Over 120 traditionally-styled properties ranging across the whole of Normandy from Rouen to Mont St Michel. Two week holidays cost from £104 to £470 per person, ferry inclusive.

Pieds-à-Terre (0622 688165)
Fourteen properties including a one-bedroomed cottage 10 miles from Lisieux with a large garden which costs from £385 to £625 per week, ferry inclusive.

Rural France Direct (0452 812294)
Half-timbered cottages and converted cider mills from £310 per week for a cottage sleeping five people, ferry inclusive.

Stena Sealink Travel (0233 647033)
Over 20 gîtes and eight self-catering apartment residences/holiday villages. Two weeks at a gîte sleeping six people costs from £453 to £612, ferry inclusive.

Westbury Travel (0225 444516)
Thirteen properties in the Manche and Calvados. A house sleeping up to five people, six miles from the beach costs from £500 in low season for two weeks, for two adults and all children under 13 years, including ferry. A converted barn, sleeping six people, with

a shared pool close to Mont St Michel costs up to £1300 in high season. The price is for two adults and all children of 13 years and under, ferry inclusive.

Provence

Blakes International Travel (0603 784141)
A two-week holiday in a six-bedroomed luxury villa with a private swimming pool for a family of 12, travelling in three vehicles, costs from £230 to £436 per person, including a short sea ferry crossing.

Crystal Holidays (081 390 3335)
Over 50 villas and seven apartment complexes. Most of the properties are coastal and have access to pool and leisure facilities. A villa sleeping six with a private pool costs from £934 to £3280 for two weeks with a short sea ferry crossing for up to six people.

Dominique's Villas (071 738 8772)
A typical mas for eight to ten people, including ferry crossings costs from £1200 to £4500 for two weeks.

European Villas (0223 314220)
Eight detached properties: a luxury villa in Grasse, sleeping six to eight people costs from £1025 to £1495, weekly rental only.

French Affair (071 381 8519)
Over 20 properties: a restored detached Provençal house near Arles, sleeping eight people with a swimming pool costs from £1739 to £4197 for two weeks. This price includes a short sea ferry crossing for up to five people and a car.

Hoverspeed Holidays (081 424 2929)
Apartments in holiday villages at Sainte Maxime, Cap Esterel and Port Grimaud and at Golfe Juan, Cannes and Villefranche. Prices start from around £81 per person, per fortnight, inclusive of Channel crossing.

International Chapters (071 722 9560)
Villas, mas, bastides and châteaux: 74 properties in Vaucluse, Gard, Lubéron, Bouches du Rhône and the Var. For example, Mas Bianca which sleeps eight, set in its own 18 acres, 15 minutes from St Rémy de Provence, with its own swimming pool and tennis court, costs from £4000 to £7550 for two weeks.

Kingsland Holidays (0752 251688)
Stone cottages and villas from around £100 per person for a two-week holiday in the lowest season.

Lagrange UK (071 371 6111)
Over 20 resorts along the Côte d'Azur and in Provence. A week in La Croix Valmer in a residence with a pool costs from £114 to £394 per studio for two adults.

Miss France Holidays (081 452 5901)
Cottages and villas: for example, a luxury villa with a swimming pool, sleeping eight to ten people near Aix-en-Provence costs around £4000 for a fortnight.
NSS Riviera Holidays (0482 42240)
Fréjus: Holiday Green is a four-star village complex. Two weeks in a holiday home costs from £292 to £797 for up to six people, ferry inclusive.
Rural France Direct (0452 812294)
Stone farmhouses and luxury villas with private swimming pools from £755 per week for a villa sleeping five people, ferry inclusive.
Something Special Travel (0992 505500)
Over 50 properties, all with pools. A three-bedroomed villa with a private pool costs from £155 to £400 per person for a party of eight people, for two weeks. This price includes a ferry crossing for two cars.
Stena Sealink Travel (0233 647033)
Over 20 gîtes, villas and 13 self-catering apartments. Two weeks at a gîte for four people costs from £655 to £1116, ferry inclusive.
Westbury Travel (0225 444516)
Fifteen Provençal houses with swimming pools and five typical cottages in regions as varied as the Lubéron and the hills behind St-Tropez. Prices range from £533 to £3760 for two weeks, for two adults and and all children of 13 years and under, ferry inclusive.

Pyrénées

Borderline (0963 250117 brochures)
Gîtes and apartments in the Hautes Pyrénées, in the Toy Valley, from £259 to £600 per week, per property.
Stena Sealink Travel (0233 647033)
Eight gîtes and two self-catering holiday villages. Two weeks at a converted windmill for two people costs from £440 to £718, ferry inclusive.

Vendée

Blakes International Travel (0603 784141)
A traditional house for a family of four costs from £136 to £211 per person, including a short sea crossing.
Crystal Holidays (081 390 3335)
Over 20 typical Vendée homes. A property sleeping five people

with a shared pool costs from £534 to £1635 for two weeks, including a short sea ferry crossing for up to five people.

Hoverspeed Holidays (081 424 2929)

Apartments in the holiday village at Port du Bourgenay. Prices start at £81 per person for a fortnight, inclusive of Channel crossing.

Pieds-à-Terre (0622 688165)

Six properties: a modern detached three-bedroomed bungalow overlooking farmland costs from £425 to £680 per week, ferry inclusive.

Westbury Travel (0225 44516)

Over 20 villas, cottages and apartments down the coast from Noirmoutier to La Palmyre. A renovated farmhouse for five people has a low seaason price of £697 for two weeks. This price is for two adults and all children of 13 years and under, ferry inclusive.

CAMPING

I blame the Boy Scouts for the fact that I long refused to face the idea of a camping holiday in France. Life under canvas in Britain has little to recommend it: that is, unless you like the idea of getting into a damp sleeping bag and waking up even damper. Even at the age of twelve, when I suppose I should have been a little less fastidious, I couldn't bear the primitive sanitary arrangements, the endless fry-up meals, washing up in cold greasy water, the insects, the cold and the damp. It's difficult to forget the damp. When it comes to holidays, I don't think it's too much to ask for a warm, comfortable bed and a decent toilet (and even a bath with adequate supplies of hot water). Camping, I would have said until recently, is definitely not for me.

So when the opportunity to take an inclusive camping package to the Dordogne presented itself, I wasn't exactly overcome with excited anticipation. I had to admit however that the camping package sounded better than the Baden-Powell gin-gan-gooley deprivation of my youth. Like the majority of inclusive camping packages to France these days, it offered a pre-erected tent equipped with a surprising degree of luxury: electric lights, a refrigerator, a double bed as well as tables and chairs, gas cooker, pots and pans and other essentials. All we had to take were sleeping bags, towels and sheets.

Even so, we would not have been persuaded had it not been for our two children, then aged four and two. In previous years when we've been to France, we've stayed in gîtes which have always suited us well. All we want from our holiday in France is peace and quiet, and somewhere to sit in the sun and read – occasionally venturing out to visit a sight or a restaurant. Unhappily this undemanding sort of holiday existence didn't impress the children. They want fun and entertainment: a swimming pool and someone to play with in the swimming pool – commodities on which gîtes tend to be rather short.

The camping package that attracted us offered a campsite with both a swimming pool and the guarantee of a certain amount of organised fun. So with heart in mouth, we drove off the ferry at St Malo one morning in May for a camping holiday in the Dordogne. From St Malo, the drive to the campsite near Domme takes about seven hours – manageable in one day but not advisable. Certainly not with our two children, who were anticipating an imminent arrival at the campsite even as we were negotiating the outer suburbs of St Malo. 'Are we there yet?' is as doleful a sound as the cry of the harpooned whale – how often must it ring out along the highways and byways of France, as fathers and mothers clench their teeth and pluckily drive on with the sort of grit and determination that saw an older generation battle their way from the coast of Normandy 45 years ago.

On the drive to the campsite we had time enough to ponder on what was waiting for us in the Dordogne. You'll find this very snooty I'm sure, but I have a horror of meeting other British people when we're on holiday in France. People who spot your GB plate and imagine you want to talk about the Test score, or where you can buy Weetabix and soft toilet paper and that the best way to beat the jams around Tours is to take the D29 or whatever. What if it's really awful, we wondered: could we really go through with it?

After an overnight hotel stop in Limoges, available as a part of the package, we arrived at the site mid-morning. The campsite was attractively landscaped and obviously well cared for, and the tents were well spaced out. The courier was there to take us to our tent and to show us how things worked and to answer any questions we had. My first concern was the toilets. No problems here: the Dutch owners of the campsite (it's apparently a well-known fact that the best campsites in France are Dutch-owned) took a peculiarly Dutch pride in the standard of the toilets which were scrubbed and cleaned once a day in the off-peak, and twice a day in the peak.

Washing facilities (with hot and cold water) were in cubicles with lockable doors, and there were showers with hot water, and large sinks for washing dishes and clothes. There was a campsite bar which offered take-away food in the evening, and the occasional 'happy hour' when campers were provided with free beer and wine. There were swings for the children – and of course, the swimming pool with a smaller paddling pool. There were 12 Canvas Holidays tents on the site – all spaced out to avoid a British ghetto. Our fellow Brits, were mostly like ourselves: families with small children – and not a roll of soft toilet paper or a box of Weetabix to be seen.

The courier ran a club for the children to provide an afternoon of fun and games. The campsite employed its own 'animateur' who arranged fun for children and adults alike: volley ball tournaments, rugby matches against a team from the nearby town, boat trips down the Dordogne river – and once a week a splendid barbecue.

And, on the whole, our camping holiday was judged a success. The weather was very good; it rained two or three times but everything quickly dried out (it rained enough to remind us that camping is complete misery if you get wet and don't dry out properly). Our children loved it; they were too young to be left entirely to their own devices but other families with older children reported that once the awning of the tent was zipped open in the morning, their kids practically vanished for the rest of the day, appearing only at meal-times. The courier would baby sit (for a fee), if parents wanted to go out for an evening meal alone; but most followed the French example and ate out in restaurants until quite late with even the smallest children in tow.

But it is still camping; and despite the luxuries that have been grafted on in the last few years by operators, it remains fairly basic and you have to be prepared to rough it a little. But any disadvantages are more than outweighed by the benefits. The children are happy, of course. And bit by bit, you begin to notice how well you feel living under canvas in the fresh air. You start to feel almost permanently hungry, everyone's cheeks blossom with health and you quickly develop a glowing tan from being out of doors all day. Other parents we spoke to said that they would choose to camp even without the children.

When we eventually said our farewells to our fellow campers and pulled out of the site for the drive back to the ferry port we felt slightly relieved and quietly pleased with ourselves – rather like first-formers who had successfully survived their first term at school. 'That was nice,' remarked the children, as we sped off with the smell of butane gas mingled with sun-baked canvas still twitching at our nostrils. Ahead lay the seven hour drive back to St Malo. The back seat fell silent for a moment, then: 'Are we there yet?'

Camping

Brittany Ferries (0752 221321)

Ready-erected tents are available or you can take your own camping equipment. Prices range from £143 to £272 per person, for two weeks, including ferry crossing for a holiday in a ready-erected tent. Two weeks in a two- three- or four-star campsite, taking your own equipment costs from £128 to £213 per person, including ferry crossing with car.

Canvas Holidays (0383 621000)

Canvas Holidays offers pre-erected tent and mobile home holidays throughout France. Prices range from around £80 to £697 for a fortnight's holiday for two adults, ferry inclusive.

Caravan & Camping Service (071 792 1944)

All regions of France – camping and caravanning holidays with clients' own equipment. A 14-night holiday costs from £292 to £460 for a family of two adults and two children under 14. Prices include a short sea crossing.

Carisma Holidays (0923 284235)

Eight-berth mobile homes and six-berth tents located on six sites along the west coast: Brittany, Vendée and Aquitaine. A fortnight's holiday for a family of four (on a beach site), including a short sea ferry crossing costs from £350 to £770 for a tent and from £490 to £1115 for a mobile home.

EuroSites (0706 830888)

Tents and mobile homes on 80 campsites all over France. Camping holidays start at £99 for 14 nights, including ferry crossing and accommodation for up to six people, and rise to about £689. Prices are per party, not per person. Mobile homes start at £239 for 14 nights for a party of eight people, including ferry crossing, rising to about £1099 in high season.

Eurocamp (0565 626262)

The market leader in holidays to pre-erected tents. It offers packages of any length to any combination of over 20 campsites. Eurocamp has children's couriers, a free children's club and baby sitting together with a range of equipment specially designed for children. Two weeks in Deauville, on the Normandy coast costs from £265 to £755 for two adults and two children (up to 14) including a short sea return ferry crossing.

Four Seasons (0532 564373)

A range of accommodation from budget-priced caravans with awnings to modern mobile homes available in Normandy, Brittany, Vendée, Languedoc, the Riviera, Dordogne and the Loire Valley. A fortnight for a family of four in a six-berth caravan, including a short sea crossing, costs £395 in low season. A fortnight's holiday for a family of four in peak season in a 28ft two-bedroomed mobile home with a shower and WC costs £1187, ferry inclusive.

Freedom of France (0989 768168)

Holidays to Normandy, Brittany, Loire, Paris, Vendée, Burgundy, Gironde, Dordogne, Landes and Mediterranean: 12-night packages including tented accommodation and ferry crossing from £190 to £659 for a family of two adults and up to four children.

French Country Camping (0923 261311)

Over 60 campsites in 43 départements of France. The length of holiday can vary, as desired, but the basic price for 14 nights accommodation for two adults and up to 4 children is from £139 to £739 including a return ferry crossing.

French Life Holidays (0532 390077)

Sites all over France: a ferry inclusive fortnight's camping package in low season in Normandy costs £170 for two adults and four children under 16.

Haven France & Spain (0705 466111)

Mobile home and tent accommodation in many areas: a two-week holiday in a tent for six people starts at £195, including a mid-week short sea ferry crossing. The most expensive high season price for two weeks in a mobile home is £1504.

Holiday Charente (081 813 5638)

Organized descents of the river Charente in Canadian canoes, camping along the route. Available for individuals, families or groups of up to 30 people. Travellers are brought back by road. The price for two adults for two weeks is £107 per person. This includes all canoes and camping equipment. Prices do not include travel to France.

Keycamp Holidays (081 395 4000)

Over 80 campsites covering 18 regions with a choice of four models of mobile homes or 'supertents'. A 12-night camping holiday starts at £55 and goes up to £188 per person. The price of a mobile home 12-night holiday ranges from £75 to £231 per person: up to four children can be taken free of charge throughout the summer.

Sandpiper Camping Holidays (0932 868658)

Tents and mobile homes on three- and four-star sites in Brittany, the Vendée, and Charente Maritime with many facilities and swimming pools. Two weeks in a tent for two adults and three children with their car, including a short sea ferry crossing costs from £199 to £699 for the complete party.

Select Site Reservations (0873 859876)

Reservations for the independent camper on camping and cara-

vanning sites throughout France. Prices for a two-week holiday for two adults range from £230 to £290, including ferry crossing.
Westents (0484 424455)
Ready-erected six-berth tents on five campsites in Brittany, Vendée and Charente Maritime. Prices range from £259 to £719 for a family, ferry inclusive.

6

ACTIVITY HOLIDAYS

Holidays in France do not begin and end at a gîte or a hotel. It is above all a place for activity holidays. There are dozens of tour operators specialising in everything from battlefield tours to improving your piano-playing.

Here we offer a selection of French specialists:

ADVENTURE HOLIDAYS FOR CHILDREN

Alpine Adventures (0451 832262)
Closely supervised activity weeks in the French Alps. A seven-night package ranges from £455 for under-12s to £490 for over-12s. This includes full board accommodation, all sports and activities and return air travel.

PGL Adventure Ltd (0989 768768)
Activity holidays for children and teenagers in Normandy, Paris, the Mediterranean, the Alps and the Ardèche. Prices start at £199 per person inclusive of travel and accommodation.

ANGLING

Maison Vacances (081 540 9680)
Holidays to every region of France. A partly accompanied fishing holiday (adhering to a good fishing charter) for six people in a special gîte in the Jura costs from around £100 to £135 for seven nights including fishing permits.

ARCHAEOLOGY

Francophiles Discover France (0272 621975)
Accompanied luxury coach holidays concentrating on history and culture in regional France, visiting one or two centres only. Destinations include Tarn, Alsace, Dordogne, Provence, Auvergne, Cévennes and Jura. A 10- to 14-day trip costs from £800 to £820 per

person in a shared room. The price includes half-board, all coach and ferry travel and the services of a bilingual courier.

LSG Theme Holidays (0509 231713)
Provence: five to eight day discovery tours in Arles and Aix-en-Provence with bed and breakfast or half-board accommodation in pleasant family-run two-star hotels, located right in the city centres. From £350 to £625 per person, including tuition, courier service and return air travel.

Specialtours (071 730 3138)
Accompanied cultural tours in various regions of France. An eight-night tour of Provence, for example, costs £1168 per person, including accommodation and most meals, air travel by scheduled services, transport by coach, guides, taxes, entrance fees, insurance and the services of a lecturer and tour escort.

ART HISTORY TOURS

LSG Theme Holidays (0509 231713)
Normandy and Île-de-France: four to fifteen day tours of the Seine Valley, Paris and the Île-de-France treasures with bed and breakfast or half-board in a three-star hotel and full board accommodation in a holiday centre. From £325 to £875 per person, including guides and visits, courier service and return air travel.

BATTLEFIELD TOURS

Galina International Battlefield Tours (0482 806020)
A five-day trip to Normandy covering the British and American landing beaches, also Bayeux and Caen costs £239 per person, staying in two-star bed and breakfast accommodation and including ferry crossings.

Major and Mrs Holt's Battlefield Tours (0304 612248)
A choice of 13 First World War tours to northern France (Somme/Picardy) and three Second World War tours to Normandy. Prices for a two-night battlefield tour including half-board accommodation and extras start at £199. A two-night history tour covering Crécy, Agincourt and the siege of Calais, based in Amiens, costs £237 per person including half-board accommodation, museum entrance fees and special events.

Middlebrook's Battlefield Tours (0205 364555)
Tours to 1914–18 and 1939–45 battlefield sites: transport is by coach and ferry and each tour is guided throughout. Prices on request.

BIRDWATCHING

Borderline (0963 250117 brochures)
Specialist ornithology weeks with local ornithologists each spring in the Haute Pyrénées. Prices range from £400 to £415 per week, per person. This price includes half-board accommodation, five-day outings and all transport.

Cygnus Wildlife Holidays (0548 856178)
Fully-guided birdwatching tour to Arles: eight days on a half-board basis costs £850 per person. The price includes all excursions, transport throughout, flights from London, and the services of an ornithological tour leader. Maximum group size is 16.

BRIDGE WEEKENDS

Hampton House Travel (081 977 6404)
Bridge weekends, with or without bridge tuition from £250 per person for two nights, including half-board and ferry.

CANAL BOATS

Alastair Sawday's Tours (0272 299921)
Barge holidays in Burgundy, Alsace, the Midi, the Charente and the Upper Loire. Prices range from £550 for a half-board charter cruise for four people to over £2000 per person for a full board cruise aboard a luxurious 12-passenger vessel.

Blakes International Travel (0603 784141)
Skipper yourself hire cruisers for parties from two to twelve people on rivers and canals throughout France. Modern boats from well-located starting points to explore the waterways of Brittany, Alsace, Burgundy, Anjou, Charente, Lot, Midi and Camargue. One way cruises are available. Seven-night packages cost from around £140 per person, including return ferry crossing, to £245 per person, by air to the south of France.

Crown Blue Line (0603 630513)
Brittany, Loire, Burgundy, Vosges, Alsace Lorraine, Lot, Charente, Aquitaine, Midi and the Camargue. More than 400 boats in 11 cruising areas with 16 starting bases. One- two- or three-week cruises. Prices range from £304 to £1773 per boat, per week, depending on the season and the size of boat.

French Country Cruises (0572 821330)
Penichettes for hire in Aquitaine, Poitou-Charente, Lot-et-Garonne, Languedoc, Camargue, Brittany, Anjou, Île de France, Franche-Comté, Burgundy, Champagne and Nord Picardie. Prices for a

four- to five-berth boat are from £1038 to £2044 for two weeks – prices are for boat hire only.

Holiday Charente (081 813 5638)
A selection of self-drive river cruisers on the river Charente. The river was re-opened to navigation in 1980 and has no more than 60 hire cruisers along its entire length of 100 miles. A two-berth cruiser costs from £215 to £395 per week, a ten-berth cruiser costs from £750 to £1550 per week. Prices do not include the cost of travelling to France.

Hoseasons Holidays (0502 500555)
Holidays on the French canals and rivers. Destinations include the Midi and the Camargue, Brittany, Anjou, Burgundy, Alsace, Charente, Lot, Marne, and the Saône. A week's boat hire for four in Burgundy, for example, costs from £350 to £581 per week excluding travel from the UK.

Riviera Sailing Holidays (0243 374376)
Motorcruisers on the Canal du Midi cost from around £350 to £1600 per week depending on size and time of year.

Sunselect Vills (061 655 3055)
Self-drive cruisers sleeping from two to ten people in Maine/Anjou. Prices range from £290 (low season for two) to £970 (peak season for nine), per week.

Worldwide Yachting Holidays (071 328 1033)
Luxury hotel barges in Burgundy, Alsace or Midi: boats have full crew and three or four cabins with high quality cuisine on board. Prices range from £766 to £828 per person for a one-week cruise. Boats are accompanied by a minibus for excursions to châteaux, medieval castles, wine tastings and exploring the local countryside. Prices are inclusive of excursions, use of bicycles (and dinghy/sailboat, where applicable).

CANOEING

Headwater Holidays (0606 48699)
Seven- and eight-night holidays on the Creuse, Loue (Jura), and Loire. An eight-night Creuse canoeing holiday on half-board costs from £419 per person, self-drive, to £595 per person by air or rail.

Holiday Charente (081 813 5638)
Organised descents of the river Charente in Canadian canoes, camping along the route. Available for individuals, families or groups of up to 30 people. Travellers are brought back by road. The price for two adults for two weeks is £107 per person. This includes all canoes and camping equipment. Prices do not include travel to France.

SVP France (0243 377862)

Unaccompanied canoeing and river running on the Dordogne or canoeing and some white water rafting on the Allier or a combination of both. Camping on the river banks. Bags transported. Prices range from £223 per person, for seven nights, ferry inclusive, to £401 by air.

CARAVANS AND MOBILE HOMES

Becks Holidays (0273 842843)

Mobile homes at Bénodet and La Baule in south Brittany, St Jean-de-Monts in the Vendée and further south at La Palmyre near Royan. A two-week stay for a family of four ranges from £328 to £852 inclusive of ferry crossings.

Brittany Caravan Hire (0454 772410)

Self-drive, self-catering holidays in mobile homes on four-star campsites in Brittany and the west coast. Prices for two weeks range from £288 to £916 for two adults and two children, ferry inclusive.

Caravan & Camping Service (071 792 1944)

All regions of France – camping and caravanning holidays with clients' own equipment. A two-week holiday costs from £292 to £460 for a family of two adults and two children under 14. Prices include a short sea crossing.

Continental Camping Holidays (0925 728975)

A two-week caravan holiday in Dinard on a three-star campsite costs from £434 to £667 for two adults and two children, including return ferry crossings from Portsmouth to Cherbourg.

Fleur Holidays (0253 301719)

Thirty mobile homes on four campsites in western France and the Côte d'Azur. A 14-night holiday for two adults costs from £339 to £995, including return ferry crossing. In May, June and September, Fleur offer one week free of charge with all 14-night bookings.

Matthews Holidays (0483 285213)

Large static mobile homes situated on campsites near the coast in Normandy, Brittany, Vendée, Royan, Arcachon and Torreilles Plage. Each mobile home will sleep six people. The price for two adults and three children under the age of 14 would range from £289 to £744 for 14 nights, including ferry travel.

Select France (086 733280)

Holidays in mobile homes on four-star campsites on the west coast. Accommodation only prices range from £149 to £466 for up to six people for seven days. A two-week holiday for two adults and up to four children ranges from £390 to £1030, ferry inclusive.

Welcome Holidays (081 398 0355)

Mobile homes in Normandy, Brittany, Vendée, Aquitaine, Dordogne, Ardèche, the Alps and Paris. Prices range from £332 for a family of four in Brittany to £975 for a family of four in the south of France. Both prices are ferry inclusive.

CITY BREAKS

Airtours (0706 260000)

Paris packages featuring a range of accommodation around the city, available for three-, four- or seven-night breaks. Prices start at £139 per person for three nights bed and breakfast accommodation, including flights and transfers, rising to around £299 for seven nights in peak season. Flight only prices are available from £89 per person.

British Airways Holidays (061 493 3344)

Bordeaux, Nice, and Paris: a two-night break to a three-star hotel in Paris, for example, costs from £167 to £234 per person on a bed and breakfast basis, flight inclusive.

Kirker Holidays (071 231 3333)

Paris: a weekend break by scheduled flights including arrival transfer and accommodation in a two-star hotel costs from £196 per person. Holidays in three- or four-star or deluxe hotels are also possible, for example a weekend at the George V costs from £489 per person.

North Sea Ferries (0482 77177)

Mini-breaks to Lille and Paris. Prices range from £131 to £166 per person. This includes return ferry crossings from Hull to Zeebrugge with dinner and breakfast on the ship and one night's accommodation.

Paris Travel Service (0920 467467)

Wide range of short-breaks to Paris. Choice of rail, coach, self-drive and scheduled flights with departures from 12 UK airports. A four-day-long weekend costs from £156 per person, flight inclusive.

Sovereign Cities (0293 599900)

Nineteen hotels in the centre of Paris and two country retreats within driving distance of the city. Three hotels in Nice. Two nights by air to Paris ranges from £128 to £340 per person on a bed and breakfast basis.

Stena Sealink Travel (0233 647033)

Self-drive packages to Paris: a two-night package to Paris, for example, costs from £68 per person including bed and breakfast accommodation and return ferry crossing.

Thomson Holidays (021 632 6282)

Monte Carlo, Nice, Bordeaux and Paris: a three-night trip to Monte Carlo, for example, costs from £355 per person, staying in a four-star hotel on a bed and breakfast basis. Holidays to Monte Carlo include transfer on arrival by helicopter from Nice.

Time Off (071 235 8070)

Paris packages: for example a seven-night holiday in a two-star hotel on a bed and breakfast basis costs from £350 to £366 per person, flight inclusive.

Travelscene (081 427 4445)

One or more night breaks to Paris by coach, car, rail or air. Hotels range from one star to the George V for a special break. A two-night trip by air from Heathrow costs from around £133 per person, on a bed and breakfast basis.

CLUB HOLIDAYS

Club Med (071 581 1161)

Holiday villages in seven different areas of France, providing activities such as golf, tennis, horse-riding, sailing, swimming, cycling and climbing. All accommodation is in two-bedded rooms. The price includes full board, wine with all meals, use of all sports facilities including equipment and tuition, childcare, entertainment and insurance. Prices range from £560 to £1632 per person for two weeks.

Mark Warner (071 938 1851)

Corsica: a seven-night full board package at one of four beach club hotels on the island, featuring free watersports, costs from around £439 to £666 per person, flight inclusive.

COACH HOLIDAYS

Cosmos Coach Tours (061 480 5799)

A 12-day Grand Tour of France costs from £388 per person. A four- to five-day stay in Paris on a bed and breakfast basis costs from £115 per person.

Excelsior Holidays (0202 309733)

From long weekends to 10-night tours. A seven-night holiday to Brittany with overnight stays at Amiens and Paris and four nights at Dinard costs from £329 per person on half-board.

Insight Holidays (0800 393 393)

An eight-day escorted tour visiting Paris, Rouen, Normandy beaches, Bayeux, St Malo, Mont St Michel and Chartres costs from £535 to £545 per person.

Leisureline Holidays (0508 88193)
Personally escorted tours by air-conditioned coach to provincial France. A six-day gastronomic tour to Normandy costs from £380 per person on a half-board basis. A 13-day tour to the Loire Valley costs from £775 per person.

COOKING HOLIDAYS

Hampton House Travel (081 977 6404)
Weekend and week long courses in Provence, Normandy and Pas de Calais, staying in three- and four-star hotels with instruction by top class chefs. From £550 per person.

Inntravel (0439 7111)
'Cook around France' programme: informal cookery tuition with hotel chefs in Normandy, Picardy, the Loire, Aveyron and Dauphine. Self-drive and fly-drive options from £149 per person for three nights on half-board.

LSG Theme Holidays (0509 231713)
Regional cookery courses in Brittany, Dordogne and Provence, and French pâtisserie courses in Brittany: from £449 to £595 per person, including full board, tuition and return transport from the UK.

SVP France (0243 377862)
One-week courses in Sospel in the mountains behind the Riviera: £477 per person half-board, flight inclusive.

CRUISES

Meon Villa Holidays (0730 268411)
Week-long Rhône cruises on board the *Princess of Provence* cost from £950 to £1205 per person, including flights, transfers and full board.

CYCLING HOLIDAYS

Alastair Sawday's Tours (0272 299921)
Burgundy, Provence, Loire and the Dordogne: prices range from £390 to £690 per person, per week. Prices include all dinners, breakfasts and accommodation; bike hire; maps; luggage carrying; support of area co-ordinator; and bike insurance. The price excludes travel to France.

Belle France (0892 890885)
Auvergne, Loire, Brittany, Normandy and Provence. Hotel-based cycling tours with all bags transported. 'Excellent quality Peugeot tourers are provided.' A three-night tour of Normandy costs from

£221 per person on half-board in a two-star hotel, ferry inclusive.

Bike Tours (0225 480130)

Cycling tours to the Dordogne, the Pyrénées and the Loire Valley. A two-week circular ride in the Dordogne from May to October costs £665 per person. The price includes 12 nights' dinner, bed and breakfast, detailed written route sheets and maps and transportation of luggage. The price excludes the cost of travel to France.

Borderline (0963 250117)

Haute Pyrénées: four levels of mountain biking for all, from beginner to expert. A week's course costs from around £400 per person, including half-board accommodation and flights.

Cyclists Touring Club (0483 417217)

A programme of organized tours led by CTC tour leaders. The *CTC Tour Guide* is published each December and provides details of CTC tours offered in the forthcoming year. A 15-day trip to Limousin, for example, costs from £451 to £600 per person. This is a moving on tour, staying half-board at hotels with 40 to 50 miles of cycling each day. It is suitable for all ages. The price includes return flights from Gatwick to Bordeaux.

Explore Worldwide (0252 319448)

Accompanied cycling holidays in the Loire Valley. A 14-night tour costs from £625 to £645 per person, including six nights' half-board accommodation and the rest bed and breakfast, cycle hire, support van for luggage and return air travel.

Headwater Holidays (0606 48699)

Six- to 14-night holidays in Provence, Burgundy, Loire, Creuse, southern Languedoc, Jura, Lot and Célé and the Western Alps. A ten-night 'Châteaux and Chablis' cycling holiday in Burgundy, on half-board, costs from £499 per person, self-drive, to £636 per person, air and rail. A ten-night 'Secret Provence' cycling trip costs from £499 per person self-drive to £740 per person by air, including half-board accommodation.

Inntravel (0439 7111)

Independent, unguided cycling in the Dordogne and Lot. Self-drive and flight inclusive options. Prices are from £460 per person for seven nights, including ferry crossings, cycle hire, full board and luggage transport.

SVP France (0243 377862)

Unaccompanied cycling holidays in Brittany, Loire, Limousin, Dordogne and Lot. Seven nights costs from £435 per person, ferry inclusive to £565 per person, flight inclusive. Both prices include cycle hire, half-board and baggage transport.

Susi Madron's Cycling for Softies (061 248 8282)

Cycling tours with accommodation in family-run hotels in nine regions of France including: Mayenne/Sarthe; Loire Valley; Venise Verte; Cognac/Charente; Dordogne/Garonne; Tarn; Beaujolais/Jura; vineyards of Rhône; Provence/Camargue. Holidays can be booked air inclusive, ferry inclusive or air/rail inclusive. Prices include use of bicycles, equipment and transport. An 11-day 'Gentle Tourer' in the Mayenne region in north west France begins with two nights in Vaiges and is followed by overnight stops in Neau, Pierre des Nids, Mayenne and Mezangers. The price, which includes the accommodation with dinner, bed and breakfast, bike hire and flights from Gatwick or Heathrow costs from £587 to £617 per person, depending on departure date.

EURO DISNEY

British Airways Holidays (061 493 3344)

A two-night stay at the Hotel Santa Fé costs from £184 to £247 per person based on four sharing. A two-night stay at the Disneyland Hotel costs from £236 to £339 per person based on four sharing. The price includes accommodation, return flights and guaranteed unlimited entry into Euro Disneyland Theme Park for the duration of your stay.

Kirker Holidays (071 231 3333)

Short breaks to Euro Disney are offered, including guaranteed entrance to the theme park. Prices on request.

Sally Holidays (0732 780440)

Seven nights bed and breakfast accommodation costs from £179 to £301 per person with up to two children free. A Euro Disney pass for a family of four – two adults and two children – for two days costs £192 extra.

Thomson Holidays (021 632 6282)

Two-, three- or four-night packages using scheduled flights from 10 UK airports; also self-drive holidays and inclusive packages using train, ferry, coach and hovercraft. Accommodation available at Euro Disney or in Paris hotels. Prices for self-drive with two nights at the cheapest Disney hotel costs from £211 per person. All holidays in the Eurofun brochure include a two-day Euro Disney passport providing unlimited use of the attractions within the theme park.

Travelscene (081 427 4445)

A two-night trip from Heathrow costs from around £269 per person on a bed and breakfast basis, staying in the Hotel Santa Fé. Prices include a pass to Euro Disney appropriate for the length of stay.

GARDEN TOURS

Merit Travel & Tours (081 653 6514)
Accompanied coach holidays visiting a variety of gardens in various areas of France. For example, 'The Great Gardens of Normandy Tour' costs £165 per person, for two nights.

GOLFING HOLIDAYS

A Golfing Experience (081 205 7138)
Holidays offer either hotel or self-catering accommodation. Seven nights' bed and breakfast with six days of golf in Bordeaux costs £356 per person, ferry inclusive. Seven nights in an apartment in southern Brittany with six days of golf costs £215 per person, including ferry crossing.

Brittany Ferries (0752 221321)
Inclusive golfing holidays in a choice of 22 locations, staying in two- and three-star hotels. A three-night stay in the Lorient area costs from £146 per person, including bed and breakfast accommodation, return ferry crossing with car and green fees.

Cresta Holidays (061 926 9999)
Inclusive golfing packages in several regions of France. One week self-catering by car costs from £167 to £252, including green fees.

FrancoLeisure (0303 276961)
Short-break golfing holidays in the Pas de Calais region. Two nights' accommodation at a two-star hotel with three days of golf costs from £86 to £110 per person, ferry inclusive.

French Golf Holidays (0277 261004)
Holidays to many regions of France. For example, 14 nights in a self-catering apartment at La Baule costs £499 for two people, ferry inclusive. The price includes five days' golf. Five nights' bed and breakfast at a three-star hotel with three days' golf and ferry crossings included costs from £351 per person.

Hampton House Travel (081 977 6404)
Short breaks and longer holidays with pre-booked tee-off times in Pas de Calais, Normandy, Champagne and Provence. Also gastronomic breaks in Normandy with free golf. Prices from £168 per person for two nights, including half-board and golf.

La France des Villages (0449 737664)
A specialist programme in most regions. A range of accommodation is offered from five-star luxury on-course hotels to simpler auberges and chambres d'hôte. On-course apartments and self-catering accommodation is also available. A week at a self-catering cottage in Burgundy for two costs from £225, including ferry.

Longshot Golf Holidays (0730 268621)
Holidays to Le Touquet, Normandy, Loire Valley, Brittany, Biarritz, Pays de Loire, Bordeaux, Languedoc, Provence and the Riviera. For example, prices from £279 to £315 per person for seven nights at the Manoir du Menec Hotel in Brittany, on a bed and breakfast basis. Price includes ferry crossing.

HORSE-RIDING

Equitour (071 602 8433)
Holidays to the Loire, Beaujolais, Languedoc, Camargue, Provence and the Ardèche. An eight-day holiday – seven days of riding – in the Camargue costs £620 per person, full board. Travel to France is not included in the price.

Headwater Holidays (0606 48699)
Riding in the Loire and the Dordogne. A seven-night holiday on half-board at Neuvic costs from £399 per person, self-drive.

Inntravel (0439 7111)
Guided and independent holidays – small groups of mixed nationalities – in Cerdagne, Corbières, Dordogne, Lot and Tarn. Seven nights from £530 per person, including ferry crossings, full board and riding.

LSG Theme Holidays (0509 231713)
Brittany, Côte d'Azur and Île-de-France: eight- to fifteen-day riding for beginners and the more advanced. From £449 to £875 per person, including full board, tuition and return travel from the UK.

Maison Vacances (081 540 9680)
Holidays to most regions of France. In Aquitaine, seven-nights' bed and breakfast in an 18th-century farmhouse set in its own large grounds with a swimming pool costs from £230 to £270 per person, including four hours of horse-riding per day.

SVP France (0243 377862)
Either day rides out from our comfortable base in the Lot or a week's independent trekking, £673 for one week with full board, flight inclusive.

HOUSE SWAPPING

HomeLink International (0628 31951)
The HomeLink directory costs £39. Members use the directory to make contact with others in order to agree an exchange holiday. No money changes hands, each member being a guest of the other and each having only to pay for air or sea travel. The directory

includes a step-by-step guide on what to do during each stage of an exchange.

Intervac International Home Exchange (0272 687431)
Home exchange holidays in most areas; properties range from small flats to mansions. Annual fee is £46.

LANGUAGE LEARNING

Accents Languages and Leisure (0606 48699)
Language and leisure: the duration of stays is varied, from three days to three weeks. Seven nights costs from £309 per person, excluding travel.

Cultural and Educational Services Abroad (0273 683304)
General language programmes, long-term courses and intensive courses. A two-week course, 20 lessons per week, with accommodation arranged in families costs approximately £640 per person on half-board, travel not included. A 12-week long term course costs around £3408 per person. Very intensive small group classes for professionals of one week cost around £1020 per person.

En Famille Overseas (0903 883266)
Paying guest holidays with over 150 host families all over France. Prices range from approximately £260 per person for two weeks demi-pension all year round, to £660 per person for two weeks full board including language tuition; both prices are excluding travel. Language courses in study centres are also offered from £280 per person, excluding travel.

Euro Academy (081 686 2363)
Family homestays in most areas of France from £385 to £479 per person for 13 nights including full board. Vacation courses which include language studies and an activity programme in Dinan, Tours, Arcachon, Montpellier and Sète from £605 to £715 per person for 13 nights including full board. Intensive study courses in Paris, Aix-en-Provence, Lyon and Nice from £590 to £905 per person for 13 nights with half-board accommodation.

LSG Theme Holidays (0509 231713)
Conversational French in Brittany, Ardèche, Île-de-France, Auvergne, Dordogne, Languedoc, Provence and the Côte d'Azur. Courses to all levels, from beginners to advanced (post A level). From eight to fifteen days. Prices range from £449 to £875 per person, including full board, tuition and travel from the UK.

VFB Holidays (0242 526338)
Four-day 'Brush up your French' courses in Normandy. Prices from £214 to £240 per person including three nights half-board

accommodation, language course, excursions and entry fees, ferry travel and insurance.

MOTOR RACING HOLIDAYS

Just Tickets & Just Motoring (0304 228866)
Packages to the French Grand Prix: one night's hotel accommodation in Montluçon, with cross Channel ferry tickets on a short sea route costs from £59 per person.

MOTORAIL

Railsavers (0253 300080)
Motorail ticket agency. In 1993 they are offering all Motorail tickets at 1992 prices. Railsavers provides all year round services including winter journeys to the French Alps. From March onwards many extra seasonal services commence and operate until October. AA Five-Star vehicle insurance for 31 days is given free with most tickets.

MOTORCYCLING

Bike and Sun Tours (0287 638217)
Accompanied motorcycle touring holidays in the French Alps and the Pyrénées. Prices are not seasonal and range from £645 for one person on a solo to £936 for two people on a solo. They include return ferry crossings, bed and breakfast in all hotels, insurance and the services of the guide.

MOTORING AND FLY/DRIVE

Time Off (071 235 8070)
Time Off runs its French Selection programme of motoring holidays in the French countryside. For example a seven-night holiday in the Loire Valley in a two-star hotel on a bed and breakfast basis costs from £206 to £246 per person, ferry inclusive.

MULTI-ACTIVITY HOLIDAYS

Freestyle (010 33 90 68 10 31)
Multi-sports holidays of one week duration. Mountain biking, rock climbing, horse-riding and canoeing in the south of France. The price per week ranges from £280 to £350 per person, including food and accommodation. Travel is not included.

PGL Adventure Ltd (0989 768768)
A programme of family holidays with activities that include archery, white water rafting, pony trekking, skiing and abseiling. Destinations include Brittany, the Ardèche and the French Alps. A seven-night holiday costs from £119 to £163 per person, self-catering accommodation and travel included.

Sun Esprit (0252 816004)
Activity-based family holidays in Morzine in the Haute Savoie region of the French Alps. The basic adult price is from £248 to £288 for one week, ferry inclusive. The first child in each family is free and the second and third child pay a percentage of the adult price dependent upon their age – from 25% to 70%. The programme features auberge-based accommodation and the price includes bed and breakfast, two family evening meals and up to three lunches and three additional evening meals for children. Also included in the basic price is three days of all-day crêche cover and two full days of activities.

VFB Holidays (0242 526338)
Independent summer activity holidays in the Alpine village resorts of Morzine and La Clusaz. Two weeks in an apartment or chalet costs from £225 to £700 per person, including self-catering accommodation, activity passport, return ferry travel and insurance. Thirteen nights in a hotel costs from £320 to £615 per person, including half-board accommodation, activity passport, return ferry travel and insurance.

Music holidays

DB Jazz Tours (0789 267532)
Escorted holidays to jazz festivals. A seven-night bed and breakfast package to the Harvey Hotel in Nice costs from £300 per week, per person, including air travel.

Music at Ladevie (071 249 7591)
Ten-day summer piano study courses in rural south west France. Full board, accommodation and tuition costs from £350 to £650 per person. Non-participating partners are welcome at a 15% discount. The price excludes the cost of travelling to France.

Travel for the Arts (071 483 4466)
Flight and hotel packages are offered at a range of three-, four- and five-star hotels in Paris with tickets for the opera at the Opera Bastille and the ballet at the Palais Garnier. Prices from £225 per person for two nights accommodation on a bed and breakfast basis, flights and a ticket in Category One or Two for a performance at the opera or ballet. Tailor-made arrangements can also be organized for many of France's regional opera houses (Lyon, Nice,

Toulouse, Bordeaux, Marseilles) and the important summer opera festivals in Aix-en-Provence and Orange.

NATURAL HISTORY

LSG Theme Holidays (0509 231713)
Provence, Languedoc, Dordogne, Auvergne: eight to fifteen day guided nature-watch holidays. From £575 to £875 per person, including full board, guides and air travel.

Simply Corsica (081 747 3580)
Seven nights full-board exploring the island's spring flowers with an experienced botanist. No single supplement. The cost is £759 per person, flight inclusive.

Snail's Pace Natural History Holidays (0943 873465)
Wildlife holidays: birds, flowers, butterflies and history. A two-week holiday based in the Central Pyrénées, touring and walking, minibus transport and half-board costs £945 per person.

NATURIST HOLIDAYS

Tamplins Travel (0865 391257)
Self-catering family caravan holidays in eastern Provence. Caravan hire for up to four persons costs from £120 to £180 per week. A two-week package for two people by air costs from £599 to £774.

PAINTING AND DRAWING HOLIDAYS

Bespoke Holidays (0732 366130)
Holidays for the over–50s. One week painting courses in Gascony with an English tutor cost £460 per person on half-board.

LSG Theme Holidays (0509 231713)
Brittany, Normandy, Ardèche, Auvergne, Île-de-France, Dordogne, Languedoc, Provence and the Côte d'Azur: four to fifteen days from £325 to £875 per person, including accommodation in two- and three-star hotels and holiday centres, tuition, and travel from the UK.

Paint at Escat (010 33 61 97 59 63)
Beginners or professionals work at their own pace in small groups, no more than six at a time. A 10-day holiday costs £315 per person, including half-board accommodation, tuition, wine with meals, tea and coffee breaks and local trips by car.

Painting School of Montmiral (0786 72023)
Individually-tailored painting and drawing courses in the Tarn region. A two-week package, including tuition, model, invited artists, visits to the Toulouse Lautrec Museum, half-board accom-

modation and collection from the airport costs £592 per person. Holidays for non-painting partners cost £368 per person.

Painting for Pleasure in France (0386 438775)
Aveyron in the south west region. An eight-day, full board painting holiday in the spring or the autumn costs £454 per person, excluding the cost of travelling to France.

Simply Corsica (081 747 3580)
Autumn watercolours: suitable for both beginners and experienced painters in a relaxed atmosphere. Two weeks full board costs £749 per person, flight inclusive.

PHOTOGRAPHY HOLIDAYS

LSG Theme Holidays (0509 231713)
Brittany, Ardèche, Île-de-France, Auvergne, Dordogne, Provence and the Côte d'Azur: eight to fifteen days from £545 to £875 per person, including full board, tuition and travel from the UK.

Photography Workshops in Provence (010 33 90 09 95 37)
Eight-day workshops in a village in the Lubéron mountains, 30 kms from Aix-en-Provence. Accommodation is in a large early 16th-century Provençal village house. The total cost, based on two people sharing a study bedroom, each with its own separate shower and toilet facilities is £280 per person. Single accommodation is available at £330 per person.

PILGRIMAGES

Kestours (081 658 7316)
Individually arranged scheduled flight-based holidays for three or seven nights. Prices range from £287 to £349 per person on a bed and breakfast basis.

RIVER RUNNING AND RAFTING

Explore Worldwide (0252 319448)
Fourteen nights rafting on the Dordogne river, camping and camp breakfasts throughout. Prices from £425 to £445 per person, including return air travel.

RUNNING HOLIDAYS

Sports Tours International (061 703 8161)
Packages for the Paris Marathon, the Paris to Versailles run and the Paris 20km. In each case travel, accommodation and entries

into the races for those who wish to compete can be arranged. Prices on application.

SAILING

Clearwater Holidays (0926 450002)
Shore-based sailing holidays in the Gulf of Morbihan, south Brittany. Accommodation in waterside Breton cottages; brown-sailed, gaff-rigged dayboats on sheltered anchorages in the bay directly in front of the cottages. A cottage for two weeks will cost in the region of £750 in the low season and £1280 in high season, ferry inclusive. Dayboat prices range from about £90 to £170 per week, according to size and season. Also a 16ft gaff topsail dayboat with camping tent is available with or without a cottage – price from £180 to £225 per week, according to season.

Corsican Places (0424 774366)
Corsica: motor boat or yacht charter with or without skipper, costs from £260 to £410 per person for seven nights, flight inclusive.

LSG Theme Holidays (0509 231713)
Brittany and Provence: eight to fifteen day courses for beginners and the more advanced. From £449 to £875 per person, including full board, tuition and travel from the UK.

Riviera Sailing Holidays (0243 374376)
Yachting holidays on the French Riviera and in Corsica. Prices range from around £450 for one week in low season for a four-berth yacht to £5000 for a week in high season in a 10-berth yacht.

Worldwide Yachting Holidays (071 328 1033)
A 73ft crewed yacht for eight people in the south of France costs from US$18500 to US$24150 per week, excluding flights.

SENIOR CITIZEN

Saga Holidays (0800 300 500)
Worldwide holidays for the over–60s. A ten-day break by ferry, coach and TGV express train to the Pyrénées costs from £479 to £539 per person on half-board. A seven-night university holiday to Reims costs from £279 per person with half-board accommodation at Reims University. A wine study holiday in the Loire Valley costs from £429 per person, for seven nights based in Orléans University. A nine-night walking holiday in Aix-en-Provence with guided walks through the forests, vineyards and fields of Aix-en-Provence costs £519 per person, travel inclusive and staying at a four-star hotel on a bed and breakfast basis.

SINGLES

SVP France (0243 377862)
Walks and hikes in small parties with a French guide. Full board accommodation staying in gîtes d'étape, chambres d'hôte or hotels from £465 with return scheduled air travel.

Solo's Holidays (081 202 0855)
Two venues in France: St Rémy de Provence and Angers in western Loire. The prices range from £475 to £569 per person for seven days at a three-star hotel on a bed and breakfast basis.

Sovereign Small World (0293 599966)
House party holidays for 'single, sociable people' in Provence. One- and two-week inclusive holidays from Gatwick – half-board with unlimited wine. Prices range from £367 to £674 per person.

SKIING

AA Motoring Holidays (0256 493878)
Self-catering accommodation in Avoriaz, Chamonix, Val Thorens, Les Menuires, Meribel, Belle Plagne and Val d'Isère. A week's self-catering for four in Chamonix costs £316, ferry inclusive.

Borderline (0963 250117 brochures)
Haute Pyrénées: downhill skiing, ski touring and cross-country skiing.

Brittany Ferries (0752 221321)
Ski-drive holidays in 19 locations in the French Alps. A one-week apartment holiday at Les Deux Alps costs from £59 to £188 per person in a party of four adults including return ferry crossing.

Crystal Holidays (081 390 3335)
Twenty high altitude resorts are featured. Seven nights in self-catering accommodation costs from £145 per person, flight inclusive.

Freedom Holidays (081 741 4686)
Ski-drive holidays to a selection of ski resorts. Fully inclusive packages to self-catering studios and apartments and small, traditional Alpine hotels with a choice of ferry routes. Prices for one week's self-catering range from £109 to £189 per person, based on four sharing. Ski weekends by scheduled air travel to Châtel in the Haute Savoie are also offered. Prices range from £269 per person, including self-catering accommodation and ski guiding.

Headwater Holidays (0606 48699)
Destinations include the Vercors, Jura, Ardèche and the Auvergne. Alpine and cross-country skiing. From £269 per person, self-drive for one week.

Hoverspeed Holidays (081 424 2929)
Self-drive hotel and self-catering accommodation in the Savoy Alps. Prices range from £111 to £657 per person for a fortnight in a studio apartment. Hotel accommodation ranges from £756 to £1042 per person for a fortnight, on a half-board basis.

Inntravel (0439 7111)
Cross-country skiing: by air and self-drive to the Cerdagne, Pyrénées, Jura and Vercors. Prices for one week start at £171 per person, self-drive and self-catering.

Jean Stanford Ski Holidays (0747 870708)
The Haute Savoie: accommodation in hotels, catered chalets and self-catering apartments. Alpine skiing and cross-country skiing, plus the opportunity to paraglide, heli-ski, snowmobile, snowshoe, ice drive, skate and curl. Prices range from £107 to £513 per person for one week, ferry inclusive.

Lagrange UK (071 371 6111)
Holidays at a number of resorts. A 'tout compris' option is offered which includes both the accommodation and a six-day ski pass – some resorts feature the added bonus of non-skiers going free. A studio for three people in Chamonix costs from £147 to £162 per person, per week.

Le Ski (0484 548996)
Catered chalet holidays in Courchevel and Val d'Isère. A one-week holiday costs from £299 to £499 per person including half-board, ski guiding service and return air travel. Self-catering apartments in Courchevel are also offered from £169 to £385 per person, flight inclusive.

Mark Warner (071 938 1851)
Val d'Isère, Meribel and Courchevel. A seven-night half-board package at a Clubhotel in Val d'Isère, with six days free ski guiding, costs from £285 to £559 per person, flight inclusive.

Meriski (081 682 3883)
A two-week holiday in Meribel in the Trois Vallées region costs from £499 to £599 per person, including return flight, private coach transfer and full-board accommodation.

North Sea Ferries (0482 77177)
Self-catering skiing holidays in six resorts. Prices for a seven-night holiday start at £159 per person, based on four adults sharing a car. The price includes overnight return ferry crossing between Hull and Zeebrugge.

SVP France (0243 377862)
Cross-country skiing in the Vosges, Jura, Vercors, Alps and the Auvergne. Seven nights full board including equipment and instruction costs from £351 to £432 per person, flight inclusive.

Also cross-country ski touring in small, accompanied groups staying in gîtes d'étape or small hotels.

Sally Holidays (0732 780440)

Self-drive ski holidays to the French Alps. A seven-night package costs from £49 per person in a self-catering studio. Fourteen nights in a three-star hotel on full board costs £776 per person. Prices include ferry crossings.

Silver Ski Holidays (0622 735544)

Fully-inclusive catered chalets in the high French Alps. Prices range from £279 per person, per week including flights from Gatwick.

Ski Enterprise (061 831 7000)

Holidays featuring self-catering and hotel accommodation. Prices range from around £145 per person for 14 nights in a self-catering apartment to £1639 per person in a hotel. All prices include flights from Gatwick.

Ski Espirt (0252 616789)

Catered chalet holidays in the Savoie and Haute Savoie regions. Chalets range from the luxurious to the more basic and are all located near lifts and ski slopes. Prices for one week range from £248 to £588 per person. This includes flights, breakfast, afternoon tea and four course evening meals with unlimited wine. Children's discounts vary throughout the season but can be up to 50% off the adult price. Ferry inclusive and independent travel packages are also available.

Ski Falcon (061 831 7000)

Resorts featured include La Plagne, La Toussuire, Les Menuires, Morzine, Val d'Isère and Val Thorens. Prices for a 14-night self-catering holiday range from £143 to £489 per person, flight inclusive. Fourteen-night packages with hotel accommodation cost from £419 to £799 per person, flight inclusive.

Ski Peak (0428 682272)

Vaujany and Dauphine: catered chalet and hotel accommodation from £325 to £450 per person for seven nights on half-board, including flights and transfers.

SkiBound (0273 696960)

Northern and southern French Alps. Hotels, catered chalets and self-catering apartments. Prices for seven nights from £159 to £505 per person, inclusive of return flight from London.

Skiworld (071 602 4826)

Destinations include Tarentaise and Dauphine. Accommodation is in self-catering apartments, chalets and hotels. A seven-night holiday costs from £159 to £499 per person, by air.

Snowbizz Vacances (0778 341455)
Southern French Alps: Serre-Chevalier, Briançon, Puy St Vincent. One week costs from £95 to £159 per person for a self-catering, self-drive holiday. By air the prices range from £169 to £309 per person in a self-catering apartment.

Snowpiper Ski Holidays (0932 868658)
Self-catering holidays in Châtel and Alpe d'Huez and hotel holidays in Flaine. Two weeks in a studio apartment in Châtel costs from £251 to £931. Prices are for four people, ferry inclusive. A seven-night half-board package at the Hôtel Aujon in Flaine in a triple north-facing room costs from £656 to £969. Prices are for three people and include a short sea ferry crossing.

Thomson Holidays (021 632 6282)
Packages to the French Pyrénées with flights from Gatwick and Manchester. Prices for four people sharing a studio at the Le Pas de L'Ours studios. Cauterets start at £133 for seven nights and £175 for 14 nights. In the French Alps packages are available with flights to Lyons from 12 UK airports. Flights also available to Geneva, Nice and Turin. Seven-night packages to the Chalet le Petit Venosc in Les Deux Alpes, for example, cost from £234 per person.

Waymark Holidays (0753 516477)
Cross-country skiing holidays: a seven-night holiday in La Fenière in the Pyrénées costs from £395 per person, full board.

Westbury Travel(0225 444516)
Hotels and self-catering available in the following resorts: Val d'Isère, Tignes, Flaine, Meribel and Courchevel. Prices range from £142 to £246 per person, self-catering and £209 to £569 per person, in a chalet run on house party lines. Both prices are for one week and both include air travel. A seven-night hotel holiday costs from £329 to £459 per person on half-board, flight inclusive.

White Roc Ski (071 792 1188)
Destinations include Morzine, Megève, Argentière, Chamonix, Meribel and Val d'Isère. Chalet and hotel accomodation is offered. One week in the Alps in a chalet on half-board costs from £279 to £479 per person, air inclusive. One week in a two-star hotel in Morzine on half-board costs from £286 to £341 per person, ferry inclusive. A weekend skiing break costs from £279 to £298 for three nights on a bed and breakfast basis, including scheduled flights from Heathrow and car hire.

STUDY HOLIDAYS

ACE Study Tours (0223 835055)
Corsica, Cévennes and the Dordogne: themes include art and

architecture, wildlife, archaeology and history. A 12-day natural history tour of the Cévennes for example, costs £895 per person, including half-board, all excursions and air travel.

Plantaganet Tours (0202 521895)

Escorted, historical and cultural study tours. For example, a 10-day French cathedrals tour costs £1450 per person on half-board. A two-week Troubadour tour to medieval Aquitaine costs £1596 per person on half-board.

Sauces Nord (010 33 63 94 05 90)

Sketching, spinning and weaving, photography and wine appreciation courses in Gascony. The cost of a full board activity holiday including the tutor's fee is £225 per person for one week. Travel to France is not included in the price.

WALKING AND TREKKING

Belle France (0892 890885)

Independent walking in the Auvergne, Brittany, Normandy, Provence, Loire, Ardèche and Cantal. A six-night gentle walking tour of the châteaux of the Loire costs from £369 per person. This price includes half-board accommodation in two-star hotels and return ferry crossings. All bags are transported.

Bespoke Holidays (0732 366130)

'Walking at an easy pace for the over-50s.' Five days walking along the Sentier de St Jacques in Gascony with visits to Lourdes and the foothills of the Pyrénées, wine tasting and an English-speaking guide. A 14-day trip on half-board costs £606 per person. A 14-day holiday in an upland village in the Pyrénées, tracing the history of the Cathar Heresy and the third crusade, with guided walks discovering varieties of orchids and other flowers costs £885 per person on half-board. Travel is not included.

Borderline (0963 250117)

Haute Pyrénées: hotel-based walking from Barèges with local mountain guides, into the National Park. There are walks for all levels. The additional price for the walking trips is £19 per day.

Explore Worldwide (0252 319448)

Walking in Provence, 14 nights camping – seven nights full board and seven nights half-board. Prices from £480 to £495 per person, including flights from London. A 14-night walking tour on the island of Corsica, staying at hotels/pensions and at village gîtes costs from £595 to £640 per person, flight inclusive.

HF Holidays (081 905 9558)

Walking holidays led by experienced, knowledgeable leaders with a daily choice of walks. Friendly atmosphere, staying in two-star hotels. Destinations include Dordogne, Auvergne, Haute Pyrénées and Haute Savoie. Prices from £565 to £718 per person for 14 nights half-board, air inclusive.

Headwater Holidays (0606 48699)

Destinations include Provence, Ardèche, Burgundy, Languedoc, Auvergne, Loire, Jura, Creuse, Lot and the Western Alps. An eight-night ridges and gorges walk in the Alps costs from £373 to £589 per person on half-board.

Hotel Treks (081 569 4101)

Hotel-based holidays for walkers. Following in the footsteps of Stevenson in the Cerdagne for seven nights costs from £405 to £639 per person, air inclusive.

Inntravel (0439 7111)

Independent, unguided walking holidays in the Loire, Cerdagne, Dordogne, Aveyron, Haute Savoie, Tarn, Cévennes, Vercors, Alsace, Alpes Maritimes and Cantal. Self-drive and flight inclusive options. Seven-night packages start from £370, including ferry crossing, full board and transport of luggage from hotel to hotel.

Quatre Saisons (0303 221135)

Walking tours in co-operation with the Fédération des Parcs Naturels in the Cévennes, the Pyrénées and the Lubéron. A seven-day tour of the Parc National des Cévennes, graded as 'easy' costs £425 per person. Hotels used are two- and three-star and all meals are included. Luggage is transported between stops. There are contributions from park guides, naturalists and botanists during the itinerary.

Ramblers Holidays (0707 331133)

Sixteen different tours and walking holidays in mountains and countryside, including Corsica. Prices range from around £350 for one week to around £650 for two weeks. This includes flights, half-board accommodation and walking programme.

SVP France (0243 377862)

Unaccompanied or small guided parties in the Dordogne, Lot, Auvergne, Pyrénées, Vosges, Jura and the Alps. Accommodation is in gîtes d'étape, chambres d'hôte or small hotels. A seven-night holiday costs £270 per person on full board, ferry inclusive. Bags are transported.

Sherpa Expeditions (081 577 2717)

Small groups travel with professional leaders; 14-day packages cost from £595 to £785 per person, flight inclusive.

Waymark Holidays (0753 516477)

Destinations include Corsica, Provence, Savoie, the Pyrénées and Languedoc: 14 nights half-board in Corsica costs from £695 per person, seven nights half-board in Provence costs from £395 per person.

WINE TOURS

Arblaster & Clarke Wine Tours (0730 266883)
Accompanied by a wine guide and a tour manager, with private visits arranged to leading estates, including meals at wineries throughout Champagne, Bordeaux, The Loire, Alsace and Beaujolais. Tours range from three days in Champagne at £199 per person, to eight days in Bordeaux and the Loire at £439 per person, and in Burgundy for eight days at £489 per person.

Hampton House Travel (081 977 6404)
Wine and Calvados tasting tours. Breaks in most wine regions, also Normandy and Pas de Calais. Prices from £198 per person for two nights in Normandy, including gastronomic dinners, Calvados tastings and ferry for car and passengers.

Inntravel (0439 7111)
Wine tasting in the Loire, Champagne and Alsace. Accommodation is in fine hotels with private vineyard visits and tastings arranged. Prices from £199 per person, self-drive.

Merit Travel & Tours (081 653 6514)
Four nights in Dijon and one night in Reims visiting a selection of vineyards in Champagne, Burgundy and Chablis costs £285 per person, meals included.

VFB Holidays (0242 526338)
Four-day wine courses in France with a qualified Master of Wine as lecturer and guide in the Bordeaux and Champagne regions. From £395 per person with return ferry travel included, to £445 with return air travel included. Prices include half-board accommodation, wine seminars, wine tastings, excursions and insurance.

Worldwide Yachting Holidays (071 328 1033)
'Quality tours' for fine wine enthusiasts, visiting leading wine estates throughout Europe. All tours led by senior wine experts with small groups. The company claims to cover every major European wine region. Prices range from £495 to £1250 per person for four to eight days.

7

HOLIDAY FRANCE

The drive from Calais south to the Riviera city of Nice is a surprisingly long one: a distance of 765 miles (much further, for example, than the distance from Plymouth to Inverness). The journey takes you from the chilly and damp northern European climate of the English Channel to the balmy, palmy Mediterranean surroundings of the Côte d'Azur.

Anyone completing this drive discovers not only a difference in temperature, but learns what an extraordinarily diverse country France is. On the journey south, every hundred miles or so the landscape seems to transform itself: from the flat lands of Picardy to the chalky, rolling hills of Champagne; from the sweeping green meadows of Burgundy to the hilltop castles of the Rhône Valley and, finally, the sweet, hot fecundity of Provence. France may be one country but it is made up of many different regions: each with its own character and displaying a particular style, a distinct climate, a special charm.

It is worth spending some time considering the various regions of France before choosing your final holiday destination. Your choice to some extent will depend on how far you wish to drive – but it will also be a question of if you want a holiday near good sandy beaches, whether you are keen on good country walks, how important it is to have plenty of hot sunshine and whether you wish to escape the crowds.

One of the extraordinary things about France is that while it may be the world's most visited country, it is still fairly easy to avoid fellow tourists. The British, like the visitors from other countries (and the French themselves!), tend to congregate in the same areas: Paris, the Côte d'Azur, Brittany and the Atlantic coast. For the French, all holidays begin and end beside the sea (or beside a river or lake – water of any sort is a vital ingredient for a French family *en vacances*). This means that by staying inland – or by searching out the less frequented stretches of coastline – you can remain far from the madding crowd. But to accomplish this you do need to do some planning and a little research.

THE BEST HOLIDAY AREAS OF FRANCE
ATLANTIC COAST

The Atlantic Coast that runs south from Île de Noirmoutier down to Biarritz and St Jean-de-Luz near the Spanish border in the south, has rapidly gained popularity with British family holiday-makers. The reasons for its success are not hard to trace. The weather here is better than Brittany – and the resorts and beaches are generally far less crowded than those of the Mediterranean coast.

There are also plenty of good sandy beaches. From the Gironde estuary, north of Bordeaux, down to the border with northern Spain, there are miles and miles of almost uninterrupted sandy beaches. It may all lack the scenic grandeur of Brittany and Normandy, but it makes undeniably good territory for family beach holidays. (A warning: don't expect the Atlantic Ocean to be as warm as the Mediterranean!)

There is no shortage of attractive towns: La Rochelle, Arcachon and the Basque port of St Jean-de-Luz are a sheer delight. Standing behind the coastline is Les Landes, a large area of pine trees planted in the 19th century as a barrier to stop the sand dunes from being driven inland by the strong winds from the Atlantic.

For wine enthusiasts, the countryside around Bordeaux is likely to provide pleasurable diversions. Wine producing places include: St Emilion, Sauternes, Château d'Yquem, Château Latour and Château Mouton-Rothschild.

Near the Spanish border is the Basque Coast with interesting ports like Bayonne, fashionable resorts like Biarritz and charming old-fashioned seaside places like St Jean-de-Luz.

Arcachon: Large, well-established resort fashionable since the late 19th century. It is pleasantly situated with a fine seafront, and bordered by sheltering pine trees. The principal tourist attraction is five miles to the south: the Pilat sand dune which stands 114m (3745ft) high.
Bayonne: A lively Basque port with a fine Cathedral famous for its stained glass and beautiful cloisters.
Biarritz: A highly fashionable resort in the 19th century (Napoleon III was a regular visitor – Queen Victoria also came). Still stylish and popular, particularly with surfers who enjoy its wide beaches and pounding rollers.
Bordeaux: Prosperous, handsome port which continues to make a good living from the wine business which still dominates the region.
Cognac: Attractive town famous for its brandy distilleries.

La Rochelle: One of the most picturesque places on the Atlantic coast (perhaps the prettiest port in France). Plenty of pavement cafés and lots of good fish restaurants. Nearby are the two popular holiday islands of Île de Ré and Île d'Oléron, both reached by bridge (Île de Ré used to be accessible only by ferry which involved an endless queue). The islands have good sandy beaches, backed by dunes and pines, salt marshes, oyster beds and picturesque fishing villages.

Royan: Resort with good beaches, now very popular with British families.

Saintes: Attractive market town on the river Charente.

Les Sables-d'Olonne: Excellent relaxed family resort with a good sandy beach. Nearby is the Île de Noirmoutier.

St Jean-de-Luz: More of a fishing port than a seaside resort: with a good beach offering safe swimming for children.

BRITTANY

The British have been fond of Brittany for well over a century. Its attraction derives partly from the fact that it is easily accessible: ferries from Plymouth and Portsmouth put in at Roscoff and St Malo respectively. Another bonus is that it offers the sort of beach holidays which we like best. There are plenty of gîtes, lots of good campsites and dozens of good modestly-priced hotels.

Our affection for Brittany must also have something to do with the fact that like the people of Cornwall, Wales, Scotland and Ireland, they have their roots in Celtic culture. Indeed, as you drive around the Breton coast, it is easy at times to imagine that you might be in Cornwall or west Wales.

For families Brittany's principal appeal is its beaches and resorts. Brittany has a long and very varied coast which seldom suffers from the sort of overcrowding that spoils the beaches further south. (But further south, it is appreciably warmer and drier than Brittany – you pays your money . . .). One of the prettiest stretches of coast – certainly one of the most visited – lies between Quiberon and Bénodet where small, pretty resorts nestle in wooded inlets and estuaries. The north coast has long, flat sandy beaches, huge rocks and well established family resorts. The best piece of northern Breton coast, known as the Pink Granite Coast, runs from Perros-Guirec to Trébeurden.

La Baule: A smart, sophisticated place that has more in common with the affluent sunspots of the Côte d'Azur than with the family resorts of Brittany. Its principal attraction for families is a perfect beach for building sandcastles.

Bénodet: Attractively situated resort on the Odet estuary, south of Quimper, very popular with the British.

Carnac: Famous for its long rows of around 3,000 megaliths or menhirs (standing stones à la Stonehenge). A good museum provides fascinating background on the period of their erection.

Concarneau: Large fishing port with a fine walled city which lies on an island in the middle of the harbour. Extremely popular with tourists but even at its busiest times, it still retains its charm.

Dinan: Picturesque Breton town in danger of being overwhelmed by its own quaintness. A good place for a meal or a shopping trip.

Dinard: A traditional resort first visited by smart English travellers in the last century. It may no longer attract the smart set but it is still an agreeable place with good restaurants and agreeable hotels.

Nantes: Within the anonymous suburbs of Brittany's largest city there lurks an historic city centre; worth visiting for an interesting ducal castle and a fine cathedral.

Perros-Guirec: A busy, attractive resort on Brittany's northern coastline particularly popular with families. The Plage de Trestraou is a huge area of excellent sand.

Quiberon: Lively resort at the centre of a good choice of beaches and a 45-minute ferry ride away from the beautiful island of Belle-Île.

Quimper: A delightful old Breton city in a choice location at the junction of the Steir and Odet rivers. There is a fine medieval quarter with timbered houses and cobbled streets.

Rennes: Not much of old Rennes remains thanks to a fire in 1720 but the city still retains a certain charm. The Museum of Brittany is worth a visit.

Treguier: A fine medieval city which overlooks the wide estuary of the Jaudy and Guindy rivers. Worth a visit for its fine Medieval cathedral.

Vannes: At the heart of the city centre lies an attractive old town with some fine half-timbered houses and a 14th-century market hall. Nearby is the beautiful Gulf of Morbihan which can be visited by boat from Vannes.

DORDOGNE

In the past 10 years, the Dordogne has become the holiday destination *par excellence* for the new Volvo-driving middle-classes. The rise of the gîte holiday and a growing interest in the small, charming French country house hotel has brought hundreds of thousands of British travellers to this strip of rural France. (And it seems that several thousand of them were so pleased with what they found, they ended up buying a house and living here permanently.)

Unlike travellers to the Spanish costas, visitors to the Dordogne do not come in search of a sun-tan and cheap booze. They are here for the scenery, the flora and fauna, the food and wine, the canoeing, the walking and the history – or in the case of the Dordogne – the prehistory.

The Dordogne maintains a careful audit of it attractions. Its promotional literature enumerates the properties: seven abbeys and 32 châteaux. But its major asset is undoubtedly prehistory: nine prehistoric settlements, two troglodyte villages, 12 caves and shelters with prehistoric paintings and four 'show' caves. The Dordogne has built a major tourist industry based largely on these prehistoric sites.

Since 1980 the number of hotels in the Dordogne has almost doubled from 142 to over 230 – campsite capacity has increased by around the same amount from 22,000 places in 1980 to around 40,000 today. There has been an equivalent growth in the number of self-catering properties available.

In an economy once dominated by agriculture, tourism is playing an increasingly important role. In the Dordogne tourism accounts for over a fifth of all commercial revenue. In this one relatively small region within Aquitaine (the Dordogne region covers an area roughly within a 40-mile radius of Périgueux), tourism directly employs over 5,000 people in the high season. There are no definite figures, however the best estimate is that the Dordogne now receives over a million tourists a year. Foreign visitors to the Dordogne account for around 40% of all hotel guests – and 31% of campers. Of hotel guests, the British are the biggest single overseas market making up almost half of the total. (The Dutch however monopolise the campsites, accounting for 50% of all campers – some achievement for a nation with a population just a quarter of Britain's.)

But while at peak periods tourists certainly arrive in large numbers, there is little evidence in the Dordogne of the sort of massive swamping which characterises British honey-pot tourist places like the Lake District. Unlike England's Lake District which is a main holiday destination for the domestic holidaying British, the Dordogne attracts relatively few French (the French have more closely defined sun and sand requirements for a summer holiday). The coach party day-out culture barely exists in France – and what there is seems to bear no resemblance to the Lake District style of cheap and cheerful charabanc trippery.

However the tourist authorities in the Dordogne deserve some credit for their efforts in managing tourism. The centrepiece for their tourism management – just as it is the centrepiece and symbol of the entire Dordogne tourist business – are the Lascaux caves.

Bergerac: A pleasant town with half-timbered houses and a fine market. Long-nosed Cyrano is immortalised with a statue.
Beynac: Magnificent medieval fortress, one of the star attractions of the region.
Brantôme: Attractive town on the river Dronne: a good base for touring the area.
Domme: Fine old hilltop village high above the river Dordogne offering towering views of the surrounding countryside.
Les Eyzies: 'The capital of prehistory' is a pleasant town often overrun by coach parties. Famous nearby caves include: Font de Gaume, Courbelles, Abri du Cap Blanc, Grand Roc and Rouffignac.
Lascaux: Situated near the town of Montignac are the most celebrated caves. The original caves are now closed to the public, but a visit to Lascaux II – which faithfully reproduces the extraordinary cave paintings – is a fascinating experience.
Périgueux: The old centre of the city has cobbled streets, good shops and plenty of alluring restaurants.
Rocamadour: This dramatically situated village has been a place of pilgrimage since the 12th century. Nearby are the popular Padirac caves which are visited by boat.
Sarlat: The tourist capital of the Dordogne, a busy market, plenty of shops and several newsagents selling English newspapers.

THE LOIRE VALLEY

At 620 miles, the Loire is France's longest river. However the part known to tourists as the Loire Valley begins where the river turns south-west at Orléans as it embarks on its final sweep towards the Atlantic. The most attractive stretch of the valley can be found between the ancient cities of Blois and Angers: the most picturesque section starts west of Tours at Chinon.
But beautiful castles seem to lie almost everywhere: Chambord, Chenonceau, Azay-le-Rideau, Amboise and dozens of others. But even if there were no castles here, the Loire Valley would still attract tourists for its charming landscape and its mild year-round climate.
While the Valley is good-looking, it has to be said that the river Loire itself is less impressive. With the building of the railways at the turn of the century, the river was allowed to silt up. Its princi-

pal use these days is to cool the nuclear power stations which can be found along its length.

Connecting with the Loire Valley are the alluring paths of other rivers such as the Cher, the Indre which flows through avenues of willows and poplars, the Vienne and the Loir (without an 'e').

Amboise: Visited for its château and the Clos Luce, a 15th-century manor house where Leonardo da Vinci, under the patronage of François I, spent the last three years of his life (Leonardo is buried in the chapel). The Clos Luce is full of models of Leonardo's inventions and reproductions of his prints.

Angers: A fascinating town with a fine castle and several good museums. The castle has the famous Apocalypse Tapestry based on the Apocalypse of St John. The old city around the cathedral has some attractive old houses with wooden shutters and amusingly-carved façades.

Blois: Beneath the high buttressed walls of the château, there are some fine old timbered buildings and a good collection of shops.

Chambord: The biggest and most ostentatious of the Loire châteaux, it has 440 rooms, nearly all of which are devoid of furniture.

Chaumont: Attractive small château in a large expanse of park land.

Chinon: Little remains of the castle where Joan of Arc confronted Charles VII. The riverside town with its cobbled alleys and the timber-framed houses is delightful. Five miles from Chinon is the Château of Ussé which is said to have inspired Charles Perrault's story of *Sleeping Beauty*.

Loches: Handsomely preserved medieval city with a small château and a remarkable Romanesque church.

Saumur: Famous for its wine and mushrooms.

Tours: Old Tours is worth a look for its huge cathedral and its network of narrow streets and attractive squares.

NORMANDY

Despite the fact that Normandy has more Channel ferry ports than any French region (Dieppe, Le Havre, Caën and Cherbourg), it is less visited than it ought to be. Perhaps it is because people always tend to dash through as fast as possible to their proper holiday destination further south.

This is a pity because Normandy is a perfect place for a holiday. It has among the best beaches in the whole of France, superb resorts like Deauville and outrageously picturesque fishing villages like Honfleur. If it is hills you want, Normandy even has its own exquisite hilly region: 'La Suisse Normande'. There are fields filled with apple trees, there is the *bocage* country with its distinctive high hedgerows, there are quaint fishing ports like Honfleur, medieval town centres like Rouen and a seemingly limitless supply of fine country towns.

Bayeux: Charming Norman town, spared serious damage during the last war, famous for its magnificent tapestry. Aside from the tapestry, will worth a visit, Bayeux has a lovely cathedral, some nicely-preserved streets and plenty of fine old houses.

Cabourg: Famous for its Grand Hotel where Marcel Proust stayed. Proust incorporated the hotel and Cabourg (renamed Balbec) into *À la Recherche du Temps Perdu*. The main attraction here is the magnificent coastline.

Caudebec-en-Caux: Delightful small market town on the right bank of the Seine.

Deauville: Still fashionable resort, now visited as much for its elegant racecourse as for its fine beach with its famous wooden walkway, Les Planches.

Étretat: Spectacular cliff-top walks and fine sea-views make this small resort well worth a visit.

Fécamp: Worth a visit if only for the free glass of Benedictine after a guided tour of the famous distillery.

Honfleur: The most picturesque of Normandy's seaside places: very touristy but generally not too tacky. Plenty of hotels at reasonable prices and no shortage of well-priced restaurants.

Lisieux: Worth visiting not so much for itself but for the splendid surrounding countryside – particularly the cheese towns of Pont-l'Evêque to the north, Livarot and Camembert to the south.

Le Mont St Michel: This extraordinary island with a fantastic steepled abbey at its pinnacle has justly been described as 'The Wonder of the Western World'. It is certainly the most visited tourist attraction outside Paris.

Rouen: Its wholly unprepossessing suburbs surround a delightful old town, at its heart lies a splendid Gothic cathedral. This is the perfect place for a casual stroll.

Trouville: A splendid, old port which is immediately next door to Deauville: not as chic as Deauville but an agreeable resort nevertheless.

PROVENCE AND THE CÔTE d'AZUR

Peter Mayle's best-selling books on his life in Provence will no doubt fuel a fresh boom in holidays to a region that has been a long-standing favourite with the British. The Côte d'Azur (the coast east of Marseille, reaching to the Italian border) was first colonised by the British as long ago as the late 18th century. But its real hey-day began in the Twenties when the smart set embraced the idea of summer holidays and sun-tans.

Today, the main coastal strip from Menton through Monte Carlo, Nice, Cannes and down to St-Tropez has become a highly-developed strip of shopping centres, apartment blocks and seaside property developments – fringed by an ever-buzzing motorway. But there are still calmer seaside places to be discovered along this busy coast.

For real peace and quiet, however, you will need to venture inland. Many of the famous hilltop villages of Provence have become highly sophisticated tourist traps but it isn't hard to wander off the beaten track and find a genuine Proven-çal village.

For those keen to escape the madding throng, the region to the west of Marseilles offers more favourable territory. Here, for example, you will discover the Camargue with its famous white horses and its ubiquitous flamingos. Inland lies the Gorges du Tarn and the marvellous Cévennes, which Robert Louis Stevenson explored in *Travels with a Donkey*.

Aigues-Mortes: Attractively-preserved medieval town complete with ramparts standing among the lagoons and marshes of the Camargue.

Aix-en-Provence: Handsome provincial city with elegant boule-vards, aristocratic mansions and bustling street cafés.

Antibes: One of the few towns in the area to preserve its identity in the face of the tourist invasion. Picasso lived and worked here: the Grimaldi museum has a good collection of his paintings.

Arles: Van Gogh spent his final years here producing some of his most famous paintings (but not one of them can be seen in the town). However it's a pleasant town with streets and squares tailor-made for strolling.

Avignon: *Sur le pont d'Avignon . . .* – not much sign of anyone dancing there these days but lots of other signs of a lively, attrac-tive city.

Cannes: Famous for its annual film festival, Cannes is a chic, elegant seaside resort with a handsome promenade (*La Croisette*) and a bevy of pricey hotels.

Grasse: The centre of the French perfume industry.

Juan-les-Pins: Busy, lively seaside resort discovered by the *beau monde* of the Twenties.

Marseille: Tourism isn't the main business of this city but worth a visit if only a boat trip to Château d'If, the prison island whence

Dumas' hero the Count of Monte Cristo was incarcerated. The countryside surrounding nearby Aubagne provided the setting for *Jean de Florette*.

Monte Carlo: Don't bet on breaking the bank, but the casino is worth a visit to catch a whiff of the high life which has made the Principality an enduring favourite. Gazing at the million pound yachts provides many hours' happy diversion – the Jacque Cousteau Oceanographic Museum is also worth a look.

Nice: Long a favourite with the British (who have the famous Promenade des Anglais named in their honour), Nice is an attractive, lively city with a fine old town with good shops and excellent restaurants.

Nîmes: An old Roman town which has a fascinating collection of Roman remains. A short drive away is the famous Pont du Gard aqueduct built by the Romans 2,000 years ago to supply water to Nîmes.

St-Tropez: Led by Brigitte Bardot, the jet set arrived in strength during the Fifties and Sixties. The smart set are still drawn by its relaxed style.

OTHER PLACES WORTH CONSIDERING

The Alps: No longer just a winter destination for skiers, the dramatic mountain scenery also offers perfect country for a variety of summer activities from mountain biking and parapenting to more relaxed walking.

Alsace-Lorraine: Strasbourg, home of the European Parliament, is the main town of a region which betrays a multitude of European influences, predominantly from neighbouring Germany.

Ardennes: East of Paris the countryside blends with the Eifel mountains of Germany and the green hills of Belgium. Nearby lies Champagne famous for its sparkling wine.

Auvergne: A place well known for its songs but now increasingly being discovered by tourists who enjoy its spectacular volcanic scenery of lakes and valleys. Its best known town is the spa resort of Vichy.

Berry and Limousin: The countryside around the old cities of Bourges and Limoges are two of the areas least visited by British tourists. They are perfect places for away-from-it-all holidays in beautiful rural surroundings.

Burgundy: Famous for its dukes and its wine, the region around Dijon is another place unjustifiably neglected by British tourists. Perfect countryside, magnificent wine and plenty of small charming hotels. The Burgundy Canal is one of the prettiest in France.

Corsica: The Corsicans would not appreciate being listed simply as a region of France. The 'Island of Beauty', as it was called by the Greeks, is in many ways a perfect holiday destination – a rugged interior marvellous for walking and gentle touring, and plenty of relaxed seaside resorts.

Île de France: The region around Paris has plenty of attractions in its own right. From the magnificent cathedral of Chartres to the châteaux and parks of Versailles and Chantilly there is plenty to keep a visitor occupied for weeks.

Jura: This region, also known as Franche-Comté, is a place of wild mountains, forests of black spruce, lakes and swift-flowing rivers. The highest region, near Geneva, is good for cross-country skiing in winter and for walks, pony trekking and water sports in summer.

Languedoc-Roussillon: The coast from Montpellier down to Perpignan on the Spanish border has suffered from recent over-development. But there are plenty of good resorts and pleasant holiday developments. Various towns just inland provide cultural diversions from the coast.

The North: The regions of Flanders, Artois and Picardy are usually rushed through en route to other holiday places further south. For those prepared to explore, however, there is plenty of attractive countryside, dozens of picturesque historic towns and cities – and on the coast there are many pleasant resorts like Le Touquet.

Pyrénées: Running 250 miles across south-western France from the Atlantic Basque country to the Catalan province of Roussillon on the Mediterranean, there are plenty of spectacular valleys offering good walking and great biking.

Rhône Valley: The fine city of Lyons offers a good base for exploring this fascinating region which includes historic towns like Vienne, Valence and St Etienne.

8

48 HOURS IN PARIS (AND A DAY IN EURO DISNEY!)

PARIS: A CAPITAL IDEA

There have probably been more romantic songs written about Paris than any other city on earth. 'The last time I saw Paris, her heart was warm and gay, I heard the laughter of her heart in every street café,' wrote lyricist Oscar Hammerstein II. And then what about: 'April in Paris', 'I love Paris in the springtime' or 'Under the bridges of Paris'? The list just seems to go on and on.

For previous generations, Paris was largely an unattainable romantic dream: a fabled city for lovers with pavement cafés, accordionists, boat rides down the Seine. Geographically it may never have been far away, but until relatively recently a weekend in Paris was way beyond the means of most British people.

In the past 10 years however the city has become a place which attracts more British package holiday-makers than traditional summer-holiday favourites such as Torremolinos and Benidorm. It is not hard to explain its success: apart from its undeniable romantic atmosphere, there is so much to see and do in Paris. *The Michelin Green Guide to Paris*, for example, awards rare three-star status to more than a dozen attractions. In a two-day stay therefore, unless you are prepared to dash around like Linford Christie there is not even enough time to see all the best sights – let alone the wealth of Michelin two- and one-star attractions.

The first-time visitors will probably want to go up the Eiffel Tower, take a look at the Mona Lisa in the Louvre, visit the cathedral of Notre-Dame, study the magnificent array of paintings in the Musée d'Orsay, see the pavement artists in the Place du Tertre in Montmartre, wander up the Champs-Elysées to the Arc de Triomphe, shop for bargains in the flea-market at Porte de Clignancourt and window shop the expensive fashion collections in the smart boutiques along the Rue du Faubourg St-Honoré.

But no-one should feel that all or any of the sights are compulsory. Don't fall victim to the belief that has grown up that you haven't 'seen' a city like Paris unless you've done the sights; if you come back from Paris and people ask you what you thought of the Louvre or the Sacre-Coeur, you're likely to be considered eccentric if you confess you didn't bother to go.

Which is a pity. Because there is much more to Paris – and most other places – than the sum total of the supposed attractions. It's enough simply to stroll along the boulevards of Paris taking in the richness of the buildings and the style of the shops. Visiting Paris and the rest of France, it's forcibly brought home just how bland the high streets of Britain have become: each with its own identikit shopping centres of chain stores. In France chain shops still seem to be in a minority. The food shops each have their own identity and are richly stocked with attractive arrays of goods in a way which one remembers British shops used to look in the far off days before supermarkets.

The least attractive aspect of Paris, it has to be said, are usually the Parisians who have their own line in spectacular abruptness and rudeness. But then Paris wouldn't be Paris without them – which is why it's probably not a good idea to visit the city in August, when many Parisians are on holiday and the city seems lifeless despite the many tourists. Spring, early summer and autumn are the best times to go.

If you are travelling to the south, you will inevitably be tempted to break your journey in Paris either on the way out or on the return journey. It makes good sense, as you can then almost enjoy two holidays for the price of one. If you have children learning French, a trip to Paris can add immeasurably to their understanding of France and its culture.

Two Days in Paris

To get the most out of a short-break in Paris, it pays to plan your time carefully. Below is a sort of sample guide to filling a weekend to show you how it could be done. After spending some time with the guidebooks (*The Michelin Green Guide to Paris* is the most useful) you might have other ideas. Don't try and overload your itinerary – remember the aim is to enjoy yourself!

Day One
Start with the Louvre: arriving early to beat the crowds. The Louvre opens its doors, or more accurately the panes of its pyramid, at 9am. Start here, marvelling at I M Pei's crystal addition to the world's largest palace. You proceed down into a subterranean space, the Hall Napoleon. Passages lead from it to the Louvre's fabulous collection of 300,000 works of art. If time is short, go for just two: the Mona Lisa and the Venus de Milo. Anyone who has

a credit card (for the automatic ticket machines) and is reasonably fit, can get in, see both and be out again in 15 minutes.

Palaces are thick on the ground in this part of Paris. The Palais Royal is occupied by civil servants; until five years ago they parked their cars in the courtyard. Today the quadrangle is filled with stripy bollards, known as the Colonnes de Burennes.
Between this mysterious former parking lot and Châtelet station you pass the Louvre des Antiquaires, a vast collection of antique shops. But save your shopping for later, and instead take the suburban RER railway to La Défense. After the 10-minute ride, follow the signs for exit E, and you emerge beneath the awesome Grande Arche. This monstrous, glittering cube is casually skewed at the end of the Grand Boulevard from the Louvre. The Arch of Fraternity takes the breath away. It is not so much the size as the sheer nerve of using a hollow white marble cube, each side measuring 380 feet, to punctuate a beautiful and historic prospect.

A glass elevator whisks you from the pavement to the proscenium, from where the whole glorious ensemble is on show. In the foreground is the crazy paving and crazed buildings of the new La Défense complex, intended as a world model for urban regeneration.

Before leaving the area, pause at the continent's largest shopping complex. Among the uninspiring Euro-shops is the extraordinary Fnac store: a big, bold bookshop that has branched out into something approaching total lifestyle support. It stages photographic exhibitions, arranges lectures and sells tickets for concerts. It also has a massive music collection.

With your image and intellect replenished, board a train at La Défense for the 20-minute ride to Versailles Rive Droite. When Louis XIV moved the French court to his new palace in Versailles, he set a fashion for grandness. The town itself is reserved rather than grand, and is certainly distinct from Paris: cars even stop for pedestrians.

Follow the tour buses to the château. With no time to spend dawdling, make straight for the Hall of Mirrors on the first floor. The most impressive of the sumptuous apartments, this is where the treaty concluding the First World War was signed. From a window, marvel at the gardens stretching out before you.

Bear right out of the gates along the Avenue de Sceaux, and head for the stylish station of Versailles Rive Gauche. Trains from here follow the historic route to the Quai d'Orsay, formerly terminus for points south and west. Today you can no longer get an away-day to Orléans at the gare, but you can enjoy the best museum in Paris.

The façade has been aggressively conserved, while the innards have been removed and replaced by works of art. The elegant design of the station architect, Victor Laloux, allows natural light to flood in, enhancing the greatest hits of Cézanne and Degas, Monet and Van Gogh. Artistically and chronologically, the Orsay bridges the gap between the Louvre and the Museum of Modern Art at the Pompidou Centre. Before inspecting the Impressionists, you may be ready for lunch. The restaurant at the Orsay offers a well-prepared meal, served in beautiful surroundings. It opens even when the museum is closed, which indicates its popularity.

Away from such oases, finding a good lunch can be a problem if time is short. McDonald's and Burger King are current favourites among Parisians, a trend which you can rebel against by buying local food. In any case, the sensible visitor should invest in food and drink to take home. The best street to shop in is Rue Cler. It is lined with beguiling stores, selling chocolate or cheese or charcuterie, in a manner designed to make you buy three times more than you need.

Stagger down to the Métro again, back across the river to the Place de la Concorde. People used to be guillotined in this huge square and it is still murderous for pedestrians, a random scattering of six-lane highways.

For yet more groceries, the French equivalent of Fortnum & Mason is on the Place de la Madeleine and stays open until 10pm. At Fauchon, a kilo of goose pâté with truffles costs £250. The city's best and most expensive restaurants are also nearby, including the Lucas Carton at number 9, opened in 1862. Maxim's is close by on the Rue Royale, but few visitors are willing to spend more on a meal than on their flight from home.

In the Latin Quarter, the medieval heart of Paris, you can eat well for a modest amount, but in the sea of Greek, Moroccan and Vietnamese it is difficult to find anywhere French.

Day Two

Next morning take an early Métro to Gambetta, and walk along Avenue de Père-Lachaise to the cemetery. The graveyard gates bear the advice 'Jim – follow the signs', a reference to Jim Morrison, lead singer of The Doors. Instead, turn left down the hill. The most moving monuments are those to the victims of Nazi concentration camps, notably the sculpture depicting the suffering of those who died at Buchenwald. At the end of the slope is the federalists' wall, against which the members of the Paris Commune were lined up and shot in 1871. They were buried where they fell. Maps in the cemetery indicate the graves of the famous, such as Chopin and Balzac. Only Edith Piaf's is hard to find: it is on Avenue Transversale No 3 and is marked with her real name, Madame Lamboukas.

Emerging on the west side of the cemetery, take the Métro at Père-Lachaise and go north five stops to Jaures. A pleasant, water-side stroll can be made along the St Martin canal, which has a weird and wonderful series of locks and swing bridges. At the southern end it dives underground; do the same by turning right for République Métro station. Take line 8 to Bastille, where you should follow the signs for line 1, which pops up for air at this point.

As well as fine murals, the platform has a view on to the ungainly Opera Bastille. Follow the signs for Rue St Antoine, and continue along it when you emerge at street level. A right turn at Rue Birague takes you into the majestic Place des Vosges, the city's first square and still the least spoilt. It is the centre of the Marais district, once a patch of marsh which became the most desirable location in Paris for the 17th century bourgeoisie. The top-left corner of the square leads, appropriately, to Rue des Francs Bour-geois, an atmospheric street too aloof to become touristy. Stop at the Marais Plus, a bookshop and salon de thé.

Turn right here past imposing dwellings and comfortable gardens to the Picasso Museum. One of the most recent additions to the city's cultural wealth, it is located in the old Hôtel Sale. An intelligent sequence of exhibits traces Picasso's life and work, from the Blue Period self-portrait to snaps of the artist in Juan-les-Pins.

Meander back to Rue des Francs Bourgeois. At the corner of Rue Vielle du Temple is Arcadi, one of the world's best postcard shops. Rue des Francs Bourgeois runs into Rue Rambûteau, lined with pâtisseries, épiceries and cafés. Its best feature is at the west-ern end: turn a corner and the backside of the Pompidou Centre, with its associated plumbing and air-conditioning, stares back at you. The Centre is visited by 20,000 people each day, but unless you have made up a great deal of time you will have no chance to visit this house of culture, whose greatest attraction is the National Museum of Modern Art. The exterior, though, is worth-while, with musicians, jugglers and mime artists competing for audiences on the piazza. The Centre faces Les Halles, formerly a sprawling market but now a shabby hole in the ground lined with ephemeral shops.

Take the Métro to a loftier place, Lamarck-Caulaincourt, where you emerge several hundred feet above the rest of Paris. To the left is a set of steps and a sign to the Vigne de Montmartre, an odd square of vineyard on the hillside. A little further on is the highest street in Paris, the narrow Rue St Rustique. Halfway along is a modest, pleasant unnamed restaurant, in contrast to the tourist traps elsewhere in Montmartre.

At the Place du Tertre you stumble upon a pastiche of the original artists' quarter, occupied by unknown painters in striped jumpers and berets. More genuine is the splendid view of the capital from the Sacre-Coeur basilica. It is best enjoyed after a few minutes spent in the austere interior of the church, from where you emerge, blinking, to the sight of Paris laid out before you. Scramble down the steps of the Rue Foyatier.

This part of the capital is downhill and downmarket. You can enjoy a funfair along the middle of the Boulevard de Rochechou-art, and buy hot chestnuts and haute-couture at cut prices. Unfortunately, the essentially charming neighbourhood of Pigalle is blighted by sex shops. Serious shoppers will be relieved to learn that Au Printemps and Galeries Lafayette are not far away, jostling each other on Boulevard Haussmann.

The day's second encounter with the dead is more chilling than a misty morning in the cemetery. Take the Métro to Denfert-Rochereau, follow the signs to the Place of the same name, cross the road and descend into the catacombs, a network of caverns under the city. After a 10-minute hike through narrowing tunnels, you reach a sign saying 'Arrete! C'est ici l'Empire de la Mort'. Two hundred years ago the city authorities became alarmed at the squalor of the cemeteries, and chose to move the remains of the dead to a labyrinthine disused quarry. Six million skeletons were moved in and arranged neatly in stacks. Visitors are free to walk through this macabre tunnel of death, which is scattered with Biblical bons mots: 'God is not the author of death' and 'The spur of death is sin'. Do not go alone.

The tunnel surfaces in a quiet surburban street. At 34 Rue Rémy Dumoncel, a guard checks your bag (apparently stealing bones is popular). Turn right along to the Avenue du General Leclerc, then left to Alesia Métro station.

Take a train five stops to Montparnasse. Here, residents have been driven out by construction work, notably the Tour Montpar-nasse, which at 700 feet was Europe's tallest building until it lost the title to London's Canary Wharf. The fee it costs to reach the top is money well spent: everything the city has is on show.

Descending one final time to ground level, board Métro line 6 in the direction of Etoile. At Passy, just across the river, disembark and take the footpath back. Halfway across you reach the Isle of Swans, in the middle of the Seine. At the far end is a modest Statue of Liberty, given by the USA in return for the original French gift to New York.

Those who are truly serious about packing as much as possible in should make a final stop on the way to the airport. Bus 350 takes you from the Gare de l'Est to Le Bourget and the Air and Space Museum, looking just like an airport terminal: indeed it was, an art deco gem with far more charm than that which replaced it. Exhibits include the world's first hang-glider, early aeronautical structures like Clement Ader's Avion no. 3, built in 1897, and the cramped-looking first Concorde.

Top Ten Must-see Sights in Paris

1. Eiffel Tower
Built for the Paris World Fair in 1889 (celebrating the centenary of the French Republic). This is the symbol of the city: whether you enjoy the view depends on the weather and your head for heights. In high summer you might not feel like standing in the endless queues. To get to the top will cost £6.

2. Louvre
At least see the famous glass Pyramid, if you don't take in the Mona Lisa and the Venus de Milo. Admission £4.

3. Notre-Dame
No sign these days of the hunchback Quasimodo, but still worth a visit. Its exterior, best seen from the Place du Parvis is as sensational as the stunning interior.

4. Champs-Elysées and the Arc de Triomphe
A walk down the wide boulevards of the Champs-Elysées, past the pavement cafés and cinemas, is one of the great free treats of Paris.

5. Montmartre and Sacre-Coeur
It may have been colonised by souvenir shops and other purveyors of tourist tack, but there is still enough of the old Montmartre to remind the visitor why it attracted a generation of poets and artists.

6. Orsay museum
Probably the finest collection of paintings in the world. The array of Impressionist and Post-Impressionist paintings on the top floor is simply breathtaking.

7. The Palace of Versailles
One of the most magnificent royal palaces anywhere in the world. Take the tour of the palace if you have the time – if not, simply stroll around the superb gardens.

8. Faubourg St Honoré
Part of the pleasure of Paris is exploring its elegant streets – and they don't come any more elegant than the Rue de Faubourg Saint Honoré. Here you will find the Elysée Palace, the home of the French President, as well as a host of famous designer shops.

9. The Pompidou Centre
The famous Paris building that wears its innards on the outside. You can simply enjoy an outside view – if you have the time you can browse its unrivalled collection of modern art.

10. Cité des Sciences, La Villette
The science-related exhibits are so compelling (a highly realistic flight simulator, for example) that children will be thoroughly absorbed all day. The science museum – rated by many as the best in Europe – has opened a new Children's Science Village (La Cité des Enfants). The interactive exhibition centre is designed for children aged from three to twelve and among other things shows them how to produce their own TV news programme allowing them to operate the TV camera or read the news. Instructions for the exhibits are printed in English as well as French.

Getting Around
The Métro is the most sensible way to travel in Paris. Buy a carnet of 10 tickets and save 40% on the price of individual journeys. Call 43 46 14 14 for information in French on the Métro, RER and bus network. Unlimited travel passes are sold for one, three or five days.

The RER is a faster version of the Métro, useful for zipping across town. Unfortunately the system is extremely complex. Finding the right platform and a train going in the right direction can be a nightmare; one pair of platforms at Châtelet station has trains to Boissy, Poissy and Roissy, each in a different direction.

Buses run 7am–8.30pm but often get snarled up in traffic. A skeleton night bus service runs from 1.30–5.30am on 10 routes from Châtelet.

Packages: See City Breaks listing on page 115.
Accommodation: The French tourist office publishes a list (in French) of more than 1,400 hotels, classified according to arrondissement.
Museums: Most close on Monday or Tuesday. The standard charge is 30 Francs for adults, with reduced prices for students, people under 25 or over 60 years, and for everyone on Sundays. The Museums Pass costs £5.50 for one day, £11 for three days or £16 for five days, and allows free entrance to most of the museums listed here plus many more. It can be bought from Métro stations or museums.

A DAY IN EURO DISNEY

When it comes to theme parks, Disney operates in a league of its own. Euro Disney is not a theme park, it must be counted as one of the Seven Wonders of the modern world. If you had to make a comparison, the only thing in Europe that comes close to Euro Disney in the hugeness of its scale and the lavishness of its execution is to be found 30 miles away on the other side of Paris – the palace and gardens of Versailles.

It took more than 30,000 workmen to build Versailles for Louis XIV and cost 60m *livres* – a phenomenal sum which practically bankrupted France. Euro Disney has not bankrupted France, though it has drained the public coffers by more than £500m in loan guarantees and investment in rail and motorway connections to the park – but like Versailles Euro Disney is a work on a truly colossal scale.

The statistics of the construction work boggle the mind: it used over 10,000 tons of cement, 132,000 gallons of paint, 2.4m cubic feet of hardcore, 'Main Street, USA' is paved with half a million red bricks, to create the site involved moving 120m cubic feet of earth.

It conjures up the images of Coleridge's poem *Kubla Khan: In Xanadu did Kubla Khan, a stately pleasure-dome decree* . . .

> *'So twice five miles of fertile ground,*
> *With walls and towers was girdled round:*
> *And there were gardens bright with sinuous rills,*
> *Where blossomed many an incense-bearing tree;*
> *And here were forests ancient as the hills,*
> *Enfolding sunny spots of greenery . . .'*

If Coleridge had travelled on 'Pirates of the Caribbean', he would probably have recognised it as an opium-generated hallucination. The Euro Disney version of 'Pirates' is better even than the two American Disney parks: a fast-paced boat trip through a Caribbean port besieged by buccaneers. The main set piece is a man of war full of audio-animatronic pirates broadsiding the harbour fort – the spectacle is breathtaking. A Frenchman sitting behind me was transfixed: '*C'est incroyable!*' he gasped. And it is incredible – the whole of Euro Disney is almost too fantastic to be true.

Look at the resort's hotels. Most people faced with the task of providing 5,000 hotel rooms would probably have been happy to get by with a few bland low-cost tower blocks. Not Disney: pursuing its Medici-like policy of sponsoring the finest artists, the company commissioned architects of the stature of Michael Graves and Robert Stern to design six distinctive hotels each reflecting a different American region and each done with delicious Disney overstatement.

Graves' skyscraper pastiche 575-room Hotel New York, complete with Art Deco-inspired rooms, faces Stern's grandiose 1,008-room Newport Bay Club hotel across a large man-made lake. Just walking around all six hotels to inspect the rooms takes you on a two-mile trek – these are big hotels in a very big setting. And they are more than hotels: they are elaborate film sets. The 1,000-room Hotel Cheyenne, for example, is a complete Wild West town, with rooms to be found in the town's various shops and offices. The 1,000-room Hotel Sante Fé has reproduction desert landscape, a crashed flying saucer and a mocked up drive-in cinema. Almost any one of these hotels on their own would be an extraordinary achievement – to produce six of them is astonishing. *C'est incroyable!*

The theme park itself is in most respects a copycat reproduction of Disney World's Magic Kingdom with a small number of modifications. Conscious of the accusations of American cultural imperialism, Euro Disney has taken account of French and European sensibilities with nods to Jules Verne, *Alice in Wonderland* and *Pinocchio*.

The best rides and attractions, however, are the familiar favourites from America: Pirates of the Caribbean, Phantom Manor (a retitled Haunted Mansion) and Big Thunder Mountain Railroad. All three are superior to the American originals. Pirates benefits from a rearrangement of its set pieces and a more thrilling boat ride; Phantom Manor tries to tell something of a story rather than just being an incoherent collection of spooky effects; Big Thunder is faster, more terrifying and much more scenic than the American varieties.

Other American favourites also certain to be popular in Euro Disney are Star Tours, a disturbingly real simulated space ride into the middle of a *Star Wars* battle, and *Captain EO*: a 3D *Star Wars*-style film starring Michael Jackson as the universe's least likely space warrior. (For those weary of a three-dimensional Jacko, Disney boss Michael Eisner has promised that a new 3D film is due to be made based on *Honey I Shrunk the Kids*).

For the £25 admission fee (£15 for children three to eleven), there is much more than 16 main rides and attractions: there are six table-service restaurants, 12 counter-service restaurants: 10 places offering light refreshments as well as food carts serving up ice cream, pop corn, stir-fry and sausages. There are also 30 shops in the park selling everything from Mickey Mouse hats for a couple of pounds to cut-glass crystal vases costing over £2,000.

Near to the main park entrance is Festival Disney with even more shops and restaurants as well as Buffalo Bill's Wild West Show, where for £30 you get a free cowboy hat, a 'chuck waggon supper', a 'rompin' stompin' Wild West spectacular' and the chance to shout 'Yiharrr!!' rather a lot.

The whole of Euro Disney is indeed *incroyable* from its huge 11,000-space car park – linked to the park by moving walkways – to the 13 scrupulously-clean toilet blocks throughout the park. And there are not just the rides and the restaurants, there are the Disney workers: over 14,000 of them – people tirelessly picking up the rubbish, pointing people to the ticket booths, dressed in Captain Hook costume, selling sticks of doughnuts, helping people on and off the rides – with badges showing that they speak English, German, Italian, Portuguese or any of 40 more different languages. This is some stately pleasure dome.

Packages
Euro Disney has negotiated a series of complex deals with tour operators for the right to sell on-site accommodation and the right to use the Disney name and related publicity material. Over 200 other operators offer a wide range of packages, featuring accommodation in towns near Euro Disney and in the centre of Paris. These include:

British Airways Holidays (061 493 3344)
A two-night stay at the Hotel Santa Fé costs from £184 to £247 per person based on four sharing. A two-night stay at the Disneyland Hotel costs from £236 to £339 per person based on four sharing. The price includes accommodation, return flights and guaranteed unlimited entry into Euro Disneyland Theme Park for the duration of your stay.

Kirker Holidays (071 231 3333)
Short breaks to Euro Disney are offered, including guaranteed entrance to the theme park. Prices on request.

Sally Holidays (0732 780440)
Seven nights bed and breakfast accommodation costs from £179 to £301 per person with up to two children free. A Euro Disney pass for a family of four – two adults and two children – for two days costs £192 extra.

Thomson Holidays (021 632 6282)
Two-, three- or four-night packages using scheduled flights from 10 UK airports; also self-drive holidays and inclusive packages using train, ferry, coach and hovercraft. Accommodation available at Euro Disney or in Paris hotels. Prices for self-drive with two nights at the cheapest Disney hotel costs from £211 per person. All holidays in the Eurofun brochure include a two-day Euro

Disney passport providing unlimited use of the attractions within the theme park.

Travelscene (081 427 4445)
A two-night trip from Heathrow costs from around £269 per person on a bed and breakfast basis, staying in the Hotel Santa Fé. Prices include a pass to Euro Disney appropriate for the length of stay.

Accommodation
Rooms can be booked directly with Euro Disney via a London telephone number: 071 753 2900: rooms cost from £55 (low season at the Cheyenne and Santa Fé) to over £200 per night (high season at the Disneyland) – or self-catering accommodation at the Davy Crockett campground starts at £90 per cabin per night. To get the best out of a visit to Euro Disney, staying at one of the Disney hotels or Camp Davy Crockett is certainly the best option.

Admission
A one-day pass costs £25 for adults, children (between three and eleven) pay £15, under-threes get in free. Once inside the park, apart from food and drink, you do not have to pay for anything. The rides are free, and you can go on them as often as you like (just as long as you are happy to queue).

How and when to visit
Avoid Continental public holidays – get to the entrance as early as you can, by 8.30am at the latest so that you are ready when the rides are opened. Head for the rides that will later be the busiest, particularly Thunder Mountain, Pirates of the Caribbean, Phantom Manor – and, for the smaller children, Dumbo.

Paris's other theme park
Parc Asterix, 60128 Plailly, Paris (44 60 60 00). A 20-hectare park based on the Asterix stories with white-knuckle rides including what it claims is the largest roller-coaster in Europe and a splash ride, as well as many attractions for smaller children.
Opening times: Until 18 October; weekdays 10am to 6pm, weekends 10am to 7pm.
Admission: £15.75; £11 (children three to eleven); under three free.
Getting there: Access from the A1 autoroute, exit at Parc Asterix. Public transport: bus from the RER station at Roissy-Charles de Gaulle (Line B).

9

TOUR OPERATOR FACT FILE

For each operator we show whether it is a member of ABTA (Association of British Travel Agents), has an Air Tour Organizer's Licence (ATOL), or whether it belongs to the Association of Independent Tour Operators (AITO): all of which guarantee that a company is bonded. Under new legislation all companies offering package travel should offer such protection but the law is patchily enforced – it would be wise to check with any operator before booking. For all purchases over £100 made with a credit card (Access or Visa), you are protected under the Consumer Credit Act. If the operator goes bust you can recover your money from the credit card company.

As well as a brief description of each company, the listing shows under which other sections of this book you can find more information about the holidays it offers.

A Golfing Experience
17 Rozel Manor, Western Road, Branksome Park, Poole, Dorset
Admin: 0202 768003
Res: 081 205 7138
Fax: 081 905 9212
AITO
VISA ACCESS
Golfing Experience is an independently-owned specialist company offering tailor-made golf holidays in France. Itineraries are arranged in all areas to suit experienced golfers and novices. 'All levels of hotel or apartment accommodation are offered. Tee times are guaranteed on pre-booked courses. The company has been established three to four years and carries around 500 people annually.'
Special interest holidays: Golfing holidays

AA Motoring Holidays
PO Box 128, Fanum House, Basingstoke, Hants RG21 2EA
Admin: 0256 493878
Res: 0256 493878
ABTA: 65626
VISA ACCESS
Holidays feature self-catering, hotel and skiing packages. Prices include return ferry crossings for car and passengers and AA Five-Star vehicle cover.
Hotel holidays: All over France
Self-catering holidays: All over France
Special interest holidays: Skiing

ACE Study Tours
Babraham, Cambridge CB2 4AP
Admin: 0223 835055
Res: 0223 835055
Fax: 0223 837394

ATOL: 616
The Association for Cultural Exchange, an independent, non-profit making educational charity, trading as ACE Study Tours, has been arranging study tours within Europe since 1958 and worldwide since 1972. 'We cater for approximately 2,200 clients a year taking part in courses varying from day courses on exhibitions to three-week-long study tours overseas, eg to China, India and Latin America. Our main emphasis is on Europe studying themes such as Art and Architecture, Wildlife, Archaeology and History. ACE is special in offering such a wide variety, and at the same time being able to examine in depth each subject or theme by using tour leaders with the right knowledge and personality.' Tours to France are either by coach or in the case of Provence by air. All leaders lecture as well as lead the excursions. Study tours are arranged on a half-board basis. Lunch hours are left for participants to feel free to explore on their own. 'Hotels used are good quality but not with an emphasis on luxury.'
Special interest holidays: Study holidays

Accents Languages and Leisure
BP 17, Artemare, 01510, France
Admin: 010 33 79 87 33 96
Res: 0606 48699
Fax: 0606 48761
AITO
VISA ACCESS AMEX
Accents has been established for eight years and offers French language tuition plus a variety of leisure activities, such as mountain biking, cross-country skiing or museum visiting. 'Our centres are in Artemare in the Jura region and Forcalquier in Provence. Teaching groups have a maximum of about eight people and we carry around 600 people each year.'
Special interest holidays: Language learning

Air France Holidays
Gable House, 18–24 Turnham Green Terrace, London W4 1RF
Admin: 081 742 3441
Res: 081 742 3377
Fax: 081 742 3459
ABTA: 63090
ATOL: 922
VISA ACCESS AMEX
Part of the Air France Group, Air France Holidays has been in business since the early Seventies. 'This year we will carry 25,000 passengers. Our destinations include all regions of France either by air, rail or self-drive. We also have a separate brochure for the French Caribbean, the Indian Ocean and French Polynesia.'
Hotel holidays: All over France
Self-catering holidays: All over France

Airtours
Holcombe Road, Helmshore, Rossendale BB4 4NB
Admin: 0706 240033
Res: 0706 260000
Fax: 0706 212144
ABTA: 47064
ATOL: 1179
VISA ACCESS
Airtours is the UK's third largest tour operator – taking over one million holiday-makers abroad every year. The company, which was set up in 1978, offers a choice of city breaks to Paris.
Special interest holidays: City breaks

Alastair Sawday's Tours
44 Ambra Vale East, Bristol BS8 4RE
Admin: 0272 299921
Res: 0272 299921
Fax: 0272 254712
Founded in 1984, Alastair Sawday's Tours is a small company specialising in group tours throughout Europe. 'Our 1993 programme includes cycling tours in France. We take care to choose the loveliest routes and the most interesting small hotels. Accommodation is en suite and the luggage is carried. We also act as independent barge bookers for luxury barges in France.'
Special interest holidays: Cycling holidays, canal boats

Allegro Holidays
15a Church Street, Reigate RH2 0AA
Admin: 0737 244870
Res: 0737 221323
Fax: 0737 223590
ABTA: 12173
ATOL: 1835
AITO
VISA ACCESS
Allegro Holidays has been specialising in Corsica for 10 years. 'We offer characterful accommodation throughout the island with flights from Gatwick to all four Corsican airports and a new service from Edinburgh to Calvi. We provide self-catering properties, inland inns and the island's finest hotels.'
Hotel holidays: Corsica
Self-catering holidays: Corsica

Allez France Holidays
27–29 West Street, Storrington, West Sussex RH20 4DZ
Admin: 0903 745033
Res: 0903 742345
Fax: 0903 745044
ABTA: A7227
ATOL: 2548
AITO
VISA ACCESS AMEX
Allez France is an independent, family-run company specialising in France. 'We have been established for 12 years and offer a wide range of villas, gîtes, hotels, holiday villages and mobile home holidays. Six in ten bookings are from regular clients or their friends.'
Hotel holidays: All over France
Self-catering holidays: All over France

Alpine Adventures
Top Lodge, Well Lane, Stow-on-the-Wold GL54 1BT
Admin: 0451 832262
Res: 0451 832262
Fax: 0451 870890
A small, independent adventure holiday company specialising in summer and winter holidays for children between the ages of eight and fifteen. 'Children join us in one of our traditionally-built Alpine chalets in Morzine for one or two weeks of closely-supervised activity holidays. We offer skiing weeks in winter with daily lessons, toboganning and ice skating. During the summer, children participate in all of the following fun sports: white water rafting, canoeing, mountain biking, rock climbing and abseiling, tennis, swimming, field games and hiking in the mountains around Morzine. We aim to encourage their use of French by playing word games and French is always spoken at dinner. Our staff ratio is one to eight. All our staff are teachers or other professionals who are experienced in dealing with children. Our maximum group size is 24.'

Special interest holidays: Adventure holidays for children

Aquitaine Holidays
Hill Place, London Road, Southborough, Tunbridge Wells TN4 0PX
Admin: 0892 516500
Res: 0892 516101
Fax: 0892 511606
ABTA: 8933
VISA ACCESS
'In business for over five years, we are now part of a larger company which is involved in short-break hotel holidays in the UK and France, and group travel both incoming and out of the UK. In 1992 we carried 1,000 people and we anticipate 1,600 in 1993. We specialise entirely in Aquitaine in south-west France. The Managing Director lived there for many years and knows it well. We have several resident local representatives who are able to help with any problems that might arise and ensure the holiday-makers' satisfaction.'
Self-catering holidays: Aquitaine

Arblaster & Clarke Wine Tours
104 Church Road, Steep, Petersfield GU32 2DD
Admin: 0730 266883
Res: 0730 266883
Fax: 0730 268620
ATOL: 2543
AITO
Arblaster & Clarke has been offering wine tours for over six years. The firm is independent and family run. 'Over 600 wine lovers a year are escorted to the major wine regions of France: Champagne, Bordeaux, Central Loire, Eastern Loire, Alsace, Burgundy and Rhône. We also go to Portugal, Italy, Spain and California. There is an extremely friendly, informal

atmosphere on the tours which are enjoyed by beginners and connoisseurs alike. The tours are escorted by a knowledgeable but approachable wine guide – often a Master of Wine or a leading specialist in the field. Visits are to well known cellars, picked by our own in-house wine expert and to rising stars. Our clients receive a warm welcome often by the winemaker himself – and we are often invited to stay for lunch and enjoy the wines with the traditional local dishes. Hotels generally have a local flavour too, often being family run.'
New for 1993 are a series of wine courses tutored by Steven Spurrier, the founder of the Academie du Vin, and staying as private guests at Château Lascombes, a top Margaux château (second growth). A self-drive programme – 'Route des Vins' – is also operated to the same French regions, with private appointments made at wineries.
Special interest holidays: Wine tours

Beach Villas
8 Market Passage, Cambridge CB2 3QR
Admin: 0223 311113
Res: 0223 311113
Fax: 0223 313557
ABTA: 1415
ATOL: 2776
AITO
VISA ACCESS
'In the 26 years that we have been involved with villa holidays, we have developed a special relationship with our villa owners and clients alike. Each and every property is chosen for its comfort, location and value for money, ranging from large villas with private pools to smaller studio apart-

161

ments. All the properties featured within our programme are intimately known to us, and our staff have first-hand knowledge of the resorts and properties.'

Self-catering holidays: All over France.

Becks Holidays
Southfields, Ditchling, Hassocks, West Sussex BN6 8UD
Admin: 0273 842843
Res: 0273 842843
Fax: 0273 842849
AITO
VISA ACCESS
Mobile home holidays on campsites in French seaside resorts. 'We handle about 1,500 holiday-makers annually with each client's holiday tailored to their requirements. About 70% of our holiday-makers are repeat bookings or friend's recommendations. At each resort we employ experienced couples who are resident throughout the holiday season who have expert knowledge of France and the local holiday area.'

Special interest holidays: Caravans and mobile homes

Belle France
Bayham Abbey, Lamberhurst TN3 8BG
Admin: 0892 890885
Res: 0892 890885
Fax: 0892 890 180
ABTA: 2231
ATOL: 2832
AITO
VISA ACCESS
Belle France has been trading for 10 years and specialises in walking and cycling holidays to provincial France. The holidays are tours from hotel to hotel or fixed locations for either groups or independent travellers. 'You are sent

highly detailed French Ordnance Survey maps (all included in the price of the holiday) which show all the tracks or lanes you may wish to explore. You also receive copious notes on places of interest, route suggestions or directions and general information about the area. Bags are transported from hotel to hotel for all holidays. Accommodation is in small family-run hotels in villages or small towns. None of the hotels cater just for tourists.'

Special interest holidays: Walking and trekking, cycling holidays

Bespoke Holidays
3 Rochester Road, Tonbridge, Kent TN10 4NU
Admin: 0732 366130
Res: 0732 366130
Fax: 0732 360634
ABTA: 3234
Bespoke Holidays runs active adventure holidays for the over-50s. 'The activity is mainly guided walking at an easy pace befitting our customers, but we also include painting in Gascony, cultural visits and wine tasting.'

Special interest holidays: Walking and trekking, painting and drawing holidays

Bike Tours
PO Box 75, Bath BA1 1BX
Admin: 0225 480130
Res: 0225 480130
Fax: 0225 480132
VISA ACCESS
Bike Tours was established 12 years ago. Destinations this year include Eastern Europe, China, Holland, Italy, Kenya, Turkey, Ireland, Cuba, Denmark, New England and France. Luggage is transported.

Special interest holidays: Cycling holidays

Bike and Sun Tours

42 Whitby Avenue, Guisborough,
Cleveland TS14 7AN
Admin: 0287 638217
Res: 0287 638217
'We are a one-man operation offering specialist motorcycle touring holidays throughout Europe. We are independent and have been in business for 10 years now. Members of the groups may have hotel accommodation or camp or a mixture of these. The tour routes and stopping places are based on my 40 odd years of touring Europe by motorcycle. They are planned ahead each year and regularly developed and improved. Our tour season is from May to October. All tours are for two weeks. I act as a guide for all groups, on my own machine, but very detailed route sheets are issued so that those riders who wish to ride alone or with a friend or two are free to do so. The groups are usually a 50/50 mix of singles and couples on solo machines and ages range from 20s to 70s with peak numbers around 30–50 years. Our routes avoid motorways and large towns in the main and concentrate on exciting scenery and good biking roads. We are currently carrying around 100 people annually.'
Special interest holidays: Motorcycling

Blakes International Travel

Wroxham, Norwich NR12 8DH
Admin: 0603 782141
Res: 0603 784141
Fax: 0603 782871
ABTA: 15966
ATOL: 2407
VISA ACCESS
Blakes International Travel is a wholly owned subsidiary of Blakes Holidays Ltd are well known for boating holidays on the Norfolk Broads and other inland waterways, as well as offering self-catering cottages throughout Britain. Blakes Holidays was established in 1908 and provides holidays for 250,000 people each year in Britain and France. Blakes Holiday Cottages in France offers just over 250 cottages, gîtes, farmhouses and villas in all the popular areas of France. Blakes also offers a wide selection of boating holidays on the canals and rivers of France in all the main cruising areas from Brittany to Alsace, Burgundy to the Camargue, and the Canal du Midi.
Self-catering holidays: Normandy, Brittany, Vendée, Dordogne, Auvergne, Provence
Special interest holidays: Canal boats

Bonnes Vacances

10 Hill Street, Richmond, Surrey TW9 1UR
Admin: 081 948 3467
Res: 081 948 3467
Fax: 081 332 1268
VISA ACCESS
Bonnes Vacances has been in business for nearly five years, working as a French travel service and agency for UK-owned property in France. 'In 1993 we are offering all types of accommodation from mobile homes, gîtes and farmhouses to manor houses, luxury apartments, villas and châteaux in all areas of France.'
Hotel holidays: All over France
Self-catering holidays: All over France

Borderline

Les Sorbiers, 65120 Barèges, Hautes Pyrénées, FRANCE
Admin: 010 33 62 92 68 95
Res: 0963 250117 brochures

Fax: 010 33 62 92 66 93
VISA ACCESS
Borderline has been trading for six years and carries up to 600 people annually. 'We offer walking, trekking, mountain biking, birdwatching and Alpine flower holidays during the summer and skiing in the winter. We are based in the spa village of Barèges in the Haute Pyrénées. We work only with qualified local guides but provide maps, bird and flower lists for clients who wish to explore on their own. During the winter we work with a local ski school. We also offer ski touring in the National Park.
Hotel holidays: Pyrénées
Self-catering holidays: Pyrénées
Special interest holidays: Walking and trekking, skiing, birdwatching, cycling holidays

Bowhill Holidays
Mayhill Farm, Mayhill Lane, Swanmore, Southampton SO3 2QW
Admin: 0489 877627
Res: 0489 878567
Fax: 0489 877872
VISA ACCESS
Bowhills is an independent, family business, started over 20 years ago featuring 300 fully-inspected farmhouses and villas in both rural and coastal France. 'Our reputation is for our product knowledge and honest descriptions which are factual not fanciful. The properties have been chosen for their situation, character and quality. We have properties at all price levels – farmhouses, châteaux, cottages, water-mills and villas – many have pools. The client has the choice of a convenient package with flexible travel arrangements or accommodation only. We carry up to 12,500 people annually, with approximately 60% of our bookings each year coming from repeat clients or client recommendation.'
Self-catering holidays: All over France

Bridgewater Travel
217 Monton Road, Monton Village, Manchester M30 9PN
Admin: 061 707 8279
Res: 061 707 8547
Fax: 061 787 8896
ABTA: 219
VISA ACCESS
Bridgewater has been trading for 12 months, carrying 2,500 passengers last year. Destinations include Italy, France, Spain and Czechoslovakia. 'All villas and apartments are personally selected'.
Self-catering holidays: All over France

British Airways Holidays
Atlantic House, Hazelwick Avenue, Crawley RH10 1NP
Admin: 0293 615353
Res: 061 493 3344
ABTA: 75416
ATOL: 2001
VISA ACCESS AMEX DINERS
City break specialist in business since 1990, providing city breaks to a range of destinations in Europe, Middle East, America and beyond. 'Paris was our top-selling destination in 1992. For 1993 we have included a range of two- three- and four-night holidays staying at the EuroDisney Resort's themed hotels. Alternatively if you would prefer to stay in one of our Paris hotels, you can purchase from us a two-day entrance pass which guarantees entrance into the Euro Disneyland Theme park.'

Special interest holidays: City breaks, EuroDisney

Brittany Caravan Hire
15 Winchcombe Road, Frampton Cotterell, Bristol BS17 2AG
Admin: 0454 772410
Res: 0454 772410
Fax: 0454 774382
VISA ACCESS
A small family business which has been running for 12 years, carrying around 1,000 people every year. 'We own all the mobile homes we rent out which are on campsites in south Brittany and the west coast.'
Special interest holidays: Caravans and mobile homes

Brittany Direct Holidays
362/364 Sutton Common Road, Sutton SM3 9PL
Admin: 081 644 7881
Res: 081 641 6060
Fax: 081 644 3068
ABTA: 94205
ATOL: 2720
VISA ACCESS
Brittany Direct was set up as a family-run business in 1985. 'Our principal accommodation is in self-catering gîtes, villas and some seaside apartments. As we have our own office in Concarneau all accommodation is regularly inspected. Before clients pay a deposit we offer our home inspection kit – this is a selection of colour photos of the inside and outside of the selected property, a floor plan and a contents inventory.' Other facilities provided for the family include babysitting at all properties.
Hotel holidays: Brittany
Self-catering holidays: Brittany

Brittany Ferries
Millbay Docks, Plymouth PL1 3EW
Admin: 0752 227941
Res: 0752 221321
Fax: 0752 600698
VISA ACCESS AMEX DINERS
Brittany Ferries operates four Western Channel routes from Portsmouth to St Malo, Portsmouth to Caen, Poole to Cherbourg and Plymouth to Roscoff. It also operates a direct ferry link to Spain between Plymouth and Santander (operated from Portsmouth during the winter) and a service between Cork in southern Ireland to Roscoff and St Malo. Linked to its routes, Brittany Ferries offers a wide choice of inclusive holidays including car touring, hotel holidays, self-catering, short breaks and mini cruises. Brittany Ferries started trading 20 years ago on 1 January 1973. It has grown from a one-ship, one-route operation to an operator with nine ships serving seven routes in 1993, carrying over 2.7 million people. 'The company has the youngest fleet on the Channel including a new generation of super-ferries to be headed in 1993 by one of the world's largest ships, the 31,000 ton *Val de Loire*. This ship will offer the very latest in luxury including comfortable cabin berths, restaurants, bars, cinemas, shops, exercise room, swimming pool and sauna.
Hotel holidays: All over France
Self-catering holidays: All over France
Special interest holidays: Camping, golfing holidays, skiing

Canvas Holidays
12 Abbey Park Place, Dunfermline, Fife, Scotland KY12 7PD
Admin: 0383 621000

Res: 0383 621000
Fax: 0383 620075
VISA ACCESS
Canvas Holidays offer ready-erected tents and mobile homes throughout France. Other countries include Germany, Austria, Italy, Spain and Switzerland. 'We are a family company and have been operating for 29 years.'
Special interest holidays: Camping

Caravan & Camping Service
69 Westbourne Grove, London W2 4UJ
Admin: 071 792 1944
Res: 071 792 1944
Fax: 071 792 1956
AITO
VISA ACCESS
A small, specialist company established seven years ago which arranges advance pitch and ferry reservations for campers, caravanners and motor-caravanners so that they can take their own equipment abroad. 'From personal knowledge of all the sites in our brochure we can advise clients about the campsites which will suit them best and can give detailed information and advice about the best routes and ferry crossings to use. Each client receives a full pack of travel documents with road maps, local maps and directions, free computer-based route plans and a European Motoring Guide.'
Special interest holidays: Caravans and mobile homes, camping

Carisma Holidays
Bethel House, Heronsgate Road, Chorleywood WD3 5BB
Admin: 0923 284235
Res: 0923 284235
Fax: 0923 284560
AITO
VISA ACCESS

Formed in 1979, the company specialises in self-drive beach holidays, with mobile homes and tents on sites with private beaches in Brittany, Vendée and the south west coast. 'We rely on 70% repeat business and recommendations and carry over 1,500 families annually. We cater specifically for families. We are a family-run business and are selective about who we take on holiday. We will not take groups of unaccompanied youngsters. Our special beach sites and organised games assure children an unforgettable holiday, where they can wander safely from beach to pools to play areas.'
Special interest holidays: Camping

Clearwater Holidays
17 Heath Terrace, Leamington Spa CV32 5NA
Admin: 0926 450002
Res: 0926 450002
Fax: 0926 450507
Clearwater Holidays has been offering shore-based sailing holidays in the Gulf of Morbihan in south Brittany for almost 20 years. 'Our traditional Breton-style cottages are situated in Bernon, near Sarzeau. Furnishing is simple but our kitchens are very well equipped. The Bernon peninsula is perfect for walking and cycling and we provide bicycles for the use of our customers.'
Self-catering holidays: Brittany
Special interest holidays: Sailing

Club Med
106–110 Brompton Road, London SW3 1JJ
Admin: 071 225 1066
Res: 071 581 1161
Fax: 071 581 4769
ABTA: 19685
ATOL: 1020

VISA ACCESS AMEX
Club Med UK is part of the
French Club Med which has been
trading for 42 years. Club Med UK
carries 25,000 people annually to
110 villages worldwide. 'In France
we have villages in Provence,
Drome, Corsica, Vosges, Limousin,
the Alps and the Pyrénées. Our
holidays are unique because they
are fully inclusive and everything
is organised in a very laid back sort
of way, so that clients can choose
between doing everything or
nothing. Children are also very
well catered for.'
Special interest holidays: Club
Holidays

Continental Camping Holidays
12 Coronation Drive, Penketh,
Warrington WA5 2DD
Admin: 0925 728975
Res: 0925 728975
Continental Camping Holidays has
been trading for 30 years. 'We are a
small, independent family-owned
company. We specialise in self-
drive holidays to France with
mobile home or caravan accommodation. Three areas of France
feature in our 1993 brochure –
Dinard in Brittany, Les Sables in
the Vendée and Argelès sur Mer
in Languedoc.'
Special interest holidays: Caravans
and mobile homes

Continental Villas
3 Caxton Walk, Phoenix Street, off
Charing Cross Road, London
WC2H 8PW
Admin: 071 497 0444
Res: 071 497 0444
Fax: 071 379 5222
ABTA: 60919
ATOL: 1886
AITO
VISA ACCESS

The company is now part of the
Travelink Group of Companies,
established in 1961, and specialises
in properties throughout Europe,
the West Indies, Florida, The Sey-
chelles and Thailand. 'All the villas
are known to the directors and
clients are dealt with personally to
ensure that the most suitable property is chosen. We have built up a
good clientele who re-book with us
over the years and the total
number of people taking villa holidays in 1992 was approximately
3,000.'
Self-catering holidays: Côte
d'Azur

Corsican Places
Great Beech, Battle, East Sussex
TN33 9QU
Admin: 0424 774366
Res: 0424 774366
Fax: 0424 774879
ATOL: 2647
AITO
VISA ACCESS
Corsican Places, now in its fourth
year, specialises in Corsica. Managing Director Janet Rankin, who has
known the island for over 20 years
and owns property there, says that
she and her staff know each villa
and hotel well and are always
ready to discuss individual
requirements to ensure that customers get the holiday which suits
them. 'Between 1,500 and 2,000
people travel to Corsica with us
each year, and a large proportion
of our custom comes from repeat
bookings or recommendations.'
Hotel holidays: Corsica
Self-catering holidays: Corsica
Special interest holidays: Sailing

Cosmos Coach Tours
Tourama House, 17 Homesdale
Road, Bromley, Kent BR2 9LX

Admin: 081 464 3444
Res: 061 480 5799
Fax: 081 466 6640
ABTA: 1395
ATOL: 1082
VISA ACCESS
Cosmos Tourama offers coach tour holidays and is part of the Cosmos travel group which has been operating for over 30 years.
Special interest holidays: Coach holidays

Cresta Holidays
32 Victoria Street, Altrincham WA14 1ET
Admin: 061 953 3006
Res: 061 926 9999
Fax: 061 953 4444
ABTA: 23996
ATOL: 606
VISA ACCESS AMEX
Cresta Holidays, part of Sun International, has provided packages to France for the past 19 years, offering both hotel and apartment holidays. Of the 120,000 passengers Cresta now carry each year, slightly over half choose France.
Hotel holidays: All over France
Self-catering holidays: All over France
Special interest holidays: Golfing holidays

Crown Blue Line
8 Ber Street, Norwich NR1 3EJ
Admin: 0603 630513
Res: 0603 630513
Fax: 0603 664298
ABTA: 3325
ATOL: 2259
VISA ACCESS AMEX
Three years ago Crown took over the Rank Blue Line operation to form the biggest British French canal operator with more than 400 boats for hire in a choice of 11 areas of France.

Special interest holidays: Canal boats

Crystal Holidays
Crystal House, Arlington Road, Surbiton KT6 6BW
Admin: 081 390 8737
Res: 081 390 3335
Fax: 081 390 6378
ABTA: 23816
ATOL: 1664
VISA ACCESS AMEX
Crystal Holidays was set up in 1980 as a specialist ski operator. 'We carry 70,000 people each year on our skiing programme and the equivalent number of passengers on our self-catering, hotels, and lakes and mountains programmes.'
Hotel holidays: Provence, Languedoc, Brittany, Normandy, Picardy, Burgundy
Self-catering holidays: Provence, Languedoc, Dordogne, Charente, Vendée, Brittany
Special interest holidays: Skiing

Cultural and Educational Services Abroad
44 Sydney Street, Brighton BN1 4EP
Admin: 0273 683304
Res: 0273 683304
Fax: 0273 683954
CESA aims to provide a comprehensive advisory service on language courses abroad. 'Operating since 1980 as an independent consultancy we have considerable knowledge of a wide range of centres throughout France. We annually arrange language programmes with accommodation, either in French families or in local apartments, for 550–600 students of all ages and abilities. Our General Language Programmes cater for those looking for two- to four-

week courses to boost linguistic confidence or brush up on the basics of the language so gaining more from future holidays. Our Long Term Courses are 20-, 16- or 12-week programmes which cater for students of all ages who wish to reach a recognised level of ability in the French language, with an Alliance Française, DELF or Chamber of Commerce qualification. Our Intensive Courses are geared to the needs of the professional with one or two week options, small groups or private tuition.'
Special interest holidays: Language learning

Cyclists Touring Club
Cotterell House, 69 Meadrow, Godalming GU7 3HS
Admin: 0483 417217
Res: 0483 417217
Fax: 0483 426994
VISA ACCESS
The CTC was founded in 1878 to promote cycling and protect cyclists' interests. It was a founder member of the Alliance Internationale de Tourisme (worldwide touring organisation) and the European Cyclists' Federation. Today the CTC has over 40,000 members worldwide. The CTC's activities and services include: specialist bicycle insurance and travel insurance; legal aid and third party insurance; information and routes for independent travellers planning to cycle in Britain and in most countries of the world; a programme of organized tours led by experienced CTC members; technical information about buying a bike and equipping a bike for touring; a network of cyclists in Britain and abroad who can assist with advice and information; and a mail order service for cycling maps, books and equipment.
Special interest holidays: Cycling holidays

Cygnus Wildlife Holidays
57 Fore Street, Kingsbridge, Devon TQ7 1PG
Admin: 0548 856178
Res: 0548 856178
Fax: 0548 857537
ABTA: 62948
Cygnus has been offering birdwatching and wildlife holidays since 1980. 'We travel to all parts of the world, but with particularly extensive programmes in Eastern and Western Europe, Russia, USA and India. Our groups are small and friendly, our objective being to provide an exciting, enjoyable holiday, by offering the chance to see and experience the birds, wildlife and culture of the country visited.'
Special interest holidays: Birdwatching

DB Jazz Tours
37 Wood Street, Stratford-Upon-Avon CV37 6ES
Admin: 0789 267532
Res: 0789 267532
Fax: 0789 414644
ABTA: 14037
ATOL: 2288
VISA ACCESS
'We have been trading for 16 years and we are an independent company carrying approximately 250 people each year to jazz festivals all around the world. In addition to arranging the travel and accommodation facilities we offer ticket reservation and information on the festival performances and programmes.'
Special interest holidays: Music holidays

Destination France
Croydon House, 1 Peall Road, Croydon CR0 3EX
Admin: 081 689 2299
Res: 081 689 9935
Fax: 081 684 8812
VISA ACCESS
Destination France is an accommodation agency specialising in supplying self-catering accommodation throughout France. 'We are able to offer a wide choice of accommodation which has not been allocated to our clients within the travel trade, direct to the public, at wholesale prices. Destination France is not a tour operator and does not organise travel or insurance requirements. The company has been trading for three years. All our properties have been carefully inspected in order to comply with the requirements of bonded tour operators. Inspection sheets are available to clients on request. We do not publish a brochure, but provide constantly updated lists of accommodation for each area.'
Self-catering holidays: All over France.

Dominique's Villas
13 Park House, 140 Battersea Park Road, London SW11 4NB
Admin: 071 738 8772
Res: 071 738 8772
Fax: 071 498 6014
AITO
VISA ACCESS
Dominique's Villas is an independently-owned company which was set up seven years ago. 'We offer self-catering holidays in villas and châteaux in many areas of France. We carry around 2,000 people each year. Dominique Wells hand picks all the properties and deliberately avoids areas spoilt by tourism.'

Self-catering holidays: Dordogne, Provence, Loire Valley, Côte d'Azur

Drive France
92–96 Lind Road, Sutton SM1 4PL
Admin: 081 395 8888
Res: 081 395 8888
Fax: 081 395 8646
ABTA: 53949
Self-drive villa and gîte holiday specialist, which offers a total of 400 properties throughout France including Languedoc-Roussillon and Alsace. 'For 1993 there is an increased selection of beach-side villas, particularly in Brittany, the Vendée and Charente Maritime, and a greater number of villas with pools in the Lot, Dordogne and on the Côte d'Azur. There is free travel for up to four children (under 14) per family on all holidays and young adults (aged 14–17) pay only 50% of extra adult costs on all holidays. Drive France, and its larger sister company, Keycamp Holidays, are part of Baldwin plc.'
Self-catering holidays: All over France

En Famille Overseas
The Old Stables, 60b Maltravers Street, Arundel BN18 9BG
Admin: 0903 883266
Res: 0903 883266
Fax: 0903 883582
The organization has arranged visits with French families for over 40 years. The stays are specifically for those not only wishing to learn the language but also for those wishing to join in French family life. A range of language holidays in house party centres is also offered for A level students and for adults at all levels. A one-to-one intensive French home tuition

scheme is also available. En Famille sent 850 holiday-makers to France in 1992.

Special interest holidays: Language learning

Equitour
14 Cromwell Crescent, London SW5 9QW
Admin: 071 602 8433
Res: 071 602 8433
Fax: 071 371 4722
Worldwide riding holidays. 'For most of the trips you must have a good knowledge of basics and some experience in riding cross country at a gallop. Your riding trip will take you far from mass tourism through landscape which is typical of the host country. All the rides have been carefully reconnoitred. Accommodation varies from place to place. It ranges from luxury hotels to small inns and tents. Your baggage is carried by vehicle to the next overnight stop.'

Special interest holidays: Horse-riding

Euro Academy
77a George Street, Croydon CR0 1LD
Admin: 081 681 2905
Res: 081 686 2363
Fax: 081 681 8850
ABTA: 6910
VISA ACCESS
Euro Academy is a specialist company which has been arranging language courses in France for more than 20 years. 'Expert advice is offered on what we believe to be the most effective and stimulating method of language training – learning the language on location. For young people we provide language experiences in line with the demands of GCSE and GCE sylla-

buses: vacation courses with leisure activities, home-stays, and university summer courses. For adults and executives the Business Class programme provides courses for all levels of linguistic ability. Choose from small group or individual tuition.'

Special interest holidays: Language learning

EuroSites
Holcombe Road, Helmshore, Rossendale BB4 4NB
Admin: 0706 240033
Res: 0706 830888
Fax: 0706 212144
ABTA: 47064
VISA ACCESS
Eurosites was set up in 1990 as part of the Airtours plc Leisure Group. 'We specialise in self-drive camping holidays to France and feature over 80 French campsites in our 1993 brochure, as well as sites in Italy, Spain, Austria, Germany and Luxembourg. We use only the highest standard of campsite – with a choice of tent or mobile home accommodation. Our holidays are primarily aimed at families, with most sites offering a wide range of leisure and entertainment facilities for children of all ages.'

Special interest holidays: Camping

Eurocamp
28 Princess Street, Knutsford WA16 6BG
Admin: 0565 626262
Res: 0565 626262
ABTA: 70677
AITO
VISA ACCESS
Eurocamp has been in business for 20 years. It is the market leader in the packaged camping business offering ready-erected three-

bedroomed tents with beds and mattresses, electric lighting, refrigerators and equipped kitchens or mobile homes with their own shower and toilet. 'Nearly 80% of our holidays last year were taken by past customers or friends booking on recommendation. We offer over 270 campsites in 14 countries.'

Special interest holidays: Camping

European Villas
154–156 Victoria Road, Cambridge CB4 3DZ
Admin: 0223 314220
Res: 0223 314220
Fax: 0223 314423
ABTA: 99694
ATOL: 2270
AITO
VISA ACCESS
European Villas has been in business for 10 years, specialising in villas with private pools in not only France but also Greece, Cyprus, Spain and Portugal. 'Our villas range from two-bedroomed family villas up to large villas for 16 people. In the new 1993 deluxe category some of the special features include satellite TV, video, microwave, dishwasher and washing machine, jacuzzi and tennis court. Holidays are available on a rental only basis, or including flights from many UK regional airports. Over 8,000 holiday-makers travelled with us in 1992.'

Self-catering holidays: Provence, Lot

Even Breaks
La Chapelle Ste Marguerite, 1 Rue Ste Marguerite, Les Chartreuses du Boulou, Le Boulou, FRANCE
Admin: 010 33 68 83 09 91
Res: 010 33 68 83 09 91
Fax: 010 33 68 83 43 14

Holidays in a 12th-century Romanesque chapel in the foothills of the Pyrénées, on the French/Spanish border. 'We combine a beautiful place with lots of sport, good food, wine and relaxation. Most of our guests are between 20 and 40 years old and come here alone.'

Hotel holidays: Pyrénées

Excelsior Holidays
22 Sea Road, Bournemouth BH5 1DD
Admin: 0202 309555
Res: 0202 309733
ABTA: 27728
VISA ACCESS
A family-owned holiday company founded in the early 1920s. It is a coach holiday company operating almost 60 coaches throughout Great Britain and on the Continent. 'All coaches are modern vehicles maintained to high standards and feature reclining seats, panoramic windows, fresh air ventilation and air suspension. In addition almost all coaches operating on the Continent have WC/wash facilities, tea- and coffee-making equipment and air conditioning. Our range of holidays depart from over 120 joining points throughout the south and south-west of England. Our capacity for 1993 is about 30,000 clients and based on previous figures at least 60% of customers will be repeat business.'

Special interest holidays: Coach holidays

Explore Worldwide
1 Frederick Street, Aldershot GU11 1LQ
Admin: 0252 333031
Res: 0252 319448
Fax: 0252 343170
ATOL: 2595
AITO

VISA ACCESS
The company specialises in running small group exploratory holidays to more remote destinations. 'Formed in 1981, our holidays include 'Ethnic encounters', wildlife safaris, easy walks, major mountain treks, wilderness experiences, raft and river journeys, sailtreks and seatreks, cultural and adventure touring. 10,000 people are carried annually, to Europe, Middle East, India, Africa, Asia, South and North America.'
Special interest holidays: Cycling holidays, river running and rafting, walking and trekking

Fleur Holidays
22 Westcliffe Drive, Layton, Blackpool FY3 7HG
Admin: 0253 301719
Res: 0253 301719
Fax: 0253 393228
VISA ACCESS
A small, independent holiday company offering French caravanning holidays since 1979. 'We keep to our maximum of 30 mobile homes, spread over four campsites on the Côte d'Azur near St-Tropez, Grimaud and Gassin and in western France near Royan. In 1993 over 78% of our mobile homes will be brand new or less than one year old. The smallness of our company allows us to pay more attention to each emplacement, each mobile home and ultimately to each visitor.'
Special interest holidays: Caravans and mobile homes

Four Seasons
Springfield, Farsley, Pudsey, Leeds LS28 5LY
Admin: 0532 564373
Res: 0532 564373
Fax: 0532 555923

AITO
VISA ACCESS
Independent company which has been selling holidays exclusively to France since 1978. 'We offer self-catering holidays in mobile homes, caravans and apartments as well as a site/ferry reservation service for caravan and tent owners. Each of the 40 locations featured in our 1993 brochure has been visited by our main reservation staff, who will be pleased to discuss the accommodation and site details as well as the best routes and ideas for overnight stays.'
Self-catering holidays: All over France
Special interest holidays: Camping

FrancoLeisure
29 Morehall Avenue, Folkestone CT19 4EQ
Admin: 0303 276961
Res: 0303 276961
Fax: 0303 221095
VISA ACCESS
In business for two years, the company operates as a members' travel club with a five pounds annual subscription, obtaining discounts from ferry operators and French establishments. 'We offer short-break golfing holidays and fishing holidays based on a Nature Reserve in the Pas de Calais.'
Special interest holidays: Golfing holidays

Francophiles Discover France
66 Great Brockeridge, Westbury-on-Trym, Bristol BS9 3UA
Admin: 0272 621975
Res: 0272 621975
Fax: 0272 622642
Francophiles Discover France has been trading for 12 years and is an independent company with two

partners, Ron and Jenny Farmer. 'We carry around 500 passengers annually on personally-escorted, culturally-based tours in regional France only. We offer one- and two-centre holidays, minimal travel by luxury coach, French cuisine and no chain hotels, as far away from 'tourism' as possible. We have 96% return business and most clients book at least one year ahead.'

Special interest holidays: Art & architecture tours

Freedom Holidays
30 Brackenbury Road, London W6 0BA
Admin: 081 741 4471
Res: 081 741 4686
Fax: 081 741 9332
ABTA: 97006
ATOL: 432
AITO
VISA ACCESS

Set up in 1970, the company is a small, privately-owned tour operator. 'In winter we specialise in weekend and tailor-made skiing holidays to Châtel in the Haute Savoie. We also offer a comprehensive ski-drive programme to most of the major ski areas in France with a choice of any cross Channel route and overnight hotels on the journey. We also operate skiing holidays by air or self-drive to Andorra in the Pyrénées. In summer we offer self-drive holidays to a chalet hotel in the Haute Savoie and windsurfing holidays on the Greek island of Lefkas.'

Hotel holidays: Haute Savoie
Self-catering holidays: Haute Savoie
Special interest holidays: Skiing

Freedom of France
Alton Court, Penyard Lane, Ross on Wye HR9 7BE
Admin: 0989 764211
Res: 0989 768168
Fax: 0989 768376
ABTA: 46875
VISA ACCESS AMEX

The company is part of the PGL group of companies which has been trading for over 30 years. 'Freedom of France offers self-drive camping holidays in a flexible framework. Clients can travel any day, stay at any number of sites, come back any day, choose any Channel crossing – all booked by us with one phone call. Freedom of France had its first season in 1989 and has seen 20% growth every year since then. In 1992 3,000 families travelled with the company, many of whom had travelled with us before. Our link with PGL gives us an advantage in offering on site activities for children. All Freedom of France children's couriers have worked at a PGL Children's Centre, which means that we offer genuine activity sessions for children rather than a token child-minding service.'

Special interest holidays: Camping

Freestyle
Impasse ML Avon, Rue du Temple, 84160 Lourmarin, France
Admin: 010 33 90 68 10 31
Res: 010 33 90 68 10 31
Fax: 010 33 90 09 72 69

A small company specialising in mountain bike and multi-sports holidays in the south of France. 'We are based at the foot of the Lubéron Hills, in the small village of Lourmarin. All our activities take place in the Natural Park of the Lubéron which offers some of the best mountain biking terrain

in the south of France. We cater for beginners and experts. Accommodation is in gîtes and farms around Lourmarin, but we can offer accommodation in hotels or chambres d'hôte. All our guides are English or English speaking. We specialise in small groups of between six and ten people.'
Special interest holidays: Multi Activity Holidays

French Affair
5/7 Humbolt Road, London W6 8QH
Admin: 071 381 8519
Res: 071 381 8519
Fax: 071 381 5423
ATOL: 2334
French Affair started operating to France in 1986. It offers self-catering properties in the Dordogne, the Lot Valley, Gascony, Languedoc-Roussillon and Provence. In addition, this year it features a programme of auberge holidays in the south of France and Corsica. There is also a small selection of waterfront hotels in Provence and Languedoc-Roussillon.
Hotel holidays: Corsica, Provence, Languedoc
Self-catering holidays: Dordogne, Lot, Gascony, Provence, Languedoc

French Country Camping
126 Hempstead Road, Kings Langley, Herts WD4 8AL
Admin: 0923 261316
Res: 0923 261311
Fax: 0923 264068
ABTA: 18470
AITO
VISA ACCESS
French Country Camping specialises in self-drive camping and mobile home holidays in France. 'The company offers high quality campsites with excellent facilites and the friendly hospitality of a family-run establishment. Our 64 campsites are selected for their genuine character, unspoilt charm and the authentic atmosphere of the real France. To maintain this, where possible, French Country Camping ensures exclusivity, with an average of only a dozen or so of our tents or mobile homes on each campsite. Our holidays can be tailor-made to suit the needs of each party. As part of our plans for developing the concept of camping holidays we provide free loan of bicycles for all the family on selected campsites. The company was formed in 1973 and the present Managing Director, Mark Hammerton, is the son of the founder. Although associated with Eurocamp, we are still essentially a family firm, providing 16,000 people with a holiday in 1992.'
Special interest holidays: Camping

French Country Cruises
Andrew Brock Travel, 10 Barley Mow, London W4 4PH
Admin: 081 995 3642
Res: 0572 821330
Fax: 0572 821072
ABTA: 16070
ATOL: 1585
AITO
VISA ACCESS
French Country Cruises is the English agent for Locaboat Plaisance – France's largest builder and hirer of canal boats, with a fleet of some 300 boats operating from 20 bases. Boats featured include the distinctive traditional-style penichettes, sleeping four to twelve persons according to model. 'With 10 years of trading behind us, sales now run at around 1,000 persons per year.'

Special interest holidays: Canal boats

French Golf Holidays
PO Box 835, Brentwood, Essex CM14 4FQ
Admin: 0277 261004
Res: 0277 261004
Fax: 0277 200460
The company has been operating since 1983. 'Much of our business comes through repeat customers and recommendations. We offer holidays in many regions, including northern France, around Paris, Rouen, Deauville, Brittany, Loire, Bordeaux and Biarritz. Accommodation ranges from family-run two-star hotels to four-star deluxe châteaux hotels. Self-catering accommodation is also available. We carried around 5,000 people in 1992.'
Special interest holidays: Golfing holidays

French Life Holidays
26 Church Road, Horsforth, Leeds LS18 5LG
Admin: 0532 390077
Res: 0532 390077
Fax: 0532 584211
ABTA: 56044
ATOL: 2694
VISA ACCESS AMEX
In business for 10 years as a specialist operator to France. 'We carry approximately 35,000 people annually. We offer all types of accommodation and all types of transport with a unique mix and match flexibility, for example one week's holiday on a campsite and one week in a gîte. Children under 16 go free on camping holidays.'
Hotel holidays: All over France
Self-catering holidays: All over France
Special interest holidays: Camping

French Villas
175 Selsdon Park Road, South Croydon CR2 8JJ
Admin: 081 651 1522
Res: 081 651 1231
Fax: 081 651 4920
French Villas is a new company with Scandinavian backing. 'It has taken over a well-established programme of villas, cottages and gîtes that has been operating for 14 years.' The company expects to handle up to 10,000 bookings this year.
Self-catering holidays: All over France

Galina International Battlefield Tours
711 Beverley Road, Hull HU6 7JN
Admin: 0482 864409
Res: 0482 806020
Fax: 0482 809717
VISA ACCESS
Galina has been trading for four and a half years. 'It is a family concern, wholly owned by Barry and Ian Matthews. We carry between 1,500 and 2,000 people a year. As a battlefield tour company the bulk of our tours centre on France and Belgium, but we also visit Holland, Germany, Italy and Poland as well as Turkey and the United States. As part of our regular itineraries we can include pilgrimages to the graves of individuals upon request. Every tour has a guide as escort. The guides themselves have a military or academic background.'
Special interest holidays: Battlefield Tours

Gîtes Plus
2 York Terrace, Exeter EX4 6QP
Admin: 0392 70873
Res: 0392 70873
A company in business for eight

years offering family holiday packages in the Ardèche. Our package includes ferries, accommodation in furnished holiday homes plus a daily programme of events and activities on an as-you-please basis – everything from canoeing, horse-riding and walking to leisurely wine tasting – and evenings at selected restaurants. We can also offer child-minding.'
Self-catering holidays: Ardèche

Gîtes de France
178 Piccadilly, London W1V 9DB
Admin: 071 493 3480
Res: 071 408 1343
Fax: 071 495 6417
ABTA: 28951
VISA ACCESS
Gîtes de France Ltd has been established in London for 15 years. The company is the official representative of an organization called the Fédération Nationale des Gîtes de France, set up over 40 years ago. It is sponsored by the French Ministry of Agriculture and the French Ministry of Tourism. In 1993 there is a selection of over 2,500 self-catering properties in 80 départements. Gîtes de France also offers chambres d'hôtes and Logis de France hotel breaks. Canoeing, cycling and rambling holidays are also featured.
Hotel holidays: All over France
Self-catering holidays: All over France

HF Holidays
Imperial House, Edgware Road, London NW9 5AL
Admin: 081 905 9556
Res: 081 905 9558
Fax: 081 205 0506
ATOL: 710
VISA ACCESS
Formerly the Holiday Fellowship,

HF has been in business for 80 years. 'Each year over 25,000 people take their holidays with us. We offer guided walking holidays throughout Europe and worldwide. All leaders are knowledgeable and experienced. Hotels are small and often family-run. The atmosphere is relaxed and informal.'
Special interest holdiays: Walking and trekking

Hampton House Travel
2–6 Queens Road, Teddington TW11 0LR
Admin: 081 977 6404
Res: 081 977 6404
Fax: 081 977 7446
VISA ACCESS
A small, independent company which has been organizing individual holidays and short breaks to France, Belgium, Switzerland and Italy for the past nine years. 'Our programme is based on a range of hotels that have been chosen for their individual character and style. The staff's knowledge of the hotels allows them to give a high level of information and to make informed recommendations to clients. A range of special interest breaks is also offered, including cookery courses, wine tasting, golf, tennis and bridge weekends.'
Hotel holidays: All over France
Special interest holidays: Cooking holidays, golfing holidays, wine tours, bridge weekends

Haven France & Spain
Northney Marina, Northney Road, Hayling Island, Hants PO11 0NH
Admin: 0705 461682
Res: 0705 466111
Fax: 0705 468521
ABTA: 30627

VISA ACCESS
Holidays in mobile homes or tents at 41 sites in France and Spain. It has been operating for 15 years and is part of The Rank Organisation. The majority of sites have a swimming pool, many with water-slides. Tennis, table tennis and cycling are among activities which are available, with extra social events organised by Haven Park Managers, such as barbecues and cheese and wine parties. The Haven Tiger Club courier on each site runs a twice daily programme for children from five to 13, organizing games and activities. Extra activities for 13 to 17 year olds are offered at the two sites owned by Haven near Montpellier and Royan – these include team sports, discos and barbecues.
Special interest holidays: Camping

Headwater Holidays
146 London Road, Northwich CW9 5HH
Admin: 0606 48699
Res: 0606 48699
Fax: 0606 48761
ABTA: 33786
ATOL: 2412
AITO
VISA ACCESS
Headwater specialises in relaxed activity holidays in France. The firm is run by its owners, Christine and Richard Bass. 'We started doing walking and canoeing holidays in 1986, in the Loire Valley. Since then, demand for our holidays has grown rapidly. We now offer walking, cycling, canoeing, watersports and multi-activity holidays in 10 regions of France. Cross-country and downhill skiing are offered in France, Canada and Norway. Our holidays are in untouristy and unspoilt places,

and we aim to keep them that way. We do not do group holidays and seldom take more than three or four rooms at any hotel. For many clients the activity bit is incidental: more a way of experiencing, at a leisurely pace, the unsuspected delights of rural France. For the more energetic there are tougher walking and cycling holidays. We have a team of 24 staff in France. Last year they drove over 280,000 miles moving bags and doing pick-ups, and spent over 3,000 hours cleaning and maintaining bikes, and giving canoeing lessons.'
Special interest holidays: Cycling holidays, canoeing, walking and trekking, skiing, horse-riding

Holiday Charente
25 New Road, Hillingdon Heath, Uxbridge UB8 3DX
Admin: 081 813 5638
Res: 081 813 5638
Fax: 0295 750900
VISA ACCESS AMEX
'Holiday Charente is a family-owned business formed in 1979, and based beside the River Charente at St Simeux, near Angoulême. Our principal activity is providing river cruising holidays on the River Charente, through a fleet of self-drive hire cruisers, and the letting of a small selection of riverside and coastal properties throughout the year. Other activities arranged by us include descents of the River Charente in Canadian canoes, fishing holidays and riverside camping. In 1992 we arranged holidays for around 1,000 visitors from the UK, plus many more from other parts of Europe.'
Self-catering holidays: Charente
Special interest holidays: Camping, canal boats

HomeLink International

84 Lees Gardens, Maidenhead SL6 4NT
Admin: 0628 31951
Res: 0628 31951
Established in 1952, HomeLink claims to be the oldest and largest home exchange holiday organization in the world, with associate companies in 25 countries, including France. It publishes an annual international Holiday Exchange Directory containing many thousands of individual listings. These describe the homes and holiday preferences of members seeking a home-swap holiday during the current year. All kinds of homes are offered, from city flats to mansions in the country. Currently, the HomeLink organisation has over 16,000 members in about 50 countries who swap homes for holidays every year. Members pay £39 for the directory which is six books of listings and house photographs.
Special interest holidays: House swapping

Hoseasons Holidays

Sunway House, Lowestoft NR32 3LT
Admin: 0502 500505
Res: 0502 500555
Fax: 0502 500532
ABTA: 3557
ATOL: 2290
VISA ACCESS
Boating holidays in France and Holland; gîte holidays in France, Italy, Spain, Holland, Germany, Belgium and Ireland. The company has been established since 1946.
Self-catering holidays: All over France
Special interest holidays: Canal boats

Hotel Treks

131a Heston Road, Hounslow, Middlesex TW5 0RD
Admin: 081 569 6627
Res: 081 569 4101
Fax: 081 572 2717
ATOL: 1185
AITO
VISA ACCESS
In 1993 Hotel Treks will be in its fifth year of trading. 'We offer a choice of over 20 classic walks across Europe including the Mont Blanc circuit, the Bernese Oberland and following in Stevenson's footsteps in the Cerdagne. Each walk can be tailored to our client's requirements and luggage is transported every day.'
Special interest holidays: Walking and trekking

Hoverspeed Holidays

Travelscene House, 11–15 St Ann's Road, Harrow, Middlesex HA1 1AS
Admin: 081 427 8800
Res: 081 424 2929
Fax: 081 861 3674
ABTA: 5956
ATOL: 34
AITO
VISA ACCESS
Hoverspeed Holidays is now part of Travelscene Ltd, a short-break tour operator which has been trading for 25 years. Hoverspeed Holidays offers three self-drive programmes: a selection of touring holidays, self-catering accommodation and hotels throughout France and the rest of Europe; ski-drive – a range of self-catering and hotel accommodation in high altitude ski resorts in France and Switzerland; and short breaks in the north of France, Belgium and Holland. Hoverspeed carries approxi-

mately 30,000 passengers annually.
Hotel holidays: Normandy, Picardy, Champagne
Self-catering holidays: Normandy, Brittany, Vendée, Aquitaine, Languedoc, Provence, Alps
Special interest holidays: Skiing

Inntravel
The Old Station, Helmsley, York YO6 5BZ
Admin: 0439 7111
Res: 0439 7111
Fax: 0439 71070
ATOL: 2644
AITO
VISA ACCESS
Inntravel is an independent, fully-bonded, family-run company which for nine years has offered a wide range of holidays for independent travellers. 'France is featured as a year round destination – in summer, Inntravel offers a range of independent hotel to hotel walking holidays, from gentle wanders in the Loire and Dordogne, to rugged walks in the Pyrénées and Alps. We have a similar formula for horse-riding and cycling. We have flexible arrangements which mean you can combine hotels and walks to make up your own itinerary, and combine France with Switzerland and Italy. Year round Inntravel offers short breaks, both self-drive and fly-drive with a range of ideas such as village festivals and cookery tuition. In winter we offer cross-country skiing in the Jura, Vercors or Mediterranean Pyrénées.'
Hotel holidays: All over France
Self-catering holidays: Aquitaine
Special interest holidays: Cycling holidays, walking and trekking, skiing, cooking holidays, horse-riding, wine tours

Insight Holidays
26/28 Paradise Road, Richmond, Surrey TW9 1SE
Admin: 081 332 2900
Res: 0800 393 393
Fax: 081 784 2808
ABTA: 18254
ATOL: 1513
AITO
The company is a specialist in escorted coach holidays throughout Britain, Europe, Scandinavia and the eastern Mediterranean. When Insight began selling tours in the UK in 1990, the company was already known to over a million passengers from Australia, New Zealand, Canada and America who had taken coach tours with Insight International Tours Ltd since 1979. Now in its third year of operation in the UK, Insight has increased its volume by 40%. The Insight Group expects to carry over 250,000 people for 1993. 'Our holidays include features such as porterage, excursions and entrance fees which are often sold as optional extras by others.'
Special interest holidays: Coach holidays

Interhome
383 Richmond Road, Twickenham TW1 2EF
Admin: 081 891 1294
Res: 081 891 1294
Fax: 081 891 5331
ABTA: 3684
VISA ACCESS
A selection of privately-owned holiday homes available for rent throughout Europe. 'We have around 20,000 homes to choose from. Properties range from castles to villas with private pools, to small farmhouses and modern flats. They can all be rented for one week or more during the

summer and winter. The company was created in London in 1965. It is now part of a large Swiss company called Hotelplan who also own the ski specialists Inghams Travel. We booked holiday homes for more than 760,000 clients during 1992, approximately 20,000 of these customers were from Britain.'
Self-catering holidays: All over France

International Chapters
102 St Johns Wood Terrace, London NW8 6PL
Admin: 071 722 9560
Res: 071 722 9560
Fax: 071 722 9140
VISA ACCESS
International Chapters has been trading for 10 years and is probably best known for its high quality Italian villa programme. 'Over the last few years however, we have been adding properties in France of a similar standard to our Italian portfolio. For 1993 we are producing a new brochure of over 100 châteaux, farmhouses, bastides and villas to rent in France, all of a high standard and with swimming pools. Most of the properties are in Provence – in the Alpilles south of Avignon, in the Lubéron hills and near Aix-en-Provence. We also have houses on the Côte d'Azur, in the Dordogne, Gascony, the Loire and the Alps. Other destinations include the Greek Islands, the Caribbean and the UK. We also have a programme of apartments to rent in the centre of Venice, Florence, Rome and Paris. In 1992 International Chapters carried around 3,000 passengers but we expect this to double in 1993 with our increased activities.'
Self-catering holidays: Provence, Côte d'Azur, Alps, Dordogne, Loire Valley

Intervac International Home Exchange
Withey House, Withey Close West, Stoke Bishop, Bristol BS9 3SX
Admin: 0272 687431
Res: 0272 687431
'Intervac pioneered the concept of home exchange holidays over 40 years ago. Now 50 countries are covered by our international team of 32 organizers. Our listings are exclusive to Intervac; we don't work with any other company. In 1992 more than 9,000 families worldwide used our services, of these 1,408 were from France. We publish three directories each year, listing our members' homes and holiday requirements. For an annual fee members receive all three directories, with their own listing included. Unlike conventional holidays, home exchange offers the opportunity to experience another lifestyle from the inside. It also brings savings (no hotel bills or rents); homes are safer while occupied; pets stay in familiar surroundings and new friendships are made.'
Special interest holidays: House swapping

Itinerary Ltd
The Old Station, Helmsley, York YO6 SBZ
Admin: 0439 71303
Res: 0439 71303
La Route des Pyrénées offers 50 hotels in the Pyrénées region. Either book as you go or reserve in advance: the minimum number of nights is three but there is no maximum.
Hotel holidays: Pyrénées

Jean Stanford Ski Holidays
Ridge House, Chilmark, Salisbury,
Wilts SP3 5BS
Admin: 0747 870708
Res: 0747 870708
Fax: 0747 871426
AITO
VISA ACCESS
Jean Stanford Ski Holidays has
been trading for eight years and is
a private company personally run
by Jean Stanford. The company
started operating in Megève and
specialised in that resort for four
winters. It now offers holidays in
Chamonix and Morzine. 'Catered
chalets are selected for general
comfort plus an adequate number
of bathrooms and a good hot water
supply. Resort staff are chosen for
their maturity and experience. The
resorts are all within easy reach of
Geneva airport, and are equally
well situated for self-drive. The
company carries around 600
people to France, it also operates
in Whistler, Canada.'
Special interest holidays: Skiing

Just Tickets & Just Mortoring
1 Charter House, Camden Crescent, Dover, Kent CT16 1LE
Admin: 0304 228866
Res: 0304 228866
Fax: 0304 225123
VISA ACCESS
'We are a small company which
has been trading for 10 years. We
specialise in the obtaining of tickets for Formula 1 Grands Prix
events, also the Le Mans 24 hour
race. We can also provide ferry
tickets and hotel accommodation
near the circuits. While we concentrate on European events, we can
also cover the Intercontinental
ones. We are also now offering
short holidays to EuroDisney.'

Special interest holidays: Motor
racing holidays

Kestours
Travel House, Elmers End, Becken-
ham, Kent BR3 3QY
Admin: 081 658 7316
Res: 081 658 7316
Fax: 081 658 9517
ABTA: 38313
ATOL: 303
VISA ACCESS AMEX
Established in 1956, Kestours
specialises in group travel worldwide. 'We also have holiday programmes for individuals to the
Caribbean and to Lourdes in
France. Our Lourdes holidays fill a
special need for those people who
do not want to travel with a group
and want to visit Lourdes at all
times of the year rather than solely
in the main season which runs
from April to October. For over 15
years we have operated this small
specialist programme using scheduled flights and a choice of three
hotels for three- or seven-night
stays. Each booking is individually
made and full documentation on
Lourdes together with a 72-page
colour guidebook to the centre is
given to our clients to enable them
to make the most of their stay.'
Special interest holidays: Pilgrimages

Keycamp Holidays
Ellerman House, 92/96 Lind Road,
Sutton SM1 4PL
Admin: 081 395 8575
Res: 081 395 4000
Fax: 081 395 8868
ABTA: 53949
VISA ACCESS
For the past 17 years Keycamp
Holidays has specialised in self-
drive camping and mobile home
holidays. 'We are an independent

tour operator – part of Baldwin plc. In 1992 we carried over 100,000 people and in 1993 we are offering 93 campsites in France, Spain and Italy. France is our main destination and we offer 18 regions, from Normandy to the Mediterranean. Campsites vary from small family-run sites to more lively holidays complexes. Most are near the beach, others are in the inland regions close to areas of outstanding natural beauty.'

Special interest holidays: Camping

Kingsland Holidays

Brunswick House, Exeter Street, Plymouth, Devon PL4 0AR
Admin: 0752 251688
Res: 0752 251688
Fax: 0752 251699
AITO
VISA ACCESS AMEX
A direct-sell, independent company featuring over 200 properties, many with pools, 'throughout some of the most beautiful areas of France'. Kingsland was started in 1988 with just seven houses in the Dordogne. The company has expanded to over 200 properties – from small cottages in Brittany, pigeonniers in Gascony to luxurious villas on the Gulf of St-Tropez. 'Although the colour brochure shows the appearance and facilities available, there is no substitute for discussing your requirements and the atmosphere of a property with someone who has actually visited the house themselves. Clients are always able to speak to someone at Kingsland who knows a property personally, and all the staff are experienced in arranging both travel and insurance, as well as advising on travelling through France. Although Kingsland carries over

3,000 passengers every year, each holiday is carefully discussed to match the clients' requirements. The time and care involved to arrange things as simple as a linen service or something as unusual as a balloon ride over the Dordogne Valley, bring clients back year after year. Over 40% of the bookings now come from previous clients or recommendations.'

Self-catering holidays: Brittany, Charente, Dordogne, Lot, Gascony, Cévennes, Côte d'Azur, Provence

Kirker Holidays

3 New Concordia Wharf, Mill Street, London SE1 2BB
Admin: 071 231 3333
Res: 071 231 3333
Fax: 071 231 4771
ABTA: 38012
ATOL: 2450
AITO
VISA ACCESS
Founded in 1986, Kirker is an independent company specialising in short breaks to European cities, taking around 15,000 people abroad each year. Christopher Kirker believes that more and more people now require flexibility and personal service with their arrangements. 'To this end, every holiday is tailor-made: any flight; any (local) airport; any time of the day/night; any hotel; any accommodation and any duration of holiday is offered. Air holidays to Paris include return flights, private arrival transfer by one of the company's own luxury seven-seater mini-buses, accommodation (with breakfast) at characterful hotels located in the centre of town, a guide to the city's museums, transportation, shopping, restaurants and the services of a local representative.'

Special interest holidays: City breaks, EuroDisney

LSG Theme Holidays
201 Main Street, Thornton, Leicester LE67 1AH
Admin: 0509 231713
Res: 0509 231713
Fax: 0509 239857
A small, independent Midlands-based organisation (average 400 clients), now in its eighth year of operation. 'We specialise in educational and activity holidays to France, lasting from four to fifteen days, between May and October. The holidays are designed specifically for people who wish to pursue their favourite interest whilst discovering the real France of the French. Over the years, LSG has developed courses such as painting, photography, creative writing, cookery, conversational French, rambling, and nature-watch. Courses take place in Brittany, Normandy, Île-de-France, Ardèche, Dordogne, Auvergne, Languedoc, Provence and the Côte d'Azur. A special feature of our holidays is that two or three different courses usually run in parallel on the same holiday to enable friends and relatives – with totally different interests – to enjoy the same holiday whilst pursuing the theme of their choice.'
Special interest holidays: Art & architecture tours, art history tours, cooking holidays, horse-riding, language learning, natural history, painting and drawing holidays, photography holidays, sailing

La France des Villages
Model Farm, Rattlesden, Bury St Edmunds IP30 0SY
Admin: 0449 737664
Res: 0449 737664
Fax: 0449 737850
AITO
VISA ACCESS
'We recognise that our clients prefer the less well trodden parts of France. We offer houses of character, sleeping from two to fifteen, many with pools. Also available are chambres d'hôte in châteaux and manoirs. We also feature activity holidays: golfing, canal cruising, hotel barges, cookery courses, photography courses and painting courses, riding treks, gypsy caravans, llama and donkey treks and canoeing/rafting.'
Hotel holidays: Normandy, Burgundy, Dordogne, Provence
Self-catering holidays: All over France
Special interest holidays: Golfing holidays, canal cruising

Lagrange UK
168 Shepherds Bush Road, Brook Green, London W6 7PB
Admin: 071 371 6111
Res: 071 371 6111
Fax: 071 371 2990
ABTA: 40120
VISA ACCESS
The company is a well-established name in Europe with offices in Paris, Brussels, Geneva and Stuttgart. Lagrange has been operating in the UK for 10 years, specialising in self-catering holidays in France. At present the London office handles around 5,000 bookings a year. 'We feature over 100 resorts and 140 residences all along the coastline of France and also in the mountains, the countryside and in major French cities.'
Self-catering holidays: Brittany, Provence
Special interest holidays: Skiing

Lakes and Mountains Holidays

The Red House, 44a Garstons Close, Titchfield, Fareham PO14 4EW
Admin: 0329 844405
Res: 0329 844405
Fax: 0329 844688
ATOL: 2859
AITO
VISA ACCESS
An independent, family-run company that arranges self-catering and hotel holidays in the Swiss, Austrian and French Alps. 'Our customers enjoy walking, touring and being away from the crowds. We have been trading since 1986. The choice of destinations covers lakeside or mountain villages, some with a lot of amenities for families, others for complete peace and relaxation. Travel options include self-drive or flights with car hire.'
Hotel holidays: Haute Savoie
Self-catering holidays: Haute Savoie

Le Ski

26 Holly Terrace, Huddersfield HD1 6JW
Admin: 0484 548996
Res: 0484 548996
Fax: 0484 451909
ATOL: 2307
AITO
VISA ACCESS
Catered chalet and apartment holidays in Courchevel and Val d'Isère in the Savoie region of France. Owned and managed by brother and sister Nick and Liz Morgan, Le Ski began operating 10 years ago in 1982 with just one chalet. Le Ski carry approximately 2,000 passengers each year.
Special interest holidays: Skiing

Leisureline Holidays

Marsh Barn, Ferry Road, Surlingham, Norwich NR14 7AR
Admin: 05088 8193
Res: 05088 8193
VISA ACCESS
The company provides a service for people who wish to see provincial France and Italy by coach at a leisurely pace and away from the normal itineraries. It has been operating for six years.
Special interest holidays: Coach holidays

Les Propriétaires de l'Ouest

34 Middle Street, Southsea PO5 4BP
Admin: 0705 872233
Res: 0705 755715
Fax: 0705 812779
AITO
VISA ACCESS
Self-catering gîtes and villas throughout Brittany, Dordogne, Ariège and Ardèche. The company also offers chambre d'hôte accommodation in Normandy, Brittany and Dordogne.
Self-catering holidays: Brittany, Dordogne

Longshot Golf Holidays

Meon House, College Street, Petersfield GU32 3JN
Admin: 0730 266561
Res: 0730 268621
Fax: 0730 268482
ABTA: 43788
ATOL: 16
AITO
VISA ACCESS AMEX DINERS
Part of the Meon Travel Group, Longshot has been in business for 20 years carrying around 7,000 passengers each year to 15 destinations including the Algarve, Lisbon coast, Costa del Sol, France, Gran Canaria, Valencia, Ireland,

Majorca, Bermuda and the USA. 'In France we offer Le Touquet, Normany, Loire Valley, Brittany, Biarritz, Bordeaux, Languedoc, Provence and the Riviera. Our staff can help you choose the destination most suitable for you and your family, and you can benefit from free or reduced green fees in most destinations. We offer both self-catering and hotel accommodation.'

Special interest holidays: Golfing holidays

Maison Vacances
86 Edna Road, London SW20 8BT
Admin: 081 540 9680
Res: 081 540 9680
The company is run by a Frenchman, Raymond Dusoulier and his English wife. 'We focus only on offering holidays in France which can be put together to meet the specific requirements of clients. We also have a portfolio of properties which we have personally vetted. Increasingly, angling and prestige bed and breakfast holidays are becoming a speciality.'
Hotel holidays: All over France
Self-catering holidays: All over France
Special interest holidays: Angling, horse-riding

Major and Mrs Holt's Battlefield Tours
The Golden Key Building, 15 Market Street, Sandwich CT13 9DA
Admin: 0304 612248
Res: 0304 612248
Fax: 0304 614930
ATOL: 2846
AITO
In business since 1985 and now part of the Green Field Leisure Group, Major & Mrs Holt's Battle-field Tours offers battlefield and history tours, ancient and modern. 'Each tour in our portfolio of over 60 destinations is researched, planned and accompanied throughout by UK-based, company trained guide lecturers. There is often a distinguished guest speaker to give additional commentary and lectures. France has always been the company's most popular destination, with tours covering Agincourt Crécy; Paris and the 1870 Franco-Prussian War; Vimy, the Somme, the Meuse-Argonne, Loos, Neuve Chappelle, Aubers and Cambrai from the First World War; Hill 112, Falaise, Calais and Dunkirk from the Second World War. A new tour is planned to Marseille to study the French Foreign Legion and plans for the important 50th-Anniversary events of 1994 are already well in hand. We offer good quality accommodation and comfortable coaches/flights. Many who travelled on the company's first tours still travel with us, some over 50 times. There is a wide age range, with companionship and participation an important element of the tours. Single people are well catered for. This year we are running 70 different tours to 28 countries worldwide.'
Special interest holidays: Battlefield tours

Mark Warner
20 Kensington Church St, London W8 4EP
Admin: 071 937 9281
Res: 071 938 1851
Fax: 071 938 3861
ABTA: 20358
ATOL: 1176
VISA ACCESS
An independent tour operator, founded in 1975, which during the

winter specialises in ski holidays to Val d'Isère, Meribel and Courchevel. During the summer it offers watersport holidays in Corsica. Each year it takes around 7,000 passengers to destinations in France. 'During the winter we feature Clubhotels and chalets on half-board, with 'premier service' available in the superior chalets.' It offers six days a week free ski guiding service in all resorts and a seven day crêche and child-minding service in Val d'Isère. During low season infants travel free of charge and pay £25 per week at all other times. Children under 14 sharing a room with two full paying adults pay half the brochure price. During the summer it offers beach club hotels in Corsica, with free watersports. Waterskiing, dinghy sailing and windsurfing are provided with free tuition.
Special interest holidays: Club holidays, skiing

Martin Sturge
3 Lower Camden Place, Bath BA1 5JJ
Admin: 0225 310623
Res: 0225 310822
Fax: 0225 447055
The company promises clients a range of 'very interesting and comfortable houses, mostly with private pools'. It has around 250 properties in Provence, Languedoc, Pyrénées, Tarn, Lot, Dordogne, Charente, Gironde, Vendée and Brittany. 'The properties have accumulated through recommendation and personal acquaintance. All are inspected by us before letting and regularly thereafter. Tenants' own comments and suggestions are sought after every holiday and carefully studied with owners in order to make each house as nice as possible.'
Self-catering holidays: All over France

Matthews Holidays
8 Bishopsmead Parade, East Horsley, Surrey KT24 6RP
Admin: 0483 284044
Res: 0483 285213
Fax: 0483 284089
ABTA: 4293
VISA ACCESS
The company is still managed by the directors who started it in 1967. 'We specialise in mobile home holidays – all the accommodation that we let has been built to our own specifications and is situated on campsites in coastal regions.'
Special interest holidays: Caravans and mobile homes

Meon Villa Holidays
Meon House, College Street, Petersfield GU32 3JN
Admin: 0730 266561
Res: 0730 268411
Fax: 0730 268482
ABTA: 43788
ATOL: 16
AITO
In business for 25 years, Meon Villas offers holidays to 16 destinations within Europe, the Caribbean and Florida. Part of the Meon Group of Companies, Meon Villas carries 15,000 people annually. 'Many of our villas are privately owned and have their own swimming pool. Short sea ferry crossings for a car and up to five adults are included in our prices.'
Hotel holidays: All over France
Self-catering holidays: All over France
Special interest holidays: Cruises

Meriski
Fovant Mews, 12a Noyna Road, London SW17 7PH
Admin: 081 682 3883
Res: 081 682 3883
Fax: 081 682 2346
VISA ACCESS
Meriski is a small, specialist, independent ski holiday company set up in 1984, offering what it describes as quality catered chalet holidays in the French resort of Meribel in the Trois Vallées ski region. Meriski carries around 1,100 people annually. 'Director and founder Colin Matthews is an expert skier and fluent French speaker. He is personally available in Meribel all season to ensure that clients get the most from their holidays, and often leads the free ski guiding sessions. All chalets are well positioned, have good views, log fires, terraces and balconies. The hosts are mature and experienced. Meriski also offers ski clinics with teaching sessions and videos. Semi-catering is a new option this year. Guests can eat out on more than one night a week and are entitled to a discount of £10 per person per meal. An experienced and fully trained nanny is available to look after children during the day, and can also babysit in the evening.'
Special interest holidays: Skiing

Merit Travel & Tours
Merit House, 79 High Street, South Norwood, London SE25 6EA
Admin: 081 653 6514
Res: 081 653 6514
Fax: 081 771 5284
ABTA: 43909
VISA ACCESS
Founded in 1980, the company offers holidays to Italy, Germany, France, Spain, USA and Poland.

About six years ago it set up a small programme of special interest holidays for gardeners and now 13 garden-interest tours are offered. Wine interest tours and château weekends are also included in the programme. Merit now handles around 1,500 bookings a year.
Special interest holidays: Garden tours, Wine tours

Middlebrook's Battlefield Tours
48 Linden Way, Boston, Lincs PE21 9DS
Admin: 0205 364555
Res: 0205 364555
Martin Middlebrook is a military historian who started taking groups to the Somme in 1984. He has since expanded his operation and now visits every important Western Front sector. Each party has around 20 clients and all tours are non smoking.
Special interest holidays: Battlefield Tours

Miss France Holidays
132 Anson Road, London NW2 6AP
Admin: 081 452 5901
Res: 081 452 5901
Fax: 081 517 1966
'I am a French woman married to an English lawyer and have been in business privately for over 10 years. I have approximately 60 properties in three regions of France: the Dordogne, Languedoc and Provence/Côte d'Azur. I know every owner personally and every property intimately. My holidays houses range from small cottages to large luxury villas with swimming pools.'
Self-catering holidays: Provence, Languedoc, Dordogne

Music at Ladevie
10 Montague Road, London E8 2HW
Admin: 071 249 7591
Res: 071 249 7591
Music at Ladevie was founded in 1991 with the aim of enabling pianists at all levels – amateur, advanced, semi-professional – to work with artists of stature and experience in a relaxed, rural setting. 'The 10-day residential courses at Ladevie provide the conditions for the highest standards of pianism to flourish, while providing an informal atmosphere in which players of more modest abilities feel inspired to contribute. The courses are residential and open to all pianists, of whatever ability, over the age of 16 (with limited space for partners or observers). Accommodation is in single, double or shared dormitory rooms in either the 18th-century Château Ladevie or in a converted farmhouse next door. Camping in the château grounds is also an option. Fees depend on the type of accommodation chosen. Masterclasses for advanced pianists provide the hub of the musical activities, with other classes tailored to suit individual needs. Piano and string ensembles are also welcome. Afternoons are for practising and private tuition, or relaxation – the countryside is perfect for walking or cycling (bicycles are available for hire) and there is a clean lake for swimming nearby. Evening activities range from recitals and lectures to poetry readings and cabaret.'
Special interest holidays: Music holidays

NSS Riviera Holidays
199 Marlborough Avenue, Hull HU5 3LG
Admin: 0482 42240
Res: 0482 42240
Fax: 0482 448905
A small, independent tour operation based in the south of France. NSS has been in operation for 39 years and NSS Riviera Holidays for 15 years. 'We offer self-catering accommodation in chalets, cottages and holiday homes. Our units are well-equipped and are set in private gardens. Some units have free places for tents. We carry around 5,000 people each year.'
Self-catering holidays: Provence

Normandie Vacances
113 Sutton Road, Walsall WS5 3AG
Admin: 0922 20278
Res: 0922 20278
Fax: 0922 725232
Established in 1982, Normandie Vacances offers self-drive, self-catering holidays in country cottages. Many properties are within a short drive of the coast. 'We offer a personalised service to our clients, many of whom re-book year after year.'
Self-catering holidays: Normandy

North Sea Ferries
King George Dock, Hedon Road, Hull HU9 5QA
Admin: 0482 795141
Res: 0482 77177
Fax: 0482 706438
VISA ACCESS
North Sea Ferries has been trading for 27 years and became a joint venture between the P&O Group and Royal Nedlloyd Group Holland in 1981. The company has its own purpose built office complex and passenger terminal at King

George Dock in Hull, while its headquarters are located in Rotterdam. North Sea Ferries offers daily overnight crossings from Hull to Zeebrugge and Rotterdam and carries around a million passengers a year. A five-course dinner and breakfast is included in the fare on all crossings. Its modern, European ships carry between 880 and 1,250 passengers and between 500 and 850 cars.'

Hotel holidays: All over France
Special interest holidays: City breaks, skiing

PGL Adventure Ltd

Alton Court, Penyard Lane, Ross-on-Wye, Herefordshire HR9 5NR
Admin: 0989 764211
Res: 0989 768768
Fax: 0989 765451
ABTA: 46875
ATOL: 1127
VISA ACCESS AMEX

The company takes its name from the initials of the man who started it all in 1957 and who is now Chairman of the PGL Group of Companies – Peter Gordon Lawrence. PGL is best known for its activity holidays for children and teenagers within the UK and abroad, but it also operates holiday arrangements and educational tours for schools in France and a range of activity and camping holidays for families in France. In 1992 PGL carried around 90,000 clients.

Special interest holidays: Multi-activity holidays, adventure holidays for children

Paint at Escat

Escat, Montastruc-de-Salies, 31160 Aspet, France
Admin: 010 33 61 97 59 63
Res: 010 33 61 97 59 63

'Paint at Escat is very small: we take no more than six guests at a time, living en famille in our own year round home. We have a large summer atelier and a small winter studio inside the house. It is a very informal holiday and you will not be hurried. The morning session starts at around 9.30. There is a choice of location each day, depending on the needs of the group and sometimes on the weather. In the afternoon we leave you to do as you please. Some people prefer to spend their time working on paintings or drawings. Local trips can be arranged for those without transport. Non-painting partners are welcome and there are may leisure activities in the area.'

Special interest holidays: Painting and drawing holidays

Painting School of Montmiral

Rue de la Porte Neuve, 81140 Castelnau de Montmiral, Tarn, France
Admin: 010 33 63 33 13 11
Res: 0786 72023

The Painting School runs two-week courses from May to September, for people of all abilities, from beginners to professionals. 'This year will be our sixth season. We try to have eight students for each of the ten courses. The school is situated in a limestone and half timbered mansion on the ramparts of Castelnau de Montmiral, a 13th-century hilltop bastide in the Tarn region of south-west France. The courses are individually tailored and open-ended. Our invited artist scheme allows contact with distinguished artists dealing with contemporary issues in painting.'

Special interest holidays: Painting and drawing holidays

Painting for Pleasure in France
Hidcote Manor, Hidcote Bartrim, Chipping Campden, Gloucestershire GL55 6LR
Admin: 0386 438775
Res: 0386 438775
Fax: 0386 438786
This is a small venture, held in the artist's home in the Aveyron. 'Tuition is tailored to the needs of the group with a maximum of eight students on each course. A large studio is available at all times. Our holiday courses are not cheap, they are not aiming to compete with budget holidays. The house, an old wine-growers Manoir, is off the tourist track, in an unspoiled region of France. The courses are fully residential – all tuition, meals, wine and excursions are covered in the cost. The cost of travel from England is not included.'
Special interest holidays: Painting and drawing holidays

Palmer & Parker
The Beacon, Beacon Hill, Penn, Bucks HP10 8ND
Admin: 0494 815411
Res: 0494 815411
Fax: 0494 814184
ABTA: 47134
ATOL: 164
Palmer & Parker has been providing villa holidays for 22 years. 'Properties featured have been built and equipped for the owners' own holidays and retirement and are therefore to a high standard. All have their own pools, some have tennis courts and many have staff. Our villas are located in Portugal, Spain, the Caribbean and France. More than half of those who travel with us have done so previously and they know they are able to talk to someone who knows the villas and can give real assistance in choosing the right holiday.'
Self-catering holidays: Côte d'Azur, Loire Valley

Paris Travel Service
Bridge House, Ware SG12 9DF
Admin: 0920 463900
Res: 0920 467467
Fax: 0920 487902
ABTA: 47276
ATOL: 267
VISA ACCESS AMEX
Paris Travel Service has been established for 37 years. 'All our hotels are individually selected, from one-star budget hotels to the very best deluxe hotels, all centrally situated. Our choice of special holidays includes gala weekends, honeymoons, haute couture fashion shows and holidays by Concorde and the Orient Express. Detailed information on Paris is sent to you with your tickets, including a Paris guide and a full colour street and Métro map.'
Special interest holidays: City breaks

Photography Workshops in Provence
Rue Basse, 84240 Ansouis, France
Admin: 010 33 90 09 95 37
Res: 010 33 90 09 95 37
Fax: 010 33 90 09 96 88
Andrew Squires is a photographer with a background in teaching photography to Art and Design students at Bristol Polytechnic and in workshops in England and France. The eight-day workshops are designed for people who are looking for a subject and ways to explore it. 'We work together through practical projects, discussion, feedback and darkroom work. At whatever level you may be, an honest desire to explore

photography will result in a very high degree of personal satisfaction. Last year those who chose to become students for a week ranged from pre- or post-foundation students to highly skilled RPS Associates who were looking for something more.'
Special interest holidays: Photography holidays

Pieds-à-Terre
Barker Chambers, Maidstone, Kent ME16 8SF
Admin: 0622 688165
Res: 0622 688165
Self-catering holidays to Normandy, Brittany, Dordogne, Vendée and the Pas de Calais. 'The houses, cottages and apartments are almost exclusively second homes to their English and French owners and, as such, each has its own individual character which reflects the tastes of its owners. Most are frequently used as holiday homes by their owners.'
Self-catering holidays: Normandy, Brittany, Dordogne, Vendée

Plantaganet Tours
85 The Grove, Moordown, Bournemouth BH9 2TY
Admin: 0202 521895
Res: 0202 521895
'We are a small, family company which has been operating since 1982. We receive about 250 customers per year on around 15 to 20 tours. Our trips are historical, cultural or literary and are conducted by specialist tour directors. In 1993 we will have tours to France, England, Germany, Italy, Spain, Denmark, Portugal, Hungary, Greece, Austria and Ireland.'
Special interest holidays: Study holidays

Quatre Saisons
The Station House, Folkestone Harbour, Folkestone, Kent CT20 1QG
Admin: 0303 221135
Res: 0303 221135
Fax: 0303 220455
The company was formed in 1991 specialising in flexible self-drive holidays to France. 'We have shunned the rather over-subscribed self-catering market in favour of a personally inspected choice of 40 or so hotels. We have increased our range in the popular areas of Normandy, Brittany, Provence and the Dordogne, whilst remaining faithful to our original selection in less well-known regions of France. Other new features include a choice of four château hotels across northern France, and a UK overnight service for clients wishing to break a long journey on this side of the Channel. The service is supported by a comprehensive transportation service including various ferry crossings, Motorail etc.'
Hotel holidays: All over France
Special interest holidays: Walking and trekking

Railsavers
22 Westcliffe Drive, Layton, Blackpool FY3 7HG
Admin: 0253 300080
Res: 0253 300080
Fax: 0253 393228
VISA ACCESS
'Railsavers is an independent specialist agency providing Motorail travel to France. It is one of the largest retailers of Motorail tickets and annually transports over 6,000 holiday-makers.'
Special interest holidays: Motorail

Ramblers Holidays
PO Box 43, Welwyn Garden City
AL8 6PQ
Admin: 0707 331133
Res: 0707 331133
Fax: 0707 333276
ABTA: 50940
ATOL: 990
VISA ACCESS
Ramblers Holidays was established in 1946 and has grown from a room shared by one man and a typist to an organization carrying over 12,000 passengers in 1992. Ramblers' parties travel all over the world in small groups of from 10 to 20 people. A large percentage of them are single, who all enjoy walking from easy rambles to tough mountain tours. 'All Ramblers holidays are graded and vary from sightseeing tours of the cities of Europe to trekking in more remote places like the Himalayas, with a great variety of other holidays in between. Trips vary in length from a week to three, so there should be something for everyone. Ramblers don't recommend their holidays for children, but providing you can convince us that you are fit enough for the trip you've chosen there is no upper age limit. The average age on a Ramblers holiday is around 50, most of whom come back feeling a lot better than when they departed!'
Special interest holidays: Walking and trekking

Riviera Retreats
11 Rue des Petits Ponts, Mougins Le Haut, 06250 Mougins, France
Admin: 010 33 93 64 86 40
Res: 010 33 93 64 00 80
From simple apartments to large and luxurious châteaux on the Côte d'Azur, Argosy Pollett has been renting out villas for over 10 years. 'About three years ago it was decided better local representation was needed and so Riviera Retreats were contracted to act as local agents. Riviera Retreats now manages nearly 100 properties on a year-round basis. The minimum rental period is two weeks, except occasionally out of season. In June and September we offer a 30% discount.'
Self-catering holidays: Côte d'Azur

Riviera Sailing Holidays
45 Bath Road, Emsworth PO10 7ER
Admin: 0243 374376
Res: 0243 374376
Fax: 0483 578880
Riviera Sailing Holidays was formed over 30 years ago to provide a reliable bare boat charter service for English people in the south of France. 'Only reliable owners with a reasonably large fleet of boats are included. We act solely as agents – we are not a tour operator, covered by the recent EEC legislation. Yachts are now available from Golfe Juan on the Riviera coast and Ajaccio in Corsica. Catamarans are available in the Gulf of St-Tropez and also from Ajaccio in Corsica. We can also arrange crewed yacht and motorcruiser charter throughout the Mediterranean and can also offer bare boat charter in Greece. For those who wish to take their holidays in the British Virgin Islands, we act as agents for the Bitter End Yacht Club who can offer holidays in apartments and/or Freedom 30 yachts. Motorcruisers are available through our agency on the Canal du Midi in the south of France.'

Special interest holidays: Sailing,
Canal boats

Rural France Direct
17 Churchill Way, Painswick, Glos
GL6 6RQ
Admin: 0452 812294
Res: 0452 812294
VISA ACCESS
RFD's proprietor Fabienne Clark is
from the Loire Valley. Having
settled in England 10 years ago she
and her husband started to send
English families on self-catering
cottage holidays in France in 1986.
'Over the last eight years we have
personally visited over a thousand
properties in order to select the 120
featured in our brochure. Our
philosophy has always been to
specialise in truly rural France
where English families can experience the traditional charm of life in
the French countryside. In this way
we deliberately avoid the expensive and often spoilt tourist centres
as well as the crowded coastline,
where holiday houses seem to us
to be overpriced. When we visit
properties we analyse them
through the eyes of a family for
practicability and value for
money.'
Self-catering holidays: Brittany,
Normandy, Loire Valley, Dordogne, Provence, Charente

SFV Holidays
18–24 Middle Way, Summertown,
Oxford OX2 7LG
Admin: 0865 311155
Res: 0865 57738
Fax: 0865 310682
VISA ACCESS
SFV Holidays was established in
1982 and offers self-catering
properties throughout France, Italy
and Spain. 'The majority of our
villas have coastal locations and
there are many with their own private pools. SFV is privately owned
and carries over 15,000 customers
per year.'
Self-catering holidays: Charente,
Brittany, Normandy, Vendée, Les
Landes, Dordogne, Côte d'Azur

SVP France
PO Box 90, Chichester PO18 8XJ
Admin: 0243 377862
Res: 0243 377862
VISA ACCESS
'SVP is now in its sixth year of
operation. We are a small, independent company offering walking,
cycling, canoeing, horse-riding and
multi-activity holidays in many
areas of France. Our holidays are
for those wishing either to travel
alone or to be part of a small,
guided group. Accommodation
can range from camping to small
hotels or holiday villages for
families.'
Self-catering holidays: Auvergne,
Alps, Dordogne
Special interest holidays: Cycling
holidays, singles, walking and trekking, canoeing, skiing, horse-
riding, cooking holidays

Saga Holidays
The Saga Building, Middelburg
Square, Folkestone CT20 1AZ
Admin: 0800 300 600
Res: 0800 300 500
Fax: 0303 220391
ABTA: 36888
ATOL: 308
VISA ACCESS
Saga has for 40 years provided
worldwide holidays exclusively
for over–60s travellers. Customers
can choose from UK and overseas
hotel stay, coach tour or cruise holi-
days, short breaks and holidays
with a theme such as bowls, danc-
ing, fitness, whist, painting,

gardens and music. Study holidays are based at UK and European universities and colleges.
Special interest holidays: Senior citizen

Sally Holidays
Basted Lane, Borough Green, Kent TN15 8BA
Admin: 0732 780562
Res: 0732 780440
Fax: 0732 884577
ABTA: 5927
ATOL: 2500
VISA ACCESS
Sally Holidays is operated by Sally Leisure Ltd and is a sister company to Sally Line, part of the Effjohn International Shipping Group which transports over five million passengers a year. Sally Holidays has been operating for four years, and specialises in motoring holidays to the most popular self-drive resorts in mainland Europe. We also offer skiing holidays and short breaks.
Hotel holidays: Dordogne, Alps, Burgundy
Self-catering holidays: All over France
Special interest holidays: Skiing, EuroDisney

Sandpiper Camping Holidays
Sandpiper House, 19 Fairmile Avenue, Cobham, Surrey KT11 2JA
Admin: 0932 868658
Res: 0932 868658
Fax: 0932 860535
AITO
VISA ACCESS
'We are a small family-run independent tour operator. For the last 10 years we have specialised in self-drive holidays to France. We have fully-equipped tents and mobile homes on west coast sites

in Brittany, the Vendée, and Charente Maritime. All are close to the sea with swimming pools and excellent amenities. Resident couriers provide activities for the children. We also arrange hotel and apartment holidays in the French Alps where activities such as swimming, rafting, tennis, riding and mountain biking are offered.'
Hotel holidays: Alps
Self-catering holidays: Alps
Special interest holidays: Camping

Sauces Nord
82120 Marsac, France
Admin: 010 33 63 94 05 90
Res: 010 33 63 94 05 90
Sauces Nord in Gascony, south west France is a residential centre providing courses in sketching, spinning and weaving, photography and wine appreciation. The centre has nine bedrooms, most of which are doubles, two self-catering kitchens and two sitting rooms. Meals are usually taken in the huge covered courtyard in summer, but picnic lunches will be provided as appropriate. The centre was set up in 1989.
Special interest holidays: Study holidays

Select France
Murcott, Kidlington, Oxford OX5 2RE
Admin: 086 733 350
Res: 086 733 280
Fax: 086 733 526
VISA ACCESS
'We have been organizing holidays in our own mobile homes on campsites on the western coast of France for over 20 years. The company formerly traded as Sparrow Holidays – the name was changed by the Brown family who purchased the company in 1988. We

carry up to 2,000 people annually to our campsites in Brittany, Vendée and Charente Maritime. Around 80% of our clients have either travelled with us before or have been recommended to us by friends. Social activities are organized on the sites for both children and adults. One of our directors visits the sites every few weeks to meet clients and ensure standards are kept high.'
Special interest holidays: Caravans and mobile homes

Select Site Reservations
Travel House, Monmouth Road, Abergavenny NP6 5HL
Admin: 0873 859876
Res: 0873 859876
Fax: 0873 859544
AITO
VISA ACCESS
Select Site Reservations is a small family-run company which makes reservations for the independent camper on 190 camping and caravanning sites spread over nine countries throughout Europe. 'We reserve individual pitches on these sites, book the ferry crossing and arrange full holiday insurance cover. We have been trading for seven years and in 1992 we made holiday reservations for over 8,000 people, several of whom made two trips in the year. The majority of the sites we use are in France and all the regions are covered quite extensively. Our service is special because our advice is based on personal knowledge of all the sites, long acquaintance with a large number of the campsite owners and detailed analysis of our customer questionnaires.'
Special interest holidays: Camping

Sherpa Expeditions
131a Heston Road, Hounslow, Middlesex TW5 0RD
Admin: 081 569 6627
Res: 081 577 2717
Fax: 081 572 9788
ATOL: 1185
AITO
VISA ACCESS
Sherpa has been organising mountain walking holidays for nearly 20 years.
Special interest holidays: Walking and trekking

Silver Ski Holidays
Conifers House, Grove Green Lane, Maidstone ME14 5JW
Admin: 0622 735544
Res: 0622 735544
Fax: 0622 38550
ABTA: 3885
ATOL: 2093
AITO
VISA ACCESS AMEX
Now almost 10 years old, Silver Ski specialises in fully catered and staffed chalets in the French resorts of Val d'Isère, La Plagne, Courchevel, Meribel and La Clusaz. Every chalet is staffed by a married couple who act as host and hostess, cook meals for their guests and in addition act as ski guides during the skiing day. 'Almost every chalet is ski door to door, and most enjoy private facilities in the bedrooms. Silver Ski is a family business and has a high percentage of repeat clients. We carry around 7,000 holiday-makers each winter.'
Special interest holidays: skiing

Simply Corsica
8 Chiswick Terrace, Acton Lane, London W4 5LY
Admin: 081 995 3883
Res: 081 747 3580
Fax: 081 995 5346

ABTA: 1281
ATOL: 1922
AITO
VISA ACCESS
Simply Corsica is part of the Simply Travel Group who started operating in Crete 14 years ago. They also offer specialist programmes to Turkey, the Ionian Islands and skiing in the French Alps. Simply Corsica is now in its third year of operation and concentrates its programme in the southern part of the island. 'Our accommodation caters for almost every need – ranging from de-luxe hotels to mountain auberges, cottages by the sea to apartments in a medieval citadel, detached villas with pools to relaxed family houses. In spring and autumn we also offer wild flower and painting tours.'
Hotel holidays: Corsica
Self-catering holidays: Corsica
Special interest holidays: Natural history, painting and drawing holidays

Ski Enterprise
Groundstar House, London Road, Crawley, West Sussex RH10 2TB
Admin: 061 237 3333
Res: 061 831 7000
Fax: 061 237 9311
ABTA: 68342
ATOL: 230
VISA ACCESS
Ski Enterprise is part of Owners Abroad, the second largest UK tour operator. Ski Enterprise has been trading for 12 years and now carries 80,000 clients annually. 'We offer a range of ski holidays from complete beginners packages in 14 resorts to ski holidays for experts and 22 resorts with ski guides for those who want to explore. Our accommodation includes chalets,

self-catering apartments and two- three- and four-star hotels. The programme now covers 83 resorts in eight different countries. Our group and child discounts are competitive, with discounts available on all dates. Our snow guarantee is comprehensive and does not depend on taking out insurance.'
Special interest holidays: Skiing

Ski Esprit
Oaklands, Reading Road North, Fleet, Hampshire GU13 8AA
Admin: 0252 625175
Res: 0525 616789
Fax: 0252 811243
ABTA: 55041
ATOL: 2096
AITO
VISA ACCESS
Ski Esprit is now in its 10th year of trading. There is also a smaller summer programme – Sun Esprit – and these come under the parent company Esprit Holidays Ltd. Ski Esprit carries around 4,000 passengers a year to France and Switzerland. It has expanded to cover eight resorts in the Alps, namely, La Plagne, Courchevel, Megève, Chamonix, Argentière, Morzine-Avoriaz, Villars and Verbier. The company specialises in family chalet-based holidays featuring in-chalet crèches run by qualified British nannies (NNEB/RGB) in all resorts. The crèches are available for babies and toddlers from four months old. Strict nanny:child ratios are adhered to and children can be booked in on a full day or part day basis. The company also caters for older children by collecting them from ski school, lunching them at a nearby Ski Esprit chalet and then returning them to ski school in the afternoon. For

children managing only a half day session at ski school, Ski Esprit runs a lunch plus afternoon activity club called Snow Club. This facility is featured in three of its resorts. Within the basic holiday price, Ski Esprit offers two free night's baby-sitting.
Special interest holidays: Skiing

Ski Falcon
Groundstar House, London Road, Crawley RH10 2TB
Admin: 061 237 3333
Res: 061 831 7000
Fax: 061 237 9311
ABTA: 68342
ATOL: 230
VISA ACCESS
Ski Falcon is part of Owners Abroad plc, the second largest UK tour operator. Ski Falcon has been trading since 1985. The company has been through several changes in this time: at present they handle around 20,000 passengers annually. 'We offer a selection of self-catering and hotel accommodation in France, Italy, Andorra, Austria, Romania and Bulgaria. The brochure is aimed more at the skier on a budget, and the resorts vary from new and relatively unknown resorts which have good ski areas to satellite resorts for a well known ski resort. Within this, Falcon does cater for every level of skier and some accommodation may be of a very high standard but we view it as exceptionally good value.'
Special interest holidays: Skiing

Ski Peak
Hangerfield, Witley, Surrey GU8 5PR
Admin: 0428 682272
Res: 0428 682272
Fax: 0428 685369
ATOL: 2697

AITO
VISA ACCESS
'We are a small, privately-owned company, in business for five years, carrying around 1,000 people a year. We are a specialist ski operator with accommodation in Vaujany, a traditional Alpine village in the Dauphine which has its own modern lift system and shares the Alpe d'Huez skiing domaine. There is excellent skiing for all abilities and local facilities include a 160-person cable car, a gondola, ski-school, day nursery and ski-kindergarten, and ice-skating rink. We have a range of accommodation, including the Hôtel du Rissiou, three catered chalets and some self-catering apartments. We are now preparing to launch a summer programme offering all the traditional sporting activities.
Special interest holidays: Skiing

SkiBound
Olivier House, 18 Marine Parade, Brighton, East Sussex BN2 1TL
Admin: 0273 677777
Res: 0273 696960
Fax: 0273 676410
ABTA: 55677
ATOL: 2165
AITO
VISA ACCESS
SkiBound Holidays was formed in 1985 and is an independently-owned and run company. It now organises over 100,000 holidays annually. It offers over 20 resorts in France as well as a selection in Austria, Italy and Bulgaria. It is possible to fly from seven UK airports or self-drive. Hotels, self-catering accommodation or catered chalets are offered. All ski essentials can be pre-booked in the UK.

SkiBound give up to one free place for every seven people booked.
Special interest holidays: Skiing

Skiworld
41 North End Road, West Kensington, London W14 8SZ
Admin: 071 602 4826
Res: 071 602 4826
Fax: 071 371 1463
ABTA: 82960
ATOL: 2036
AITO
VISA ACCESS
Skiworld is a specialist company in its 12th year of operation, taking around 10,000 skiers each season to France, Andorra and America. Initially Skiworld's programme concentrated on self-catering apartments but has developed to include a wide range of chalets and also Clubhotel properties. 'We focus on high altitude snow-sure resorts and offer a complete range of travel options. We are happy to take children of any age in any of our chalets or Clubhotels without requiring you to book the whole chalet.'
Special interest holidays: Skiing

Snail's Pace Natural History Holidays
25 Thorpe Lane, Almondbury, Huddersfield HD5 8TA
Admin: 0484 426259
Res: 0943 873465
Fax: 0943 873349
ATOL: 917
Snail's Pace began five years ago offering holidays to look at birds, flowers, butterflies and general natural history as well as history and archaeology. 'Our customers have many interests and vary from experts to beginners but are happy to follow the philosophy of hurrying slowly! Most of the holidays

are personally led by Stephanie Coghlan. The holidays aim for a friendly atmosphere with plenty to do but also time to relax and stand and stare. Holidays are offered to Europe, Crete, Greece, Portugal, France, UK, Borneo, Western Australia and Costa Rica.'
Special interest holidays: Natural history

Snowbizz Vacances
69 High Street, Maxey, Peterborough PE6 9EE
Admin: 0778 341455
Res: 0778 341455
Fax: 0778 347422
ABTA: 2007
ATOL: 2463
AITO
VISA ACCESS
Snowbizz Vacances are a husband and wife partnership offering skiing holidays to the southern French Alps in the resorts of Puy St Vincent, Serre Chevalier and Briançon. Having been in operation for seven years, Snowbizz now carry 2,000 people per year. 'Although all grades of skiers are catered for, with a free ski guiding service in all resorts, perhaps the most special part of the service provided is our own crêche with qualified British staff. We also provide a free après ski club for ages two to ten and our own ski school for ages three to six years.'
Special interest holidays: Skiing

Snowpiper Ski Holidays
Sandpiper House, 19 Fairmile Avenue, Cobham, Surrey KT11 2JA
Admin: 0932 868658
Res: 0932 868658
Fax: 0932 860535
AITO
VISA ACCESS

'We are a small, family-run independent tour operator organising self-drive skiing holidays to Châtel, Alpe d'Huez and Flaine. Accommodation is in self-catering apartments and hotels which have been carefully chosen. We can adapt holidays to meet clients requirements wherever possible. Our aim is to provide good value holidays without compromising on quality.'
Special interest holidays: Skiing

Solo's Holidays
41 Watford Way, Hendon, London NW4 3JH
Admin: 081 202 1922
Res: 081 202 0855
Fax: 081 202 4749
ATOL: 559
AITO
VISA ACCESS
Solo's Holidays has been trading for over 10 years handling around 10,000 bookings a year. 'Our overseas programme covers virtually the whole world and we also have an active UK weekend programme. We provide holidays only for single people. We have two age groups, 30–50 and 50–69. A tour leader accompanies each group, acting as a social host as well as an organizer. We make an effort to achieve a good social mix of people without in any way operating as a match-making outfit.'
Special interest holidays: Singles

Something Special Travel
10 Bull Plain, Hertford, Herts SG14 1DT
Admin: 0992 552231
Res: 0992 505500
Fax: 0992 587057
ABTA: 99336
ATOL: 2136
AITO
VISA ACCESS AMEX
Something Special has been operating for 12 years to destinations such as the Algarve, Corfu, Costa Blanca and Florida. 'Now we are offering over 65 villas with pools in France – in the Dordogne, Provence and along the coastline of the Alpes Maritimes. We offer our clients flights from the nearest or most convenient airport and a range of cross-Channel ferry routes which can be checked and confirmed immediately.'
Self-catering holidays: Dordogne, Provence, Alps

Sovereign Cities
Astral Towers, Betts Way, Crawley, West Sussex RH10 2GX
Admin: 0293 560777
Res: 0293 599900
Fax: 0293 543414
ABTA: 68342
ATOL: 230
VISA ACCESS AMEX
Sovereign has been trading for 21 years – the city-break programme was first introduced in 1985. Sovereign Cities is a division of Owners Abroad Holidays, the UK's second largest tour operator, and carries over 12,000 passengers a year. The programme offers a range of 24 destinations including Paris, Nice, Amsterdam, Prague, Istanbul and New York. 'We use a range of scheduled flights with a choice of timings, regional departures and airlines. We also feature rail and sea and self-drive holidays to selected destinations, including Paris.'
Special interest holidays: City breaks

Sovereign Small World
Astral Towers, Betts Way, Crawley,
West Sussex RH10 2GX
Admin: 0293 588207
Res: 0293 599966
Fax: 0293 543414
ABTA: 68342
ATOL: 230
VISA ACCESS
Small World was founded by Colin
Murison Small more than 30 years
ago. Now known as Sovereign
Small World, it is part of the
Owners Abroad Group and offers
house party and cruising holidays
for 'sociable, single people'. The
majority of people are in their 30s
and 40s who are keen to visit
places slightly off the beaten track,
away from mass tourism. House
party holidays are like ski chalet
holidays – staffed and catered – but
in the sun. Guests have single
rooms or share a twin with someone of the same sex. Resort staff
prepare meals – half-board with
unlimited wine. 'The emphasis is
on meeting people, good food and
wine and enjoying local life. Destinations include the Algarve, Provence, Tuscany, the Greek Islands
and Turkey. There are also gulet
and caique cruises in Turkey and
Greece and all cruises operate
along the same lines as house
parties.'
Special interest holidays: Singles

Specialtours
81a Elizabeth Street, London SW3
4RD
Admin: 071 730 2297
Res: 071 730 3138
Fax: 071 823 5035
ATOL: 715
Specialtours has over 20 years'
experience in arranging escorted
cultural tours to Europe, the
United States and the Middle East,
with the emphasis on art and
architecture or archaeology. 'Privi-
leged private visits to houses, collections or gardens are often
included in our itineraries and
each tour is created on a one-off
basis, with a different selection of
themes and destinations each year.
The tours, accompanied by a lecturer and/or experienced guide,
are for members of the National
Art Collections Fund but others
may book provided that they take
out membership (£15) before
departure.'
Special interest holidays: Art &
architecture tours

Sports Tours International
91 Walkden Road, Walkden,
Worsley, Manchester M28 5DQ
Admin: 061 703 8161
Res: 061 703 8161
Fax: 061 703 8547
ABTA: 406 2711
VISA ACCESS
Sports Tours sends runners and
non-runners to more than 30 differ-
ent races worldwide and its staff
include experienced runners. In
1992, Sports Tours sent more than
500 British runners to the London
Marathon, carried 886 people from
the UK to the New York Marathon,
over 200 people to the Barcelona
Olympics and over 2,500 people to
the sporting complex – Club La
Santa in Lanzarote. 'The Paris
Marathon, Paris/Versailles and
Paris 20km are all mass participation events and have proved
particularly popular with our customers.'
Special interest holidays: Running
holidays

Stena Sealink Travel
Charterhouse, Park Street, Ashford
TN24 8EX

Admin: 0233 647022
Res: 0233 647033
Fax: 0233 623294
ABTA: 16920
VISA ACCESS AMEX DINERS
Stena Sealink Travel is part of the ferry company, Stena Sealink Line. 'We have five holiday brochures for the independent motorist: Holiday France and Europe; Short Breaks (to Northern France, Holland, Belgium and Ireland); Family Fun (theme parks in France, Holland and Belgium); Holiday Ireland; and the Holland, Belgium and Germany brochure. Our accommodation in the Holiday France and Europe brochure 1993 includes over 400 gîtes, villas with pools, apartment residences, Club resorts such as Pierre et Vacances and a go as you please touring programme with five hotel chains. Motorail is available to many destinations and can be booked separately or in conjunction with a main holiday.'
Self-catering holidays: Normandy, Brittany, Loire Valley, Charente, Dordogne, Pyrénées, Languedoc, Provence, Alps
Special interest holidays: City breaks

Sun Esprit
Oaklands, Reading Road North, Fleet, Hampshire, GU13 8AA
Admin: 0252 816004
Res: 0252 816004
Fax: 0252 811243
ABTA: 55041
AITO
VISA ACCESS
Sun Esprit is the sister programme to Esprit Holidays Ltd's Ski Esprit which has been in operation for 10 years as a specialist in family chalet holidays. Sun Esprit's lakes and mountains programme is based, for 1993, in Morzine, in the Haute Savoie Alps. It offers auberge-based family holidays following the theme developed by Ski Esprit where children are cared for by NNEB/RGN British nannies. A week's holiday includes three days where the nannies will run an all-day activities club or provide crèche care for children aged from four months to nine years old. There are also two evening family meals and three nights' babysitting. All these services are included in the basic holiday price.
Special interest holidays: Multi-activity holidays

Sunselect Villas
60 Crow Hill North, Middleton, Manchester M24 1FB
Admin: 061 655 3055
Res: 061 655 3055
Fax: 061 655 4055
VISA ACCESS
'We are an independent, family-run company specialising in organizing self-catering holidays to Brittany. We have been established for 10 years, during which time we have gradually built up a selection of good quality holiday cottages and villas, always conscious of our responsibility to the many past customers who re-book with us. If we would not be happy to spend a holiday in a property ourselves we do not feature that property in our brochure. We carry about 500 families annually so that we can continue to offer every family a personal and informed service, helping them choose a suitable property depending on their individual requirements, even to the extent of turning down bookings if we do not feel we can offer something suitable.'

Self-catering holidays: Brittany
Special interest holidays: Canal
boats

Sunvista Holidays
5a George Street, Warminster
BA12 8QA
Admin: 0985 217373
Res: 0985 217373
Fax: 0985 219874
ABTA: 56858
AITO
VISA ACCESS
Sunvista Holidays has been established for 14 years and offers a
selection of country cottages, villas
and some apartments. 'Some of the
villas have swimming pools and at
some others there is a pool shared
with holiday-makers in neighbouring properties. We regularly
visit all our properties and our
clients can always speak to someone who has seen the cottage or
villa they are interested in and
knows the region near to it. Sunvista also arranges self-drive touring
holidays with hotel accommodation. Hotels are chosen either
from own experience or from the
France Accueil Hotel group or
from the Logis en Liberté organization.'
Hotel holidays: All over France
Self-catering holidays: Brittany,
Dordogne, Côte d'Azur

**Susi Madron's Cycling for
Softies**
2–4 Birch Polygon, Rusholme,
Manchester M14 5HX
Admin: 061 248 8282
Res: 061 248 8282
Fax: 061 248 5140
VISA ACCESS
In business since 1981, the com-
pany offers two main types of cyc-
ling holiday. The first provides

planned routes with pre-arranged
stays in family-run hotels. The
second allows clients to make one
hotel their home base and take day
trips into the surrounding countryside. A choice of travel arrangements is offered: direct scheduled
flights, air-rail, air-coach and
self-drive.
Special interest holidays: Cycling
holidays

Tailhos
Route de la Salvetat, 34220 Saint-
Pons de Thomières, Herault,
France
Admin: 010 33 67 97 27 62
Res: 010 33 67 97 27 62
Tailhos is a new ferme-auberge in
the Haut Languedoc region of
southern France. The farm was
bought by Penny and Gerard Hin-
singer in 1988. They combined
their respective qualifications to
run an agricultural and tourist
enterprise producing foie gras,
fruit and vegetables for the restaurant and providing accommodation in the converted stone
buildings. Gîte and chambre d'hôte
accommodation is offered.
Hotel holidays: Languedoc
Self-catering holidays: Languedoc

Tamplins Travel
16 Bailie Close, Abingdon, Oxford-
shire OX14 5RF
Admin: 0235 526855
Res: 0865 391257
Tamplins Travel is a very small
company, now in its fifth year,
specialising in naturist holidays at
just one naturist holiday centre in
France. It is situated in the hills
of eastern Provence at about 900ft
above sea level. The centre has
been in existence for nearly 20
years, but has recently changed
hands. The new owners are carry-

ing out improvements to the site. The proprietors of Tamplins Travel are resident on the site during the summer.
Special interest holidays: Naturist holidays

Thomson Holidays
Greater London House, Hampstead Road, London NW1 7SD
Admin: 071 387 9321
Res: 021 632 6282
Fax: 071 387 8451
ABTA: 58213
ATOL: 152
VISA ACCESS
Thomson Holidays, Britain's largest holiday company, is part of Thomson Travel, which also owns travel agency chain Lunn Poly and charter airline Britannia Airways. Thomson arranges holidays for around three million people each year.
Special interest holidays: City breaks, EuroDisney, skiing

Time Off
Chester Close, Chester Street, London SW1X 7BQ
Admin: 071 235 8070
Res: 071 235 8070
Fax: 071 259 6093
ABTA: 58374
ATOL: 2315
AITO
VISA ACCESS
Time Off is an independent company founded 25 years ago in 1967. 'We started with individual, inclusive holidays to Paris. In 1968 we added Amsterdam. We subsequently added other cities: Brussels, Bruges, Luxembourg, until today we can offer a choice of 22 European cities plus New York and Istanbul. We also offer motoring holidays in a range of accom-

modation in the French and Irish countrysides. We offer our clients flexibility in where to stay and how to get there. We give them accurate itineraries, maps, helpful guides and a feeling that they are travelling independently, although we put it all together.'
Special interest holidays: City breaks, motoring and fly/drive

Travel for the Arts
117 Regent's Park Road, London NW1 8UR
Admin: 071 483 4466
Res: 071 483 4466
Fax: 071 586 0639
ABTA: 98916
VISA ACCESS AMEX
Travel for the Arts was set up in 1988 and is wholly-owned by Blair Travel & Leisure Ltd. Travel for the Arts operates a programme of specialist holidays for music lovers including tickets for the opera, ballet and concert performances in many of the major venues in Europe and North America. The programme comprises 40 to 50 tours a year during the opera season and the summer music festivals. The maximum number of participants on any tour is 30. 'The emphasis is on looking after the requirements of individuals who are travelling together as a group. A cultural theme underpins the itinerary which includes sightseeing and, in some cases, special visits such as theatre backstage tours, access to ballet classes etc. A professional tour manager accompanies the groups. As an extension of this service in 1992 we launched our à la carte service offering tailor-made itineraries to individual specifications with fully inclusive travel arrange-

ments and ticket reservations for musical events.'
Special interest holidays: Music holidays

Travelscene
11/15 St Anne's Road, Harrow HA1 1AS
Admin: 081 427 8800
Res: 081 427 4445
Fax: 081 861 3674
ABTA: 5956
ATOL: 34
AITO
VISA ACCESS
'Travelscene is an independent company, established for over 25 years specialising in short breaks to European cities.'
Special interest holidays: City breaks, EuroDisney

VFB Holidays
Normandy House, High Street, Cheltenham GL50 3HW
Admin: 0242 235515
Res: 0242 526338
Fax: 0242 570340
ATOL: 1403
AITO
VISA ACCESS
Established in 1971, VFB introduced the concept of gîte holidays to Britain and it is for this programme that the company is best known. There is, however, a wider range of holiday programmes available today: Cottage Holidays; Auberge Holidays – touring holidays using two- and three-star hotels; City Sorties – trips by air to French cities; Freewheelers – short breaks to Normandy, Picardy and Bruges; Outdoor France – activity-based holidays and Faraway France – long-haul holidays to French overseas departments and ex-colonial territories. 'We currently carry 27,000 passengers each

year: 75% of our business comes from previous customers and their friends.'
Hotel holidays: All over France, Corsica
Self-catering holidays: All over France
Special interest holidays: Language learning, Multi-activity holidays, wine tours

Vacances en Campagne
Bignor, Pulborough RH20 1QD
Admin: 07987 461
Res: 07987 433
Fax: 07987 343
ATOL: 2433
AITO
VISA ACCESS
Vacances en Campagne is a specialist in self-catering holidays in almost every region across France, including Corsica. It has been established for 17 years and has over 600 properties. Spain and Mallorca are now also featured.
Self-catering holidays: All over France

Voyages Ilena
7 Old Garden House, The Lanterns, Bridge Lane, London, SW1 3AD
Admin: 071 720 0111
Res: 071 924 4440
Fax: 071 924 4441
ATOL: 2770
AITO
Voyages Ilena is an original Corsican specialist, a family partnership established six years ago to offer tailor-made self-catering and hotel holidays that will particularly appeal to those wanting to get to know Corsica and its people. 'We offer a wide range of accommodation, from country cottages and mountain gîtes to luxurious mansions and small friendly

hotels. We only offer places that we know well and would like to stay ourselves. All of our properties and hotels are in the quieter areas, away from the crowds. We send only 1,200 people on holiday each year and all our holidays involve a high level of personal service.

Hotel holidays: Corsica
Self-catering holidays: Corsica

Waymark Holidays
44 Windsor Road, Slough SL1 2EJ
Admin: 0753 516477
Res: 0753 516477
Fax: 0753 517016
ATOL: 624
VISA ACCESS
Specialists in walking and cross-country skiing holidays. 'Waymark has been trading since 1973 and is privately owned. In 1992 we carried around 1,800 skiers and 2,200 walkers. We feature most countries in Europe plus Canada, Peru, Bolivia, Argentina, China and Turkey. Holidays are designed for small groups with a leader, staying at family-run hotels or guest-houses. Instruction and equipment are included in our skiing holidays.'
Special interest holidays: Walking and trekking, skiing

Welcome Holidays
1st Floor, 54 High Street, Thames Ditton, Surrey KT7 0SA
Admin: 081 398 0355
Res: 081 398 0355
Fax: 081 339 0446
AITO
VISA ACCESS
Welcome Holidays specialises in self-drive holidays to France. Accommodation is in very modern mobile homes on campsites with swimming pools, restaurants and bars. 'For 1993 we have four new campsites which makes a total of 16 campsites to choose from. We are an independent family-run company. We have operated for 16 years.'
Special interest holidays: Caravans and mobile homes

Westbury Travel
1 Belmont, Lansdown Road, Bath BA1 5DZ
Admin: 0225 445732
Res: 0225 444516
Fax: 0225 444520
ABTA: 64746
ATOL: 1383
AITO
VISA ACCESS
Westbury Travel operates two main holiday programmes. 'Just France specialises in summer holidays in villas, country cottages and hotels throughout France, either by ferry or fly/drive and Ski West offers a choice of chalet party, hotel or self-catering skiing holidays in French and European resorts with flights from five UK airports. The company has traded for 12 years, the last seven as part of the Bladon Group plc, and carries 14,000 people in the summer and 12,000 in the winter.'
Hotel holidays: Normandy, Brittany, Loire Valley, Dordogne, Provence
Self-catering holidays: Normandy, Loire Valley, Brittany, Vendée, Dordogne, Gascony, Provence, Côte d'Azur, Alps, Les Landes, Languedoc, Ardèche
Special interest holidays: Skiing

Westents
88 New North Road, Huddersfield, West Yorkshire HD1 5NE
Admin: 0484 424455
Res: 0484 424455
Fax: 0484 424622

AITO
VISA ACCESS
Westents is a small, family-run business selling self-drive camping holidays to ready-erected tents in France. 'This year will be our 10th season. The holidays are aimed at families and there is a resident courier and children's Squirrel Club on each campsite throughout the season. In 1992 275 families holidayed with us. We use one of the biggest tents on the market and there is a strong emphasis on a personal service. Our couriers spend a lot of time looking after families on holiday and this leads to a very high percentage of repeat business.'
Special interest holidays: Camping

White Roc Ski
69 Westbourne Grove, London W2 4UJ
Admin: 071 792 1188
Res: 071 792 1188
Fax: 071 792 1956
AITO
VISA ACCESS
White Roc Ski has been established for seven years, offering 'quality chalet holidays in some of the best ski resorts in France. Travel is by scheduled Swissair flights or self-drive – with an en route hotel booking service for our clients. The resorts range from the pretty and traditional, such as Megève, to the high altitude resorts of Val d'Isère and Meribel. By giving a personal service, with a friendly and informed approach to enquiries, our clients can rely on being provided with accommodation which exactly suits their requirements. We offer weekend skiing in addition to seven or fourteen day holidays and now almost 25% of our clients travel on non standard

holidays. Free ski guiding is offered in all resorts.'
Special interest holidays: Skiing

Worldwide Yachting Holidays
35 Fairfax Place, London NW6 4EJ
Admin: 071 328 1033
Res: 071 328 1033
Fax: 071 328 1034
'Since 1974 Worldwide Yachting Holidays has been providing professionally crewed sailing and motor yacht holidays, bareboats and canal barge holidays. Destinations include France, Corsica, the French West Indies and French Polynesia.'
Special interest holidays: Canal boats, sailing

FACT FILE

Advice
Theoretically the best place to go for all information and advice about holidays in France is the French Government Tourist Office, 178 Piccadilly, London W1V 0AL (071 491 7622; fax: 071 493 6594). Unfortunately it is hard to get through on the phone, and it is difficult to get a specific response to questions sent in by letter. However the office publishes a good range of helpful guides, particularly *The Traveller in France Reference Guide* which is an invaluable source of good information. If you can get to London, you might find it useful to call at the office in Piccadilly.

If you want information on a specific place in France, contact the relevant local tourist office in France. The *Michelin Red Guide to France* lists all the local tourist offices in France, providing their address and telephone number. Many tourist offices have an English speaker, so you could try telephoning. Alternatively you could write: it would be a good idea to enclose an International Reply Coupon available from post offices.

Customs Allowances
These are the new duty-free allowances which came into force on 1 January 1993:

	Duty Free	**Duty Paid**
	Goods obtained anywhere outside the EC or duty and tax free within the EC, including purchases from a UK duty free shop	Goods obtained duty and tax paid in the EC
Cigarettes, or	200	800
Cigarillos, or	100	400
Cigars, or	50	200
Tobacco	250g	1kg
Still table wine	2 litres	*see below

	Duty Free	**Duty Paid**
	Goods obtained anywhere outside the EC or duty and tax free within the EC, including purchases from a UK duty free shop	Goods obtained duty and tax paid in the EC
Spirits, strong liqueurs over 22% volume, or	1 litre	10 litres
Fortified or sparkling wines, other liqueurs, or	2 litres	*20 litres of fortified wine, or 90 litres of wine (of which no more than 60 litres of sparkling wine)
An additional still table wine allowance	2 litres	
Perfume	60cc (2 fl oz)	no limit
Toilet water	250cc (9 fl oz)	no limit
All other goods including gifts and souvenirs	£32 worth, but no more than 50 litres of beer, 25 mechanical lighters	no limit except for the beer allowance, which is increased to 110 litres

Electricity

While the electricity supply in France (even in camping sites) is very similar to that in Britain, French sockets and plugs are quite different. You can buy adaptors which will allow British three-pin plugs to fit French sockets.

Emergencies

To contact the police in France dial 17; for the fire brigade dial 18. For ambulances, if no number is given in the telephone box, call the police. Following car accidents, police are usually only called if someone is hurt, one of the drivers is drunk, or if you're holding up the traffic. Before you move your car, you and the other driver should fill in a European Accident Statement Form or the French equivalent *constat a l'amiable*.

Guidebooks and Maps

The Michelin Red Guide to France (Michelin, £12.50) is more than a list of hotels and restaurants. There are good town centre maps – now in colour – as well as brief guides to the main sights, address of the tourist office, local car dealers and much more. *The Michelin Green Tourist Guides* (£7.25 each) are a model of conciseness, presenting useful information in a user-friendly format. The areas of France covered by English language Green Guides are: Brittany, Burgundy, Châteaux of the Loire, Dordogne, French Riviera, Île-de-France, Normandy, Cotentin, Normandy Seine, Paris and Provence. Michelin has now also produced a Green Guide to the whole of France. You will also need a Michelin map of some sort to guide you around France. The *Michelin Motoring Atlas of France* (£11.99) is excellent whether you want to stick to the autoroute or venture off the beaten track.

Other guides worth a look include *The Rough Guide to France* (£9.99) as well as the separate Rough Guides to Paris; Brittany and Normandy; and Provence and the Côte d'Azur.

For a more scholarly account of France, the *Blue Guide: France* (A&C Black, £14.95), runs to almost 1,000 densely-printed pages concentrating on history and architecture.

Richard Binns has an infectious enthusiasm for the pleasures of France. Following the success of his *French Leave* series, there is a brand new self-published book *French Leave Encore* (Chiltern House, £9.99) which he claims is his best yet. With 400 closely-printed pages – and dozens of invaluable maps – the book is certainly excellent value. It is an invaluable companion for any visitor to France. There are excellent guides to hotels and restaurants but it is much, much more than a simple guidebook. There is a list of 'who's who in French cuisine', an introduction to the wines of France, an index of cheeses, specimen letters of reservation for booking hotels and a guide to hotels on French autoroutes. But best of all are the host of Binns' *bons mots* and instructive comments and observations which make his guides so readable. Copies of *French Leave Encore* are available from bookshops or direct from Chiltern House, Honeywood House, Avon Dassett, Leamington Spa CV33 0AH (send £9.99 including postage and packaging).

Understanding France (Papermac, £7.99) by John Harris is a marvellous guide to France for the independent traveller, offering a concise introduction to the manners and method of daily French life.

Specialist travel bookshops include: Daunt Books for Travellers, 83 Marylebone High Street, London W1 (071 224 2295); Stanfords, 12–14 Long Acre, London WC2E 9LP (071 836 1321); Travel Bookshop, 13 Blenheim Crescent, London W11 2EE (071 229 5260); Travellers' Bookshop, 25 Cecil Court, London WC2N 4EZ (071 836 9132); Waterstones, 121–125 Charing Cross Road, London WC2 (071 434 4291).

Radio

It is surprising how far south in France you can pick up BBC Radio 4 on Long Wave during the day and night. The Dordogne is about the southern limit of daytime reception – at night, depending on atmospheric conditions, reception should be possible anywhere in France.

Telephones

Unlike Britain's complex system of STD area codes, the French system has only two areas: Paris and everywhere else. Paris numbers are shown with a '1' at the beginning; you don't need to dial this when dialling within Paris. When dialling from Paris to the provinces or vice versa, you always preface the number with 16. Numbers are always written in groups of two.

When phoning Britain from France, dial 19 to access the international exchange; wait for a new dialling tone; then dial 44 to get Britain; then your STD code without the first 0; then the number itself. For reverse charge calls, use the UK Direct service by telephoning: 1 900 44.

To phone France from Britain dial 010 33 to get France (with a '1' prefix for a Paris number); then the eight-figure number.

Telephone boxes: The ones that accept coins take 1, 5 and 10 Franc coins. As in Britain, in France an increasing number of phone boxes will only accept phone cards (*Telecartes*): these cost 40 Francs and 96 Francs and are available from post offices, SNCF counters, tobacconists and France Telecom offices. You can also make pay calls from many post offices; you make the call and pay after you finish.

Walking

Le Sentier de Grande Randonnée, 'GR' for short, is the French network of long-distance footpaths. There are three separate types of GR:

Grandes Randonnées: The main long-distance footpaths that form a network that covers the whole country.

GRs de Pays: Regional walking routes offering a walk of one or two days.

Petites Randonnées: Departmental routes in the regions, walks of a couple of hours up to ones lasting a whole day.

The supervising French authority is the Fédération Français de Randonnée Pedestre (FFRP), 9 Avenue George V, 75008 Paris (010 33 1 47 23 62 32). It produces a series of Topoguides which cover particular GRs in great detail.

These guides written in French have black and white reproductions of the relevant IGN (Institut Geographique National) map. The guides provide details of things to see on the route and information about accommodation available en route. Some of the Topoguides have been translated into English for the Robertson McCarta series. The guides in English cover Normandy and the Seine; Walking through Brittany; Walks in Provence; Coastal Walks: Normandy and Brittany; Walking the Pyrénées; Walks in the Auvergne. Unlike the Topoguides, the Robertson McCarta books have colour maps but cover the walks in one direction only. The *Walks in Provence* (£9.95) guide, for example, offers a guide to over 300 kilometres of footpaths through the hills of Provence and down to the sea.

The IGN maps are reckoned to the best for walkers. Map 903, *France, Sentiers de Grande Randonnée* (£4.95) shows the full network of GR footpaths. The IGN *Série Bleue* maps (£4.95) are larger scale maps which show GR paths in greater detail.